Shakespearean
Constitutions

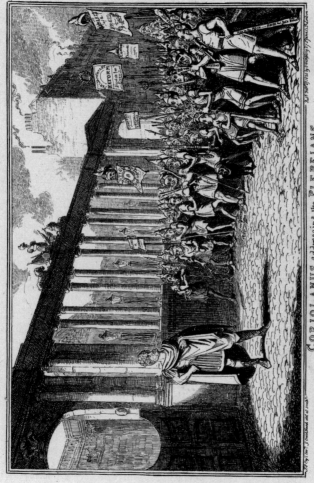

George Cruikshank, *Coriolanus addressing the Plebeians* (British Museum)

SHAKESPEAREAN CONSTITUTIONS

Politics, Theatre, Criticism 1730–1830

But Shakespeare one gets acquainted with without knowing how.
It is a part of an Englishman's constitution.

Mansfield Park

JONATHAN BATE

CLARENDON PRESS · OXFORD

1989

Oxford University Press, Walton Street, Oxford OX2 6DP
Oxford New York Toronto
Delhi Bombay Calcutta Madras Karachi
Petaling Jaya Singapore Hong Kong Tokyo
Nairobi Dar es Salaam Cape Town
Melbourne Auckland
and associated companies in
Berlin Ibadan

Oxford is a trade mark of Oxford University Press

Published in the United States
by Oxford University Press, New York

© Jonathan Bate 1989

British Library Cataloguing in Publication Data
Bate, Jonathan
Shakespearean constitutions: politics,
theatre, criticism 1730-1830
1. English literature, 1558-1975.
Influence of Shakespeare, William
I. Title   820'.9
ISBN 0-19-811749-3

Library of Congress Cataloging-in-Publication Data
Bate, Jonathan.
Shakespearean constitutions : politics, theatre, criticism,
1730-1830 / Jonathan Bate.
p.   cm.
Bibliography: p.
Includes index.
1. Shakespeare, William, 1564-1616—Criticism and interpretation—
History. 2. Shakespeare, William, 1564-1616—Stage history—
England—London. 3. Shakespeare, William, 1564-1616—Political and
social views. 4. Politics and literature—England—History.
5. Literature and society—England—History. 6. England—
Civilization—18th century. 7. England—Civilization—19th
century. 8. Theater—England—London—History. I. Title.
PR2965.B38   1989
822.3'3—dc19   89-2869
                                          CIP
ISBN 0-19-811749-3

Typeset by Downdell Limited, Oxford
Printed in Great Britain by
Courier International Ltd
Tiptree, Essex

For
Hilary

Acknowledgements

I AM grateful to Cambridge University Press for permission to incorporate in this book my article 'Hal and the Regent' (*Shakespeare Survey*, 1985), and to the editors of the *Journal of Popular Culture*, the *Journal of the Warburg and Courtauld Institutes*, and *Prose Studies* for permission to use much-revised versions of material that originally appeared in their publications. I am grateful to the librarians of the institutions where I have worked, especially the Cambridge University Library, the English Faculty Library, Cambridge, and the print room of the British Museum. For their comments on all or part of the typescript, I am deeply indebted to Stanley Wells, Christopher Ridgway, Adrian Poole, Jeremy Maule, Reginald Foakes, Juliet Dusinberre, and David Armitage. Roy Porter cast an historian's eye over sections of Part I; Leo Salingar, Richard Luckett, and James Engell helped me in the very early stages of my work on Shakespeare's 'afterlife'. The support of Kim Scott Walwyn at Oxford University Press and Peter Holland at Trinity Hall has been invaluable. I would like to thank the Master and Fellows of Trinity Hall and the Mistress and Fellows of Girton College for sabbatical leave which enabled me to write this book.

J.B.

Contents

Illustrations

All illustrations are reproduced by permission of the Trustees of the British Museum, with the exception of Plate 1, which is by courtesy of the Dean and Chapter of Westminster, Plate 2, which is by courtesy of the National Portrait Gallery, and Plate 35, which is by permission of the Governors of the Royal Shakespeare Theatre.

A Note on References

WITH a few exceptions, references are keyed by author and date to the bibliography. The exceptions are Shakespeare and my two principal sources, the *Catalogue of Political and Personal Satires Preserved in the Department of Prints and Drawings in the British Museum* (11 vols., 1870–1954), edited by F. G. Stephens (vols. i–iv) and M. Dorothy George (vols. v–xi), and *The Complete Works of William Hazlitt*, edited by P. P. Howe (21 vols., 1930–4). Titles of caricatures are followed in my text by their number in the *Catalogue* (abbreviated hereafter as BMC); quotations from Hazlitt are followed by volume and page number in *Works* (abbreviated hereafter as HW). For ease of consultation, Shakespearean quotations are followed by line reference to *The Riverside Shakespeare*, general editor G. Blakemore Evans (Boston, 1974), though since I am considering late eighteenth- and early nineteenth-century readings of the plays, the text quoted is a widely used edition of the period, that of Alexander Chalmers; first published in 1803, this is based on the final text of George Steevens, but the eight-volume reprint of 1823, which I have used, also takes into account the variants of Edmond Malone.

. . . he wrote the text of modern life . . .
Ralph Waldo Emerson, 'Shakespeare'

Prologue

THIS book is an account of how Shakespeare was constituted in England in the eighteenth and early nineteenth centuries, and how cultural life during that period was by constitution Shakespearean. Although self-contained, it was conceived as a sequel to *Shakespeare and the English Romantic Imagination* (Bate 1986): where that was a study in poetic influence, this turns to society at large and the public history of the dramatist's 'afterlife'. The century from 1730 to 1830, and in particular the reign of George III, was especially important in that afterlife, but at many points the book refers both back and forward. Recent criticism has said much about the Renaissance Shakespeare and the modern Shakespeare, but has failed to bridge the two.[1] This book attempts to hold together Shakespeare's historicity and his modernity by showing that our century has not been the first to make him contemporary.

The term 'afterlife' is taken from the idea of *Nachleben* formulated in that tradition of scholarship, associated with the Warburg Institute, which concerns itself with the endurance and the transformation of the artistic achievements of classical antiquity. In his book *Subsequent Performances*, Jonathan Miller uses the word with reference to the performance of a play after its author's death: 'By submitting itself to the possibility of successive re-creation, however, the play passes through the development that is its birthright, and its meaning begins to be fully appreciated only when it enters a period that I shall call its *afterlife*' (Miller 1986, p. 23). The theatre was, naturally, one place where Shakespeare's eighteenth- and nineteenth-century afterlife was played out, so throughout this book there is reference to the stage. There was, however, a wider presence: not only in such projects as David Garrick's Shakespeare Jubilee and John Boydell's Shakespeare Gallery, but also in the political discourse of the time.

---

[1] Witness the gulf between pt. 1 ('Recovering history') and pt. 2 ('Reproductions, interventions') of the collection *Political Shakespeare* (Dollimore and Sinfield 1985). There is a similar lack of material on the eighteenth- and nineteenth-century Shakespeare in Howard and O'Connor 1987 and Holderness 1988.

The subject of Shakespeare and politics in Georgian England is a vast and neglected one. I have viewed it through the distorting lens of caricature: in an age without photography and television, when newspapers were not illustrated, caricature was the principal medium through which the public derived their images of politicians and State affairs. A study of the presence of Shakespeare in caricature in that period is the nearest equivalent to a study of his presence in television in our period; that is to say, it is a study in popular iconography. Furthermore, Shakespeare's life in Georgian graphic satire evinces not only the centrality of the plays to English culture, but also the process whereby they are forever being re-created, *appropriated* in the name of conflicting political and aesthetic ideologies.[2]

'Appropriation' will be a key term. In his important essay 'Literary History as a Challenge to Literary Theory', Hans Robert Jauss writes that a literary text 'can continue to have an effect only if those who come after it still or once again respond to it—if there are readers who again appropriate the past work or authors who want to imitate, outdo, or refute it' (Jauss 1982, p. 22). *Shakespeare and the English Romantic Imagination* examined authors who wanted to imitate and outdo, though not necessarily refute, Shakespeare; this book is concerned with the appropriation of the plays by certain readers, most notably James Gillray and William Hazlitt. For Jauss, the act of reading is essentially a private affair, whereas for an East German critic like Robert Weimann, the relationship between a literary work's 'past significance' and its 'present meaning' cannot be separated from its social function. For Weimann, both the act of writing and the act of reading are activities which involve 'the socializing of the individual and the personalizing of the social'; both partake of the 'process of *Aneignung*, the imaginative appropriation of the world and the nature of one's own existence in it' (Weimann 1977, p. 9). Whilst—for ideological reasons—the West German critic emphasizes the individual and the East German one the social, they both see literary history as the history of *Aneignung*, appropriation, 'making things one's own'. Weimann's 'socialized' model is, however, the

---

[2] I say 'political and aesthetic ideologies' because throughout this book I wish to argue that whilst responses to Shakespeare are inevitably political they are not solely political. I use the word 'ideology' because it has a political charge, but would wish to retain the broader sense of the term as a 'body of implicitly held ideas' or a 'way of thinking'; *OED*'s new sense of the word, 'A systematic scheme of ideas, usually relating to politics or society' (1976 Supplement) catches precisely what I mean— much virtue in *usually*.

more useful in approaching readers such as Gillray and Hazlitt who, in making Shakespeare their own, also make him their society's.

Weimann's best-known work is concerned with how Shakespeare's plays are produced out of a social mode, 'the Popular Tradition in the Theatre' (Weimann 1978). My concern here is with reception rather than production, with the appropriation of Shakespeare rather than Shakespeare's appropriations, because by moving from the writing of the plays to the reading of them at a particular historical moment we may see especially clearly how art 'is both a force in history and a source of value that can survive the changing conditions it originally reflected' (Weimann 1977, p. 11). Much valuable work has been done in recent years on Shakespeare's writing of history and his place in the history of his own times; this book turns attention to the reading and performing of Shakespeare in history, to his place in the history of a later time. The variety of responses to the plays in the late eighteenth and early nineteenth centuries forces one to ask whether any interpretation or ideology can claim exclusive 'right' or 'truth' to 'Shakespeare'. The history of appropriation may suggest that 'Shakespeare' is not a man who lived from 1564 to 1616 but a body of work that is refashioned by each subsequent age in the image of itself.

Weimann uses the term 'appropriation' in a broadly Marxian sense, but in the early nineteenth century the word could apply to any application of a literary text to a particular referent outside that text, as when Emma Woodhouse speaks of the application of Mr Elton's charade to Harriet Smith: 'But take [the couplet] away, and all *appropriation* ceases'.[3] Shakespeare was appropriated in the nuanced world of Jane Austen as well as in the cut and thrust of political debate: in the same chapter of *Emma* there is a discussion about the validity of a line in *A Midsummer Night's Dream* when applied to Harriet's experience of love. Emma believes that the course of Harriet's love is running smoothly and that Shakespeare's famous line is therefore wrong—'a Hartfield edition of Shakespeare would have a long note on that passage'—but of course neither Harriet's love nor her own *does* run smoothly, so Shakespeare is right, as usual, and Emma wrong, as usual.

Whilst there are, then, kinds of appropriation that should not be read solely in terms of dialectical materialism, Marxist aesthetics have made a major contribution to the study of cultural history. A key

---

[3] *Emma* (1815), vol. i, ch. 9, Jane Austen's italics.

figure in this respect is Walter Benjamin. The essay 'Eduard Fuchs, Collector and Historian', first published in the journal *Zeitschrift für Sozialforschung* in October 1937, crystallizes many of the ideas of this most suggestive and undogmatic of Marxist thinkers. Eduard Fuchs was a leading figure in the German Social Democratic movement and, like Benjamin, became an exile in Paris when Hitler rose to power. He was also an art historian, and it was his concern with the relationship between politics and the practice of cultural history that attracted Benjamin.

The essay on Fuchs begins with Engels's formulation of Marxism's fundamental objection to treating art, or any other sphere of thought, in isolation from its effect on people and the economic processes of its production. It is in this context that Benjamin first makes his much-quoted assertion that art 'owes its existence not just to the efforts of the great geniuses who fashioned it, but also in greater or lesser degree to the anonymous drudgery of their contemporaries. There is no cultural document that is not at the same time a record of barbarism' (Benjamin 1979, p. 359). One consequence of this critique is that the work of art is wrested from its creator; emphasis is switched from its creation and internal organization to its effect, from functioning to function. Works of art, Benjamin contends, 'incorporate both their pre-history and their after-history—an after-history in virtue of which their pre-history, too, can be seen to undergo constant change. . . . their function can outlast their creator, can leave his intentions behind' (Benjamin 1979, p. 351). Benjamin himself introduces Shakespeare as his exemplar here: 'This is what Goethe intimated to Chancellor von Müller in a conversation about Shakespeare: "Nothing that has had a great impact can really be judged any longer" ' (ibid.). Shakespeare cannot be approached directly; he has been modified by his own after-history. It is not entirely a joke when a character in David Lodge's novel *Small World* (1984) proposes to write a book about the influence of T. S. Eliot on Shakespeare.

For Benjamin, the reconstruction of a work of art's 'after-history' (*Nachgeschichte*) is not a disinterested activity. He believes in the necessity of the abandonment of the contemplative approach characteristic of traditional historicism: 'Historicism presents an eternal image of the past, historical materialism a specific and unique engagement with it' (Benjamin 1979, p. 352). In the last years of the eighteenth century, the researches of Edmond Malone, such as his 'Historical Account of the English Stage', were beginning to recover

Shakespeare's original cultural context. This historicism had its counterpart in John Philip Kemble's stage productions of the time, with their obsessive re-creation of 'authentic' period costume. Such approaches ran the risk of preserving Shakespeare in amber. More 'materialist' engagements were provided by the raids on Shakespeare in political satire and the radical refashioning of certain plays in the performances of Edmund Kean and the criticism of William Hazlitt. The best readings on both stage and page will always have, to use another phrase of Benjamin's, 'recourse to a consciousness of the present'.

Fuchs argued that the 'history of reception' was an area that had been ignored in art history: 'This omission is a failure in our overall appreciation of art. And yet it seems to me that uncovering the real reasons for the greater or lesser success of an artist, for the duration of his success, and no less so for the opposite, is one of the most important problems of art' (quoted, Benjamin 1979, p. 353). Shakespeare's survival and continuing influence may be put down to his exceptional capacity to be appropriated. That peculiar quality in his plays which Hazlitt denoted 'sympathy' and Keats 'negative capability' enables him to speak to every age and sect (in the West at least), whereas a writer like Milton speaks only to certain ages and sects. This relationship between endurance and the capacity to absorb new appropriations is central to the question 'What is a classic?': in Frank Kermode's words, 'A classic is required, in short, to be a piece of wisdom literature, but also to be a nature susceptible to an indefinite number of physics, some rational, some not' (Kermode 1971, p. 178).

Kermode has been much influenced by the Warburg approach to cultural history, which shares Fuchs's and Benjamin's interest in reception but not their belief that it is a political matter. My sense of 'appropriation' is close to Kermode's term 'accommodation', which he defines in *The Classic* as 'any method by which the old document may be induced to signify what it cannot be said to have expressly stated' (Kermode 1975, p. 40). I endorse Kermode's view that 'the books we call classics possess intrinsic qualities that endure, but possess also an openness to accommodation which keeps them alive under endlessly varying dispositions' (p. 44), but prefer the term 'appropriation' because it suggests greater activity on the part of the appropriator—appropriation may slide into misappropriation—and because it has stronger political overtones than 'accommodation'.

Fuchs's preoccupation with the politics of reception and the popularization of knowledge took him into the area of mass art or what we would now call popular culture: he devoted himself to a multi-volume history of caricature, an art-form that he took to be dependent on mass circulation and cheapness. His knowledge of the subject became prodigious: 'For the first volume of *Caricature of the European Peoples* alone he brought together no fewer than 68,000 items' (Benjamin 1979, p. 373). From the point of view of historical materialism, caricature is an especially attractive form because the mechanics of its printing, distribution, and pricing give it the potential to reach and politicize an unusually large audience. As Fuchs writes early in the first volume of his *Honoré Daumier* (Daumier, engaging as he did with the polarization of class in nineteenth-century France, was for Fuchs the pre-eminent caricaturist):

Every age has its own quite specific techniques of reproduction. They represent the technological potential of the period concerned and are . . . a response to the requirements of the time. It is therefore no cause for wonder that every major historical upheaval that brings other classes to power than those who have ruled hitherto, also regularly produces a change in the techniques of graphic reproduction. (cited, Benjamin 1979, p. 384)

Thus the development in eighteenth-century England of a recogniz-ably 'modern' political system was accompanied by the growth of caricature as an influential medium in the shaping of public opinion, and in particular as a manifestation of the (comparative) freedom of the Press and the opposition's right to criticize governments and ministers. And caricature developed at this time because of the change in technique from expensive and time-consuming copperplate engraving to forms of etching which were quicker and cheaper, making for wider and more immediate distribution.

For Benjamin, Fuchs was a pioneer in the analysis not only of reception and of the technology of reproduction, but also of icono-graphy. Caricature relies on a variety of iconographic codes; allusion is one of them, and in English caricature Shakespearean allusion is especially central precisely because Shakespeare is iconic, is, as Jane Austen's Henry Crawford remarks, 'part of an Englishman's con-stitution. . . . His thoughts and beauties are so spread abroad that one touches them every where, one is intimate with him by instinct.'[4] The process and the consequences of Shakespeare's assumption of the status of England's patron Poet, even its patron Saint, are among my

---

[4] *Mansfield Park* (1814), vol. iii, ch. 3.

major themes—it is no coincidence that during the eighteenth century it was agreed that Shakespeare's birthday should be celebrated on St George's Day. Modern 'demythologizing' critics like to mock the tradition of Bardolatry and to dismiss it as jingoistic: Shakespeare is élitist, an instrument of the ideological State apparatus, the National Poet who must be usurped.[5] This critique of the 'fetishizing' of Shakespeare seems to me to be misguided because, as I shall show, there is a strand within Bardolatry which turns Shakespeare against the power of the State and repossesses him in the name of liberty.

Art, nevertheless, does tend to have a sympathy with power. It was Hazlitt who observed that a lion is more poetic than the herd it hunts, that poetry is 'a very anti-levelling principle'. His clear-sighted statement of this problem is one of the reasons why he is at the heart of my enterprise: this book moves from a general consideration of the appropriation of Shakespeare in caricature and other satirical forms to an attempt to make the case for Hazlitt as the exemplary English Shakespearean critic. That case rests on the claim that no other critic has been so attuned at one and the same time to the theatre, to the plays as literary objects, to Shakespeare's capacity to illuminate a later age, and to the difficulty of being liberal-minded in politics yet committed to the power of art. Hazlitt is exemplary in his ability to cut across boundaries, as C. L. R. James, one of our century's boundary-crossing writers, has seen:

Hazlitt was an intellectual to his fingertips, and a militant, an extreme democrat who suffered martyrdom for his opinions. Yet he is not a divided man, he has no acute consciousness either of class or of divided culture. He discusses with equal verve the virtues of a classical education and the ignorance of the learned. It is impossible to distinguish any change in his style whether he writes on William Cobbett, on his First Acquaintance with Poets, on John Cavanagh, the Fives Player, or on the Fight between Bill Neate and the Gas-man. . . . He takes his whole self wherever he goes; he is ready to go everywhere; every new experience renews and expands him. He writes as freely and as publicly of a most degrading love-affair as of Elizabethan literature. The possibility of such completeness of expression ended with him and has not yet returned. (James 1963, p. 158)

Hazlitt took his whole self wherever he went: to the annoyance of some of his contemporaries, this meant that he never left his politics behind. His criticism of Coleridge's *Biographia Literaria*, for example,

---

[5] Evans 1986 provides an especially virulent example of writing of this sort.

was aimed squarely at his old intellectual mentor's political apostasy. It was in the *Biographia* that the phrase 'practical criticism' was coined, and there is a sense in which Hazlitt's critique of Coleridge foreshadows the attack by politically minded critics of the 1980s on the practical criticism which treated literary texts as self-contained organisms, 'words on the page' in glorious isolation from any social or historical context. But Hazlitt was too catholic in his interests to go to the opposite extreme and imply that there is nothing but politics: today's more strident 'materialist' readers of Shakespeare would do well to remember the warning that 'he who pretends to fit words to things, will much oftener accommodate things to words, to answer a theory' (HW xii. 250). Hazlitt lived and wrote not only by his political principles, but also by a passionate belief in the value of reading and the theatre. So it is that, while this book is concerned with politics and with theory, it aims never to lose sight of art and of practice. I have tried to keep in mind both Benjamin's praise of Fuchs's work as 'the practical man's answer to the paradoxes of theory' (Benjamin 1979, p. 353) and Hazlitt's words about rigid political theoreticians in his essay 'On Egotism':

A man is a political economist. Good: but this is no reason he should think there is nothing else in the world, or that every thing else is good for nothing. Let us suppose that this is the most important subject, and that being his favourite study, he is the best judge of that point, still it is not the only one—why then treat every other question or pursuit with disdain as insignificant and mean, or endeavour to put others who have devoted their whole time to it out of conceit with that on which they depend for their amusement or (perhaps) subsistence? (HW xii. 159)

Whilst it is important to recognize that literary works are *productions* and to keep in mind the means of production, the labour that is necessary for literature to be disseminated, the weight of Benjamin's dictum that there is no cultural document which is not at the same time a record of barbarism, it is necessary also to acknowledge, as Hazlitt did, that there are other forms of barbarism: 'To stop at the *mechanical*, and refuse to proceed to the *fine arts*, or churlishly to reject all ornamental studies and elegant accomplishments as mean and trivial, because they only afford employment to the imagination, create food for thought, furnish the mind, sustain the soul in health and enjoyment, is a rude and barbarous theory' (HW xii. 162). That is why not all the constitutions of Shakespeare which I consider are political ones: I have tried to give some sense of the philosophy of sympathy and the sensitivity to form as well as the politics of liberty in Hazlitt's criticism, and the aesthetic as well as the economic issues at stake in Boydell's Gallery.

The one premiss shared by all the appropriators of Shakespeare whom I discuss, otherwise so different from one another, is that his plays matter, that they are to be valued—which is why they are worth appropriating. Hazlitt comes to the heart of the matter in some rousing words of gratitude to Shakespeare in 'The New School of Reform', the most devastating of his many attacks on Jeremy Bentham and the theorists of his day:

People would not trouble their heads about Shakespear, if he had given them no pleasure, or cry him up to the skies, if he had not first raised them there. The world are not grateful *for nothing*. Shakespear, it is true, had the misfortune to be born before our time, and is not one of 'those few and recent writers,' who monopolise all true greatness and wisdom (though not the reputation of it) to themselves. He need not, however, be treated with contumely on this account: the instance might be passed over as a solitary one. We shall have a thousand Political Economists, before we have another Shakespear. (HW xii. 187)

Part I

CARICATURE AND THE AGE

1

Caricature

The print-shops are actually so many galleries of painting. To
the number of privileges enjoyed by these islanders may be
added that of publishing caricatures, which ridicule the occur-
rences of the times.

The French compose songs; the Dutch, of a duller cast, strike
medals; but the English have chosen engravings as the most
proper vehicle for their satire.

(Archenholtz 1790, p. 96)

THUS Johann von Archenholtz, formerly a Captain in the Service
of the King of Prussia, recorded his impression that caricature was
the distinctively English mode of satire prevailing in the last years of
the eighteenth century. The period is now known as the golden age
of English caricature: unusually, this was a golden age that was
acknowledged at the time, not invented after it had passed.

There can be no surer sign that a form has come of age than that
someone should write its history. So it was that in 1813 one J. P.
Malcolm claimed that 'the Art of Caricaturing having reached a
degree of perfection which has rendered it one of the means for the
correction of vice and improper conduct, it became a fit subject for an
historical sketch of its progress' (Malcolm 1813, p. iii). Malcolm
shared von Archenholtz's sense that graphic satire was peculiarly
English, though his grounds for doing so were distinctly political and
patriotic; after all, as he was writing his *Historical Sketch of the Art of
Caricaturing*, England was at war with Napoleonic Europe. He asserted
that a history of caricature must necessarily be a history of English
caricature 'for the obvious reason, that in no other country has the art
met with equal encouragement, because no other portion of the globe
enjoys equal freedom' (p. iv). The Englishman argues (complacently)
that the very existence of caricatures which attack government and
ministers is proof of the superiority of the English mode of government. Significantly, whilst Malcolm approves of caricatures which
upbraid political hypocrisy and corruption, he has no time for criticism
of actual English political institutions: when he writes of caricature in

the 1790s, he singles out such engravings as James Sayers's *Loyalty
against Levelling* (1792, BMC 8138), with its resolute caption from the
end of *King John* '—nought can make us rue | If England to itself do
rest but true'.[1]

There were, then, ideological reasons for claiming that graphic
satire was a peculiarly English form, but there was little justification
for the claim—caricature played an important enough part in the
French Revolution for Jacques Marie Boyer-Brun to begin publishing an *Histoire des caricatures de la révolte des Français* as early as 1792.
The project was considered sufficiently inflammatory for the author
to have been guillotined while still working on volume three.[2]
Malcolm's historical sketch is less exceptionable as an account of the
evolution of English caricature. It argues that William Hogarth had
firmly established the engraver's art, then his successors turned it
from social to political ends. The 1770s are seen as the take-off point:
'The administration of Lord North gave fresh vigour to the Caricaturists; and the manner in which the different ruling parties appear to
have viewed their labours, encouraged them to proceed, till they
became a kind of allegorical history of public events, which is continued with unabated zeal to the present moment' (Malcolm 1813,
p. 102). Broadly speaking, modern scholarship has endorsed these
findings. In the early eighteenth century, English graphic satire was
still under a strong Dutch influence, and relied more on emblem than
physiognomic representation. The publication of Hogarth's *Harlot's
Progress* in 1731 is rightly seen as a landmark. Although Hogarth
himself gave the appearance of standing above the cut and thrust of
party politics, he was largely responsible for the advances in both the
technique and the status of graphic art which enabled it to play a
major role in the political dialogue of the time.

The subversive potential of satire during the years of Walpole's
supremacy was apparent to caricaturists from the success of Gay's
Beggar's Opera in the late 1720s and the government's action in
restricting new plays through the Licensing Act of 1737. A native
tradition of political satiric engraving thus evolved in the 1730s;
Herbert M. Atherton argues cogently that 'The development of the
political print was, in part, the result of the emergence of a con-

---

[1] A favourite quotation of Sayers's: he also etches it beneath the title of *Mr Burke's
Pair of Spectacles for Short Sighted Politicians* (BMC 7858), his allegorical representation of
the argument of *Reflections on the Revolution in France*.

[2] Mitchell 1978 provides a good introduction to caricature in Jacobin Paris.

stitutional Opposition, committed more to the task of persuasion than
to violence and conspiracy. The prints shared with Opposition
pamphlets a common stock of ideas, themes, and a mythology'
(Atherton 1974, p. vi).

I will be arguing that the leading opposition publication of the
Walpole years, the *Craftsman*, may have led graphic satirists to the use
of Shakespearean allusion, but it needs to be pointed out here that
caricature was not at this stage as influential as pamphleteering. I do
not think that caricature exercised an overriding pressure on public
opinion until the beginning of the reign of George III; the campaign
in the early 1760s against the influence of John Stuart, third Earl of
Bute, was the first in which caricature was in the vanguard, not least
because of the iconographic possibilities of Bute-Boot-Jackboot.
Thomas Wright, J. P. Malcolm's successor as historian of English
caricature, contended that 'With the overthrow of Bute's ministry,
we may consider the English school of caricature as completely
formed and fully established' (Wright 1865, p. 453). So it was that in
1765 a worried correspondent in the *Public Advertiser* blamed caricature
for the developing political consciousness of the metropolitan lower
orders: 'Prints are a universal Language, understood by Persons of
all Nations and Degrees. He that runs may read . . . Every Window
of every Printshop is in a Manner glazed, and the Shop itself papered
with Libels' (quoted, Langford 1986, p. 30). Tellingly, the campaign
against Bute was also the first in which Shakespearean allusion
became widespread.

The notion of prints as a universal language, appealing to all
nations and degrees, was widely shared. Another foreigner visiting
England, this time in 1802, said that a viewing of the new caricatures
in the print-shop windows was as essential a part of a man of fashion's
morning perambulation as a visit to Tattersall's; he also records that
one had to fight one's way through a crowd in order to catch a
glimpse of the window, and that every day whole bales of caricatures
were sent abroad.[3] This last fact would account for the description of
James Gillray in a German magazine of 1806 as 'the foremost living
artist in the whole of Europe'.[4] The same magazine had reported in
1798 that the 'whole of London' regarded Gillray with a mixture of
approval and fear, and in 1803 that he was to be found 'all over the

---

[3] C. A. G. Goede, *A Stranger in England*, quoted, Ashbee 1928, p. 47, and Hill
1965, p. 2.

[4] *London und Paris* 1806, 17: 7, quoted, Hill 1965, p. 2.

place, following the troubled élite like the ghost of Hamlet's father'.[5]
And although London dominated the print market, just as it dominated political life, engravings were not confined to fashionable
centres. Of Sayers's 'Carlo Khan' prints, Nathaniel Wraxall wrote,
'It is difficult to conceive the moral operation and wide diffusion of
these caricatures through every part of the country' (Wraxall 1884,
iii. 254); Gillray's works 'were bought up with unparalleled eager-
ness, and circulated not only throughout England, but all over
Europe' (Wright and Evans 1851, p. xi). 'All over Europe' is an
exaggeration: the fiercely anti-Gallic Gillray was inevitably far more
popular in Germany, especially after it fell under the yoke of
Napoleon, than he was in France.

Statistics as to the increase in the quantity of political engravings
published in the period support the impressionistic testimony of
contemporaries. In the 1760s about one print appeared per week, in
the 1770s 50 per cent more than this, in the 1780s to early 1800s an
average of four per week, in the Regency years and 1820s 20 per cent
more than this, and in the two years up to the Reform Bill seven to
ten per week (see Dickinson 1986, pp. 13–15). Furthermore, in each
year prior to 1788 more social caricatures were published than
political ones, whereas thereafter it was the other way round. Weekly
averages do not give a full sense of the influence of caricatures, since
there would often have been many quiet weeks when very few were
published, then a short period of intense political activity or crisis
when dozens appeared. It must also be borne in mind that these
figures are based on numbers of prints preserved in the British
Museum collection, which cannot be thought of as complete—in
particular, it underrepresents the work of the more radical engravers,
partly because their work was more likely to have been suppressed
and partly because the origins of the collection were genteel.

Despite the great increase in production revealed by these statistics,
numbers of copies remained limited, especially in comparison with
those of popular newspapers such as Cobbett's *Political Register*.
Although some crude prints sold for a halfpenny, the usual price was
sixpence for a black-and-white engraving, one shilling for a coloured
impression, and up to five shillings for the larger, finer pieces. Precise
circulation figures are hard to establish, but it seems that the average
print run was about five hundred; a peak was reached with George

[5] *London und Paris* 1798, 1: 196; 1803, 11: 158.

Cruikshank's *The Political House that Jack Built* (December 1819), of which over 100,000 copies were sold.[6] But caricatures were seen by many more people than those who could afford to buy them: the display in the window of Mrs Humphrey's print-shop attracted so many people that iron railings had to be erected in front of it. Gillray's *Very Slippy-Weather* of 1808 (BMC 11100) shows a bustling scene outside the shop, with fifteen of his own prints in the window. Richard Dagley's poem of 1821, *Takings*, suggests that there was still public interest in the print-shop windows at the end of the Regency period:

> They walked together, and in all the shops,
> The pictures noted, read th' appended rhyme,
> Made in their promenade repeated stops,
> To criticise, applaud, quiz, *taking time*.

> (Dagley 1821, p. 96)

The twofold response is worth remarking: first the pictures are noted, then the 'appended rhymes'—sometimes invented, sometimes consisting of adapted quotations—are read. A picture, especially a funny one, will always attract attention where a newspaper or broadsheet might not; often, in the caricature of the period, the design draws in the 'readers', who then attend to the text as they might otherwise not have done. One must posit a multiple audience for the caricatures in the print-shop windows, varying from those, including the illiterate, who simply enjoyed the grotesque physiognomy and the sometimes scatological postures, to those who appreciated every nuance of iconographic and verbal allusion.

The major shops were centres of high society. There was strict competition as proprietors boasted of their attractions: 'In Holland's Exhibition Rooms may be seen the largest collection in Europe of Caricatures Admittance one Shilling' (BMC 7678); 'S. W. Fores . . . who has just fitted up his Exhibition in an entire Novel Stile admittance one shilling. NB Folios lent out for the Evening' (BMC 8632). The lending system meant that engravings could be perused—be *read* —at leisure. But, according to *London und Paris* (1806, 17: 7), it was

---

[6] According to *London Journal*, 20 Nov. 1847, quoted Jerrold 1882, i. 90. *The Political House* went through 50 edns by the end of 1820; it may have been outsold by *The Man in the Moon* of Jan. 1820, which reached its 51st edn. by 1821. These are not, of course, individual prints, but pamphlets by William Hone, each with a series of cuts by Cruikshank. They sold for 1*s*.

neither Fores's nor Holland's but Hannah Humphrey's that was the print-shop where 'upper-class people with taste and knowledge' were to be found—presumably they would sit inside, while a less privileged audience looked at the window display. Mrs Humphrey was a considerable patron and an extremely influential figure: the Prince of Wales held an account with her and she received regular visits from figures such as Charles James Fox, especially after she entered into her liaison with Gillray. This suggests that the butts of Gillray's satires, such as Fox, viewed his attacks with considerable indulgence; according to one commentator, 'the King was frequently incensed, sometimes gratified, and generally inclined to be amused by the sallies of Gillray' (Grego 1873, p. 13). But the reaction was not invariably amusement: although prosecutions were almost unheard of, owing to the ridicule that would result from a court case, individual plates were sometimes suppressed, and, most remarkably, in 1820 George Cruikshank was paid £100 'in consideration of a pledge not to caricature His Majesty in any immoral situation'.[7]

Prints could damage political careers. According to Lord Eldon, 'Fox said, that *Sayers's caricatures* had done him more mischief than the debates in Parliament or the works of the press. . . . These and many others of these publications, had certainly a vast effect upon the public mind' (Twiss 1844, i. 162). Fox's remark cannot be taken at face value—it is, after all, a neat way of dismissing his parliamentary opponents as ineffective—but Eldon's perception of the political potential of caricature is what matters. Von Archenholtz was amazed at the high level of political consciousness in England; caricatures give a remarkable sense of rapid and incisive response to events both major and minor. It must, however, be pointed out that, for all its politically educative and hence subversive potential, English caricature of this period cannot be seen as a true 'mass' art.[8] Graphic satire often seemed to participate in a dialogue of the political *cognoscenti*, as is apparent from Fox's role as both object and consumer of caricatures. As for the wider audience, it consisted primarily of the metropolitan middle ranks, that broad band of consumers, many of them from a dissenting background, highly attuned to both cultural and

[7] Receipt in Royal Archives, Windsor Castle, dated 19 June 1820.

[8] This does not, as it might at first appear to, invalidate the argument of Eduard Fuchs which I cited in my prologue: from a Marxist point of view, caricature could be seen as a bourgeois form at the time of the bourgeois Revolution but a proletarian form a hundred years later as Fuchs participates in preparation for the proletarian revolution.

1. Peter Scheemakers, statue of Shakespeare in Westminster Abbey (1741)

2. Thomas Gainsborough, Garrick leaning on Shakespeare (1769)

GVLIELMO SHAKSPEARE
ANNO POST MORTEM CXXIV
AMOR PVBLICVS POSVIT

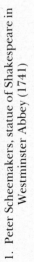

WILLIAM SHAKESPEARE 1564 - 1616
BURIED AT STRATFORD - ON - AVON

3. W. H. Watts, Kean as Shylock (1814)

4. Anonymous caricature of Mrs Siddons (1790)

political events, who were so crucial to the debates of the 1790s. Both government and radicals fought for the souls of this audience, enlisting caricaturists in the battle, in the knowledge that these were the potential English Jacobins.

It was common practice in eighteenth-century caricature to include satirical verses beneath an engraving, most frequently in couplets. As the century unfolded, captions came to rely increasingly on quotation and adaptation instead of invention. By the 1780s the use of allusion to provide points of reference that either reinforced or ironically undercut the thrust of a caricature had become a favourite, and often very sophisticated, device. What seems to have happened is that first the great satirical works of the century—above all, *The Dunciad*, *The Beggar's Opera*, and *Gulliver's Travels*—were appropriated, and then the repertoire was extended to other works. The literary sources used reflect some of the reading habits of the period: Shakespeare was far and away the most quoted, but Milton, Bunyan, and *Tristram Shandy* were also especially popular; there was also a strong current of biblical allusion, but, as will be seen in the case of William Hone, this was something that had to be handled with caution.

There was also a development, analogous to that within the poetry of the time, from classical allusion in the early part of the century to allusion to the English classics in the later part. Indeed, the earliest Shakespearean allusions in political caricature had a distinctly classical flavour in that they came from *Julius Caesar*.[9] Shakespearean quotations were thus given an elevated status, yet on other occasions they appeared beside popular songs: certain speeches had a dual identity as both 'classical' texts and widely known saws which had entered the popular consciousness and, for many, were not 'literature' in an élitist sense. The shift from the ancients to Shakespeare was symptomatic of both the forging of a distinctively national culture and the broadening of the appeal of caricature: one did not have to be a 'gentleman' to appreciate an allusion to, say, Falstaff.

The plays were frequently appropriated for political purposes. The young Henry Brougham advised that 'different people should at their spare hours be reading Shakespeare and Swift with a view to selecting passages suitable to the time, as descriptions of base courtiers, particular characters of bad ministers, hits at bishops (if safe) etc.' (quoted, Wardroper 1973, p. 187). A fascinating insight into the way

---

[9] See my discussion in Ch. 3 below, of BMC 2454 and 2458.

that Shakespearean quotation could be used is provided by a letter of December 1797 sent to Gillray by Revd John Sneyd, an amateur caricaturist who had links with the Canning circle and gave Gillray a number of ideas:

Though I have not the power of describing it by drawing, I think in your hands a good thing might be made by putting Hamlet's exclamation (with a little variation) in the mouth of John Bull (or Britannia) on their perceiving Bonaparte at Dover (or the Royal Exchange) when he (or she) least expected him. ('Doctors and Ministers of Disgrace defend me.') (quoted, Bagot 1909, i. 139)

The end product of Sneyd's advice was Gillray's *Physical Aid* (BMC 9972): he chose to put the words into the mouth of Britannia; the 'Ministers of [dis]grace' defending her are Addington, Hawkesbury, and Sheridan.

Perhaps the best summary of the characteristics of Gillray and his peers is that of the Goncourt brothers; they point not only to what they took to be the essential Englishness of the art, with its outlandishness, wit, and penetration, but also to its Shakespearean character: 'caricature is the English art, an inimitable, impulsive, unique art, which has the fantastic imagination, the strangeness, the unruliness, the philosophy, the laughter, the eloquence, the bantering majesty of Shakespeare'.[10] Caricature is thus invested with precisely the qualities which made Shakespeare so central to that taste for the irregular, the imaginative, and the profuse which became so characteristic in the second half of the eighteenth century. Shakespeare and caricature were twin weapons in the hands of English readers and critics waging chauvinistic battle against the neoclassicism associated with Voltaire and the French. That kind of imaginary inventiveness which the Goncourts termed 'la fantaisie' was especially popular in this respect: as will be shown, the Shakespearean supernatural became a frequent reference point in caricature.

The association between Shakespeare and graphic satire may have had its origin in the achievement of Hogarth, who, although he did not like to think of himself as a mere caricaturist, had raised the status of satirical engraving from ephemera to art. By the turn of the century, his art was being treated very seriously: in Germany, Lichtenberg's commentaries were published; in England, Lamb spoke of *reading*

---

[10] Goncourt 1854, p. 279, my translation. I am grateful to Mr Timothy Clayton for this reference and for a number of others.

him, and Hazlitt found it natural to list 'Hogarth's prints' beside the names of the great English writers among the topics of conversation at Lamb's famous literary evening parties.[11] The Shakespearean link becomes apparent when it is recalled that Lichtenberg's other English obsession was Garrick's performance of the plays, and that Lamb's remark was inspired by a gentleman being asked which books in his library he most esteemed and replying, first Shakespeare, then Hogarth. Neither Lamb nor Hazlitt doubted that Shakespeare and Hogarth were the two great English comic geniuses. Any caricaturist who could prove himself a worthy descendant of Hogarth would be guaranteed not merely a large public, but also readers willing to attend to the literary nuances of his work—especially if his range of allusions showed that he was himself, as *London und Paris* (1798, 1: 196) took Gillray to be, 'an extremely literate man who read a lot'.

Another reason for Shakespeare's prominence in caricature was that certain cultural activities in the period kept him in the public eye. The plays were not merely a resource in political caricature: their contemporary life was also a subject in social satire. Once one has a sense of this cultural presence, as manifested in the Garrick Jubilee, the Boydell Gallery, and the Ireland forgeries, it is easy to see how Shakespeare was carried over into politics. My discussion of particular engravings will accordingly begin with overtly Shakespearean matters.[12] This will also show how important the theatre and its actors were in constituting the age's Shakespeare.

---

[11] Lichtenberg's 'Ausfürliche Erklärung der Hogarthischen Kupferstiche' first appeared in the *Göttingen Taschenkalender*, from 1784 to 1796, and were published separately, enlarged and revised, between 1794 and 1799. For Lamb's and Hazlitt's remarks, see 'On the Genius and Character of Hogarth' (Lamb 1912, i. 82) and 'On the Conversation of Authors' (HW xii. 36). Lamb's essay includes an extended comparison between Shakespeare and Hogarth as tragi-comic artists.

[12] I follow BMC in using the word 'engraving' to cover line-engraving, etching, and stipple-engraving; although etching came to predominate over line-engraving, many prints of the period used a combination of techniques.

2

Shakespeare

IF it is granted that English caricature came of age some time between the accession of King George III and the administration of Lord North, then it is a contemporary of English Bardolatry, for it was at Stratford-upon-Avon in 1769 that the deification of Shakespeare took place.[1] But since a god is made not born, the idolatry of Shakespeare has a long history prior to David Garrick's (in)famous Jubilee. Ben Jonson honoured Shakespeare's memory 'on this side Idolatry'; many men and women fostered his reputation before Garrick finally took it over on to the other side of Idolatry. A history of Shakespeare's apotheosis might begin in the late seventeenth century with the vocabulary of Dryden's immensely authoritative criticism—'our *reverence* for Shakespeare', 'the *venerable* shade of Shakespeare', Thomas Rymer's '*blaspheming* Shakespeare'[2]—but it would have to attend particularly to the burgeoning of editions and stagings in the first forty years of the eighteenth century.

Until 1709, when Jacob Tonson published Nicholas Rowe's six-volume octavo edition, the complete works of Shakespeare could only be read in the bulky, scarce, and expensive Folios of the previous century. Historians of Shakespeare's text tend to follow the example of Dr Johnson's 1765 preface and concern themselves with questions of accuracy, of the movement towards a 'better' text. Standard accounts work through the succession of editors that runs Rowe–Pope–Theobald–Warburton–Johnson–Capell–Steevens–Malone. But, by emphasizing the *quality* of texts, textual historians lose sight of the *quantity* of texts. There is, to my knowledge, no study of how many and what kind of people bought and read editions of Shakespeare in the eighteenth century. From the point of view of Shakespeare's reputation, the landmarks are not so much the expensive new editions

---

[1] Though the word 'Bardolatry' was only coined when George Bernard Shaw took exception to the practice. The first recorded use of 'Bardolatry' is in the preface to *Plays for Puritans* (1901), of 'Bardolater' in the dedicatory epistle to *Man and Superman* (1903). The words 'Shakspearolatry' and 'Shakespearolater' date from the 1860s.

[2] Dryden 1962, i. 239, ii. 160, ii. 178, my italics.

as the cheaper reprints. Pope's six-volume quarto edition (1723–5), of which 750 sets were printed at a price of six guineas, did not make much impression outside aristocratic circles. Pope's text only reached a wide public with an edition produced a decade later for theatrical and provincial consumption. It is the now neglected 'stage editions' that were really important for Shakespeare's dissemination in the culture.

Rowe's 1709 edition will always occupy a special place in the Shakespearean pantheon, since it was the first text to derive from the collation of editions and the first to include illustrations and a biography of the dramatist. But an equally exalted position should be given to Tonson's duodecimo reprint of Rowe, published in 1714. It was with this edition that Shakespeare first gained a wide reading public; Tonson's motive for reprinting was the desire to sell the works 'in a more convenient and less expensive form to a play-going and reading clientele' (Ford 1935, p. 3). The 1714 edition is now scarce precisely because it was popular; copies would have been bought to be read, not to be preserved: 'in the large mansions in town and country the 1709 edition reposed in state in the library, but often the owners of these were again customers for the smaller and cheaper edition, either for their own use or for the amusement of the then large household staff attached to their residences: some copies do turn up marked specifically for "The Housekeeper's Room" ' (Ford 1935, pp. 3–4). One suspects that the purpose of such purchases was edification as much as 'amusement'. The 1714 edition was sold at the theatres and distributed to pedlars or 'running booksellers' for sale in rural districts; furthermore, individual plays were sold separately, so the popular ones could be obtained extremely cheaply. Like modern paperbacks, they would be read until they fell to pieces.

So too with the Pope edition: in 1734–6 Tonson junior produced the plays separately for sale at the theatres and to pedlars. That demand was increasing by this time is demonstrable from the fierce battle that took place between the Tonson empire and the rival publishing house of Robert Walker. Like modern newspaper proprietors undercutting each other, Tonson began selling plays at a shilling each, Walker sold his editions at fourpence each, Tonson brought his down to threepence. Eventually the reading public could obtain a Shakespeare play for a penny. The two publishers vigorously attacked each other's products on grounds of quality: in Walker's *Two Gentlemen of Verona* (1735) we are told that 'each volume of Tonson's may be

called a gallimaufray of scraps and nonsense'. Tonson's volumes
came with an advertisement that mixed incentive and invective; it
gives a fine sense of how hot a property Shakespeare was in the
mid-1730s:

Advertisement.—J. Tonson and the other Proprietors of the Copies of
Shakespear's Plays, designing to finish their Edition now publishing, with all
speed, give notice, That with the last Play they will deliver Gratis general
Titles to each volume of the whole Work, so that each Play may be bound in
its proper Place: and also do give further Notice, That any play of Shake-
spear's that now is, or hereafter shall be out of Print, will be reprinted without
Delay; so that all Gentlemen who have bought these Plays shall not be dis-
appointed, but may depend on having their Sets compleated.
    N.B. Whereas one R. Walker has proposed to pirate all Shakespear's
Plays, but thro' Ignorance of what Plays are Shakespear's, did in several
Advertisements propose to print Oedipus King of Thebes, as one of
Shakespear's Plays; and has since printed Tate's King Lear instead of
Shakespear's, and in that and Hamlet has omitted almost one half of the
genuine Editions printed by J. Tonson and Proprietors: the World will therefore judge how likely they are to have a compleat Collection of Shakespear's
plays from the said R. Walker. (quoted, Ford 1935, p. 44)

The jibe at Walker for printing Tate's *King Lear* instead of Shakespeare's is especially interesting in view of the fact that these editions
were to be sold at the theatres: Tonson clearly expects the discerning
gentleman to want to *see* Tate's version but *read* Shakespeare's. The
massive discrepancy between the text as spoken on the stage and as
sold in the foyer is testimony to the extraordinary multiplicity of
Shakespeare's identities in the eighteenth century.

It should, however, be noted that Tate's *Lear* and such acting
versions as Davenant's quasi-operatic *Macbeth* were to some extent
exceptional. The prevalence of Shakespearean adaptation can easily
be exaggerated: three of the four plays most frequently performed in
the first half of the century (*Hamlet, Othello*, and *1 Henry IV*) were
given in versions that, whilst marked by some cutting and local verbal
alteration, were close to their originals. So it is that the many versions
of *Hamlet As It Is Now Acted* which were popular from the time of
Betterton onwards (new texts of this sort appeared, mainly for sale at
the theatres, in 1676, 1683, 1695, 1703, 1718, 1723, and subsequently)
were somewhat abbreviated but by no means mangled. There may be
a correlation between the lack of textual interference and the massive

popularity of Hamlet and Falstaff—to butcher their parts would have been beyond the pale.

The competition between Tonson and Walker is not the only sign that the mid-1730s marked a turning-point in the history of Shakespeare's popularity: the development of the repertory in the theatre tells the same story.[3] Indeed, the increasing centrality of the plays to the repertory provides the strongest evidence of their rise in cultural status. In the first decade of the century Shakespeare's plays constituted about 11 per cent of the total number of performances in the London patent theatres; in the second decade this rose to about 14 per cent, but in the third, mainly owing to the popularity of new plays such as Gay's *Beggar's Opera*, Vanbrugh and Cibber's *The Provoked Husband*, and Lillo's *The London Merchant*, the percentage dropped back to about 12. It then doubled in the 1730s, so that when Garrick made his London debut in 1741, one in four London performances were of Shakespeare.[4]

The sharp increase in the mid-1730s was due to a combination of circumstances, the most interesting of which was the establishment in 1736 of a 'Shakespeare Ladies Club', formed with the specific aim of persuading the theatre managers to put on more Shakespeare. There is considerable evidence for the existence of the Club (see Avery 1956): in January 1737 playbills for Shakespearean revivals began to be headed 'At the Desire of several Ladies of Quality'; newspapers and magazines began complimenting the ladies on their contribution to the improvement of taste (on 4 March 1737 the *Daily Advertiser* published a letter signed 'WILLIAM SHAKESPEAR, from Elisium, to

---

[3] I am conscious that in what follows I refer exclusively to London. Very little work has been done on Shakespeare in the eighteenth-century regional theatre (though Rosenfeld 1939 testifies to his predominance in the repertory), and to have undertaken research of this sort would have been beyond the scope of the present study. We all assume that eighteenth-century cultural life was synonymous with London; Johnson and Garrick walking together to the metropolis is an iconic image of the age—and an especially relevant one for Shakespeare, in that only by going to London can the century's great critic-editor and its great actor-Bardolater prosecute their ambitions. Everything seems weighted towards London: politics, publishing, galleries, the productions of engravers from Hogarth to Gillray, actors from Garrick to Kean, writers from Johnson to Hazlitt. Cultivated assumptions, such as a facility in the recognition of Shakespearean allusion, are London assumptions. A detailed study of 'Shakespeare in the provinces' might change all this. It is certainly the case that regional Shakespeare was not confined to fashionable centres such as Bath: in 1793 the Mayor of Derry asked for a performance of *Lear* on behalf of the city poor (*Londonderry Journal*, 5 Feb. 1793; see further, Clark 1965).

[4] The above figures are based on Scouten 1945 and 1956, and the relevant vols. of the *London Stage*.

the Fair Supporters of Wit and Sense, the Ladies of Great Britain',
thanking them for their work on his behalf); and prologues to revivals
were ecstatic in their praise. That the Ladies persuaded John Rich,
manager of Covent Garden and most celebrated pantomimist of the
age, to forsake Harlequin for Shakespeare was a mark of their success
—the letter from the grave in the *Daily Advertiser* said that their
example had 'prevail'd upon the Town to neglect and despise Harlequin and his Harlot Columbine, for Shakespear and his lawful
Spouse Common Sense'. The vogue for Shakespeare is apparent
from the fact that plays hitherto unacted in the century were revived.
In 1738 Lillo's adaptation of *Pericles*, entitled *Marina*, extolled the
virtues of the Shakespeare Ladies in its epilogue (while at the same
time casting a derogatory eye over pantomimes and Italian opera):

> But, Sirs, what e'er's your fate in future story,
> Well have the British Fair secured their glory,
> When worse than barbarism had sunk your taste,
> When nothing pleas'd but what laid virtue waste,
> A sacred band, determin'd, wise, and good,
> They jointly rose to stop th' exotick flood,
> And strove to wake, by *Shakespear*'s nervous lays,
> The manly genius of *Eliza*'s days.

> (Lillo 1738, p. 60)

But who were this 'sacred band'? Vivid testimony to the erasure of
women—even aristocratic ones—from the historical record is provided
by a defeated footnote of the scholar who collected the evidence for
the existence of the Club: 'An extensive search of poems, essays,
newspapers, periodicals, correspondence, and diaries for the years
from 1736 through 1739 has failed to yield the names of any of the
women who organized or who belonged to the Shakespeare Ladies
Club' (Avery 1956, p. 153 n.).

Once the fashionable female theatre-goers had forced more Shakespeare on to the stage, other developments conspired to keep him
there. The Licensing Act of 1737 restricted new plays and led the
managers to rely still more on trusted favourites. Then in 1740–1 a
complicated set of rivalries brought several comedies back into the
repertory. Henry Giffard reopened his theatre at Goodman's Fields
in defiance of the Licensing Act, so in order to entice audiences back
to Covent Garden John Rich showed off the figure of his beautiful
new leading lady, Margaret Woffington, in male costume in such

roles as Sir Harry Wildair in Farquhar's *The Constant Couple*; Drury Lane then sought to cash in on the vogue for actresses in 'breeches' parts, and revived *As You Like It* for the first time since the Restoration, with Mrs Pritchard as Rosalind; a revival of *Twelfth Night* followed, and for a time two of the three theatres often produced Shakespearean plays on the same night. 1741 also saw the advent of Charles Macklin in his ground-breaking performance as a 'natural', as opposed to a burlesque, Shylock. One begins to see that David Garrick, usually seen as the pivotal figure in the history of Bardolatry, came to London at a propitious moment.

Garrick burst on to the scene in October 1741 with his Richard III, but he had in fact made a brief anonymous appearance on the London stage that spring. There is an association here with an object that Garrick was subsequently to appropriate: the statue of Shakespeare in Westminster Abbey. There had been agitation for recognition of Shakespeare in the national shrine as far back as the mid-1720s; a benefit performance of *Julius Caesar* in 1738 raised much of the necessary capital (the Shakespeare Ladies may have been behind this); William Kent was commissioned to design the statue and Peter Scheemakers to sculpt it; and in January 1741 it was dedicated in the Abbey. It is a competent rather than an outstanding piece of work (pl. 1), but it effectively marks the canonization of Shakespeare. Garrick would preside over the translation from canonization to apotheosis, so it is fitting that he made his début under the shadow of the statue: one of the most successful new shows of the year was *Harlequin Student; or, The Fall of Pantomime*, performed at Goodman's Fields, which ended with the expulsion of pantomime and a representation on stage of the new Westminster Abbey monument, and it was in this burletta that Garrick stood in for one night when Richard Yates, the Harlequin, was taken ill ('Yates last Season was taken very ill and was not able to begin the Entertainment so I put on the Dress and did 2 or three Scenes for him, but Nobody knew it but him and Giffard', Garrick 1963, i. 34).

There is a further connection. *Harlequin Student* was not the only example of the somewhat oxymoronic genre of burletta attacking burletta. The most celebrated was Garrick's own *Harlequin's Invasion*, his only pantomime, which was loosely based on the 1741 Goodman's Fields extravaganza. It also ended with Harlequin being beaten off, and here Garrick took the opportunity to include a procession of Shakespearean characters of the sort that would be planned as the

centre-piece of his Jubilee. What is significant about this pantomime
is its date, 1759: it was performed at the height of the Seven Years
War, so Shakespeare was made to stand for England and its values,
the invasion for the French. The high point of the show was a patriotic
sea song with words by Garrick and music by William Boyce—'Heart
of Oak'. This was one of the first instances of what would become a
recurring tactic: the patriotic appropriation of Shakespeare in time
of war.

By about 1760, then, a complex set of forces had combined to give
Shakespeare an extraordinary pre-eminence. He had penetrated
Westminster Abbey, the most potent symbol of the established
Church; he had furnished the literary establishment with a model of
distinctively English (un-French, un-neoclassical) genius; he was
coming to serve as a cultural icon for the expanding section of the
population, of both sexes, who were newly literate but not schooled in
the classics. And, more tangibly, certain of his plays were becoming
texts for the articulation of patriotic identity at key moments in the
life of the nation: thus *Henry VIII* was given pride of place at coronation time in 1761, and *Henry V* performed every season during the
Seven Years War, its playbills usually including the pointed subtitle
'with the Conquest of the French at Agincourt'.[5] Garrick's entrepreneurial skills did not exist within a vacuum: the climate was right
for his Bardolatrous projects.

As the eighteenth century progressed, caricaturists more and more
frequently viewed politics as theatre, producing engravings on such
subjects as *Europe in Masquerade or the Royal Farce* (May 1747, BMC
2858) and *The Present State of Europe; A Political Farce, of Four Acts. as it is
now in Rehearsal* (1761, BMC 3820). Hogarth's celebrated *Southwark
Fair* (1733), with its panoply of popular dramatic entertainments, was
seminal here, but it was also the case that caricaturists came to treat
politics as theatre because the theatre itself was a constant point of
reference in their work. The association derived both from the fact
that the audience at whom caricatures were aimed overlapped with
the theatre-going public and from the analogy between the posturing
art of the caricaturist and that of the actor. So it is that a concern with
the politics of theatre—the choice of plays, the promotion of new
actors, and so on—is apparent in engravings throughout the century.

As early as 1724 Hogarth showed the works of 'Shakspere' being

---

[5] The performance of 5 Nov. 1757 was by Royal Command. After the war, the play
dropped out of the repertory for over two years. See the *London Stage*.

wheeled off in a barrow as 'Waste paper for Shops' while *Masquerades and Operas* hold the stage (BMC 1742). This initiated a genre: *The Stage Medley* of April 1728 included a large pair of scales in which 'The *Beggers Opera*, weighs Shakespear down' (BMC 1806), and *Punch Kicking Apollo* had a figure of Shakespeare consigned to the background (BMC 1832). John Rich was a frequent butt of satire; there are many prints with captions like 'Lo! *Shakespear's* Head is crush'd by *R—h's* Heels' (BMC 1834). If it was not Rich's pantomimes, it was the vogue for opera—'And Shakespear to the Itallian Eunuchs Yield' (BMC 2148). Despite Rich's reverses at the hands of the 'ladies of quality' and Garrick's successes in bringing Shakespeare to the centre of the repertoire, 'low' theatrical entertainment was still perceived as a threat in the 1770s (BMC 5063–4) and again in the early nineteenth century: *The Monster Melo-drama* (December 1807, BMC 10796) has a four-headed monster resting its hind foot on 'Shakespear's Works'; Samuel De Wilde's *Feast of the Board of Management* (February 1809, BMC 11438) shows mice or rats nibbling at 'Jonson, Shakesp, Beaumont and Fletch', books that have been cast under a table. Perhaps the two finest examples of this genre are George Cruikshank's *The Rehearsal or the Baron and the Elephant* (January 1812, BMC 11935), where an elephant crushes a bust of Shakespeare, and *Spirits of the British Drama* (BMC 13042), which has the ghosts of Shakespeare and another dramatist fleeing from the stage, crying 'Murder—Murder'. Both are attacks on the vogue for performing animals: a scroll hanging from Cruikshank's elephant is inscribed 'Royal Menagerie Covent Garden This Evening performd The Murder of Shakespeare a Tragedy with the Farce of Joh[n] Bull *in Extacy* Principal Performers Two Bears An Ass etc.' (note the attack here on the poor taste of John Bull, the archetypal boorish Englishman). In verbal as opposed to visual caricature, perhaps the most notable attack on the preference for pantomimes over Shakespeare was 'Punch's Apotheosis', the last of Horace and James Smith's celebrated *Rejected Addresses* of 1812, which begins with 'PUNCH *on a throne, surrounded by* LEAR, LADY MACBETH, MACBETH, OTHELLO, GEORGE BARNWELL, HAMLET, GHOST' and travesties Shakespearean tragic plots in order to suggest that they are being degraded by the modern age.

Caricaturists responded to Shakespeare being performed badly as well as in travesty or not at all. Especially provoking was the tendency of actors to arrogate to themselves a 'truth' to Shakespeare, or an intimate companionship with him, that others were supposed to lack. The supreme example of such arrogation was Garrick's Jubilee.[6] The Jubilee was a fiasco in itself, but it set the seal on a number of developments. After the Jubilee it was universally acknowledged that Shakespeare was at the very least *the* National Poet and for many people not merely a poet but a god; that Stratford-upon-Avon, little visited before 1769, was a shrine and a place of pilgrimage; and that, whether or not one approved of his activities, Garrick was Shakespeare's self-proclaimed representative on earth.

The creation of a special relationship between Garrick and Shakespeare is nowhere more apparent than in Gainsborough's portrait (pl. 2), which Garrick gave to the town of Stratford at the time of the Jubilee. In this image, iconography is deployed to create the desired 'meaning' that Garrick and Shakespeare are now synonymous: the actor reclines on a bust of Shakespeare in a posture that seems to be both proprietorial and fraternal; the impression that Garrick has become an incarnation of Shakespeare is achieved by the way that his legs are crossed exactly like those of the Bard on the Westminster Abbey monument (it is noteworthy that Shakespeare's iconographic power was such that the cross-legged posture of the Abbey monument was imitated in numerous portraits of the period).

Garrick, then, was a superb publicist on both his own behalf and Shakespeare's. The Jubilee marked the culmination of a series of inflationary public pronouncements. At the opening of the theatre in Drury Lane in 1747 he spoke Johnson's specially commissioned prologue, which emphasized the centrality of Shakespeare to the English theatrical tradition, and on the first night of the season of 1750 he declaimed his own prologue, which made Drury Lane into a temple dedicated to the Bard: 'Sacred to SHAKESPEARE was this spot design'd, | To pierce the heart, and humanize the mind' (Vickers 1974–81, iii. 365). In 1765, in a celebrated letter to the editor of the *Gazette Littéraire de l'Europe*, he made a stand for English values against Voltaire's strictures on the Bard's irregularity by calling Shakespeare 'the God of my Idolatry' (Garrick 1963, ii. 463). The phrase recurs, along with 'that demi-god', in the central text of the Jubilee, Garrick's 'An Ode upon Dedicating a Building and Erecting a Statue, to Shakespeare, at Stratford upon Avon' (Vickers 1974–81, v. 344).

---

[6] Of the many accounts of the Jubilee I am most indebted to Deelman 1964. Testimony to the endurance of Bardolatry is the fact that 3 different books on the Jubilee were published in the quatercentenary year of 1964.

When visiting Stratford to make preparations for the Jubilee, Garrick invoked the language of divine incarnation in order to encourage people to undertake the pilgrimage:

> The Gothic glories of the ancient Church, the modern elegance of the Civic Hall, cease to be regarded, when it is remembered that the humble shed, in which the immortal bard first drew that breath which gladdened all the isle, is still existing; and all who have a heart to feel, and a mind to admire the truth of nature and splendour of genius, will rush thither to behold it, as a pilgrim would to the shrine of some loved saint; will deem it holy ground, and dwell with sweet though pensive rapture, on the natal habitation of the poet. (quoted, Halliday 1957, pp. 67–8)

It is an important characteristic of Bardolatry that it should enact the perennial significance of Shakespeare by praising him in his own words. Thus, as 'the God of my Idolatry' is a quotation from *Romeo and Juliet* (II. ii. 114), so 'gladdened all the isle' is an echo of 'lighten all this isle' (*Henry VIII*, II. iii. 79) and 'natal habitation' of Theseus' famous 'local habitation' in *A Midsummer Night's Dream* (V. i. 17).

Garrick succeeded in making his Jubilee *the* talking-point in polite society in the summer of 1769. Whether one thought it was a proper tribute to the great dramatist—'The whole will conclude with the apotheosis of Shakespear,' as the *Gentleman's Magazine* laconically put it in its August issue—or a farrago designed entirely for the gratification and self-advancement of Garrick, one could not ignore it. The three-day jamboree in Stratford was widely reported, especially in the monthly magazines aimed at a 'gentle' audience, and London cultural life felt its repercussions for years to come. There were spin-off publications, such as books of jokes with titles like *Yorick's Jests* and *Shakespeare's Jests: or the Jubilee Jester*; a miniature pamphlet war was fought (*Garrick's Vagary: or, England Run Mad, An Essay on the Jubilee*; *Anti-Midas: A Jubilee Preservative from Unclassical, Ignorant, False and Invidious Criticism*; and so on); in 1770 *Harlequin's Jubilee*, a burletta by Henry Woodward, had 'Lun' (John Rich) getting his revenge and triumphing over Shakespeare's statue; and as late as 1785 in Cowper's *The Task*, that immensely popular repository of the taste of the age, there are the lines

> For Garrick was a worshipper himself;
> He drew the liturgy, and framed the rites
> And solemn ceremonial of the day,

> And call'd the world to worship on the banks
> Of Avon famed in song. Ah! pleasant proof
> That piety has still in human hearts
> Some place, a spark or two not yet extinct.   (vi. 678–84)

A more immediate, less flattering, and for a time most influential response to the Jubilee was a definition inserted into Samuel Foote's popular play at the Haymarket, *The Devil upon Two Sticks*:

A jubilee, as it has lately appeared, is a public invitation, urged by puffing, to go post without horses, to an obscure borough without representatives, governed by a mayor and aldermen who are no magistrates, to celebrate a great poet whose own works have made him immortal, by an ode without poetry, music without harmony, dinners without victuals, and lodgings without beds; a masquerade where half the people appeared bare-faced, a horse-race up to the knees in water, fireworks extinguished as soon as they were lighted, and a gingerbread amphitheatre, which like a house of cards, tumbled to pieces as soon as it was finished. (*Town and Country Magazine* 1769, 1: 477)

This extemporization was not included in the published text of Foote's play, but it was reported in a number of magazines. Indeed, it is from the magazines that one gets a sense of the impact the Jubilee made, the detail in which it was reported, and the debate it provoked.

The September number of a recently established monthly, the *Town and Country Magazine*, provides a good example. It included 'Particulars of the Jubilee at Stratford': an account of the succession of meals, orations, musical performances, dances, and other events (notably the firework display and the horse-race) that constituted the entertainment. Special emphasis is given to the 'persons of distinction' who were present. But the account ends in bathos:

The great rains, which several people considered as a judgment on the poetical idolatry of the jubilites, were a material prejudice to the entertainment; they prevented the theatrical procession, and also Mr Garrick from reciting his ode a second time. Besides this, they spoiled the fireworks, the masquerade, and the race, and occasioned the procession and crowning of Shakespeare to be omitted; but it is the opinion of many, especially the admirers of Mr Garrick, that they were more than overpaid for their fatigue, expence, and disappointment, by that gentleman's recital of the ode. (*Town and Country Magazine* 1769, 1: 475)

As far as the quality of the ode itself was concerned, readers were given the opportunity to judge of that themselves, for the poetry pages of the magazine were given over to it ('To what blest genius of the isle, | Shall Gratitude her tribute pay, | Decree the festive day, | Erect the statue, and devote the pile?') and the other airs and songs, nearly all by Garrick, that had been performed at Stratford. The latter included 'Shakespeare's Mulberry-Tree. Sung with a Cup in his Hand made of the Tree'—the Jubilee had been marked by brisk trade in holy relics—and 'Warwickshire', with its rousing chorus 'the lad of all lads was a Warwickshire lad', 'the bard of all bards was a Warwickshire bard', 'the Will of all Wills was Warwickshire Will', 'the wag of all wags was a Warwickshire wag'. But, on turning the page from the account of the masquerade, the reader of the *Town and Country* would have been faced by a cut of a singing man stuck in the top of a bottle on a tripod inscribed 'Stratford Jubilee' (BMC 4309). This is an allusion to a celebrated incident twenty years earlier when a man had claimed that he would get into a quart bottle at the Haymarket Theatre and there sing songs. A large crowd turned up and were disappointed. Garrick's spectacle is thus dismissed as a similar imposture. On the opposite page there is a letter, under the ominous running head 'The other Side of the Question', from a disgruntled 'Jubilite'[7] classing the whole event 'among the political and m——l humbugs of the present aera'. The correspondent claimed that every event had misfired, that the cancellation of the procession and crowning of Shakespeare had been an outrage, and that attendance had been a waste of £49. 2s. (itemized under expenditure for travel, tickets, board and lodging, and so on). The letter ends with the passage from *The Devil upon Two Sticks*.

What all this demonstrates is that the Jubilee had as much to do with the promotion of Garrick in polite society—the sums of money quoted show that attendance was confined to the well-to-do—as with the idolatry of Shakespeare. Barely a line of Shakespeare was spoken in the three days at Stratford. Paradoxically, however, the very deficiencies of the Jubilee and the attacks on Garrick for serving himself and not his master led to precisely the apotheosis of Shakespeare which was supposed to have, but conspicuously had not, taken place at Stratford. Shakespeare's pre-eminent status was the premiss of the entire debate: the accusation that Garrick had not done justice to the plays carried the implication that honouring Shakespeare was the actor's primary duty. The point is especially clear in a pair of

[7] Those who went to Stratford were frequently called 'Jubilites', an appellation coined especially for the occasion (not in *OED*).

caricatures in the *Oxford Magazine* entitled *The Procession at the Jubilee at Stratford upon Avon* (pl. 5, BMC 4311–12), a jibe at the procession which 'was obliged to be declined on account of the wetness of the weather': the effectiveness of the piece depends on the contrast between the bedraggled pantomime figures portrayed and the reader's ideal image of Shakespeare's characters. Typically, Shakespearean quotation is deployed for satiric purposes—Poor Tom is 'a Cold' because of the weather, Richard III cries out for a horse because he is having to go on foot, the 'Tyrant' about whom Caliban complains is by implication Garrick, and the ghost crying 'Revenge his foul and most unnatural Murder!' becomes a representative of Shakespeare himself, murdered by Garrick's folly.

So, despite the fact that the Jubilee was like *Hamlet* without the prince, it did more than anything else to give Shakespeare his cultural prominence in the period. There was further demand for cheap texts in the next few years, a demand met by Charles Jennens's issues of individual plays between 1770 and 1774, and Bell's much-used performance-based texts of 1773–4.[8] On stage, soon after the career of Garrick came to an end, those of Sarah Siddons and her brother John Philip Kemble began (Garrick's last performance was in 1776, Siddons's first in 1782, and Kemble's a year later). The appearance of engravings satirizing their idiosyncrasies provides further evidence that the question of who owned Shakespeare and how he was mediated to the public had become a matter of considerable concern.

Kemble's style was essentially statuesque, marked by firmness of posture and slowness of delivery. *How to Tear a Speech to Tatters*

---

[8] As far as issues of the complete works were concerned, a number appeared shortly before or simultaneously with the Jubilee. Numbers of issues of the complete works provide a good guide to Shakespeare's popularity among the reading classes. By my calculation, there were 5 in the 1730s, 7 in the 1740s, 6 in the 1750s, 15 in the 1760s, 10 in the 1770s, 6 in the 1780s, 23 in the 1790s, and 30 between 1800 and 1809. In 1811 alone, 9 different issues appeared in London. The early years of the nineteenth century saw no new recensions—Malone's Variorum was sufficient—but a wide choice of texts. In 1800, for example, Sharpe produced the first miniature (16mo) Shakespeare, and the plays penetrated to the furthest provinces with a nine-vol. edn. appearing in Berwick-on-Tweed. The variety of kinds of edn. give a sense of how, although there was little new editorial work being done by this time, publishers were exploring the possibilities of marketing Shakespeare in new forms; e.g., in 1807 a six-vol. Stockdale edn. with copperplates by J. Heath after designs by Stothard and Fuseli met the demand for illustrated texts, Francis Douce produced the first facsimile of the 1623 Folio (Keats and B. R. Haydon annotated their copies of this), and in Bath 'Victorian' Shakespeare reared his (clean-shaven) head with Henrietta Bowdler's first 'Family' text of 20 plays.

(December 1789, BMC 7590) shows him as a stiff Henry V, reciting 'From—this—day—to—the—end—ing—of—the—world— —Ti—tum—tum—ti—ti—tum—ti—'. A companion piece of the following year, *How to harrow up the Soul* (pl. 4, BMC 7716), gives similar treatment to Mrs Siddons, singling out her handling of the sleep-walking scene in *Macbeth*. This scene had been the subject of much controversy, since Siddons had broken with convention and changed the business. In Garrick's production Mrs Pritchard had carried a candle throughout the scene, so subsequent actresses were expected to do the same. Hearing a rumour that on her début Mrs Siddons was going to put the candle down, manager Sheridan hurried to her dressing-room shortly before the performance to try to dissuade her; angry at being disturbed, she refused and went her own way, thus freeing her hands to rub off the imagined spot of blood. Sheridan came to her afterwards and admitted it had been an effective coup (see Siddons 1834, ii. 37). One of the most admired touches introduced by her revision was an impassioned delivery of Lady Macbeth's cry, 'Oh—h—h!' Hazlitt wrote later that 'it was in bursts of indignation, or grief, in sudden exclamations, in apostrophes and inarticulate sounds, that she raised the soul of passion to its height, or sunk it in despair' (HW v. 198). One G. J. Bell, who wrote careful notes on his impressions of Siddons's performance, singled out the 'convulsive shudder' as she delivered 'O, O, O!' at the end of the line 'all the perfumes of Arabia will not sweeten this little hand' (quoted, Jenkin 1887, i. 66). The caricaturist was less impressed: in *How to harrow up the Soul* the exclamation seems to result from the tight fit of her bodice. Mrs Siddons's attempt to squeeze the maximum passion from the moment is dismissed as fakery.

In exercising their role as watch-dogs, guardians of the sacred Bard against the excesses of actors, caricaturists could, then, be sufficiently iconoclastic to take on even the incomparable Siddons, most admired actress of the age. Every age thinks that it has refined and naturalized acting technique, cast off the excesses of the previous age, but in every age the accusation of overacting recurs. The Cruikshanks' undated *The Effect of Over-Acting* carries an epigraph that neatly sums up the satirists' attitude to the practice: 'Oh, the offence is rank.'[9] *Hamlet* is the appropriate play to quote here in that the Prince's advice to the players is the most famous of all attacks on overacting.

[9] Not in BM; see Krumbhaar 1966, No. 306 and Cohn 1924, No. 1082.

Kemble seems to have been particularly susceptible to attack, probably because he was the kind of 'Establishment' figure—manager of first one, then the other, of the two major theatres, arbiter of taste, classicist in style—who was ripe for debunking. In the first decade of the new century more of his idiosyncrasies were parodied. Sayers's *Hamlet Act V Scene Ist* (BMC 10322) addresses itself to his obsession with 'authentic' costume: Gravedigger and Skull claim that Hamlet looks 'Like a Ninepin dress'd up in a Blanket & hat'; Kemble replies, 'Ye Num sculls be silent how dare ye presume To find fault with my Dress tis your Danish Costume'. Kemble's search for historical accuracy was a major influence on the productions of William Macready and Charles Kean a generation later. It went with a taste for elaborate stage machinery, which is satirized in another print by Sayers, *Macbeth Act VI* [*sic*] *Scene II* (BMC 10323). Shakespeare, strongly irradiated, stands on a cloud and points to a scroll on which is written 'Pray Sir dont boil my Spirits in this manner some of them are of ye Lobster kind & will boil red[.] the Cauldron is intended for the purpose of Incantation not as a Stew pot for Ghosts[.] Pray open your Trap doors and let them rise in a more natural Way.' The criterion of 'naturalness' begs a lot of questions: whether on the stage or in an engraving, especially in a self-consciously distorting form such as caricature, there can be no unmediated 'natural' style, for technique is always determined formally, generically, and by audience expectation. Caricature works with the unexamined premiss that there is a norm ('truth' to a 'natural' Shakespeare) from which the person or tendency under attack (Kemble, pantomimes, Jacobins) departs. Thus the 'true' Shakespeare, in the form either of a quotation or an irradiated figure who is ignored by the self-indulgent moderns who fill the print and the stage, is brought on to chide those satirized.

This technique offers a particularly strong instance of Shakespeare's status as an object of appropriation. The irradiated Bard admonishing the contemporary misappropriator has an oddly ambivalent status as both icon and cipher. He is introduced as a figure of authority, but he may be made to authorize almost anything. Ironically, the fact that the figure of the 'true' Shakespeare is used to support and to attack so many different positions in so many different campaigns throws into question whether there really is a 'true' Shakespeare. Each time he is cited as a figure of authority, he takes on more of a force in the culture at large. And with each appropriation it becomes more difficult to occlude the 'afterlife' and recover the 'original'. The 'truth' of Shakespeare thus comes to reside in the very multiplicity of his manifestations.

Impatience with Kemble in the early years of the nineteenth century was also due to the fact that, together with his sister, he had dominated the London stage for many years. The public were ready for a new star. They were given one with the advent in 1804 of the child prodigy 'Master Betty', otherwise known as 'the Young Roscius'. In a development altogether characteristic of the form, caricature first helped to engineer this need for a new departure by drawing attention to the deficiencies of the established norm, then the moment it happened set out to debunk it as a mere nine days' wonder. *The Extinguisher* (BMC 10457) by Charles Williams, a follower of Gillray who became Fores's leading caricaturist, shows the Young Roscius as a comet blazing across the sky, extinguishing Kemble and other leading actors; but the inscription undercuts him by juxtaposing two lines from *Hamlet*:

> POLONIUS. When Roscius was an Actor at Rome.
> HAMLET. Buzz! Buzz! Buzz!——

What is really one of Hamlet's lines is given to Polonius, with the implication that the admirers of the Young Roscius have the theatrical judgement of Polonius; the reply invites the reader to join the caricaturist in damning Master Betty by aligning himself with that most authoritative of theatre critics, Hamlet.

The enthusiastic amateur, Robert Coates, met with more derision. After his London début in December 1811 he was the victim of many caricatures. Perhaps the most pointed of them was published in the *Satirist* on 1 January 1812; entitled *An Amateurs Dream* (BMC 11934), it shows Coates reclining on a sofa with visions of greatness, saying, in the words of Romeo, 'O heavy lightness! serious vanity | Misshapen chaos of well seeming forms!' But there is an even sharper thrust than that 'serious vanity', for behind him Shakespeare rises saying 'Oh Romeo! Romeo! wherefore art *thou* Romeo?' The *Satirist* (1811, 9: 317) also published a poem that made much of Coates's motto, 'While I live I'll crow': 'Your *Romeo* is not worth a d—n!—Let | Your next part be—the Cock *in Hamlet*' (1811, 9: 317). In Charles Williams's *A Cart Load of Young Players on their Journey to London* (BMC 11771), published the following month, there is a

'Cock for Hamlet'. 'Romeo Coates', as he became known, was singled out for the special scorn of professional caricaturists because he was a wealthy amateur who got on to the London stage through money rather than talent. The professionalization of culture went with the rise of the middle-ranking mercantile classes; Coates was attacked as a throw-back to the aristocratic dilettantism of an earlier age.

Edmund Kean was less easy to ridicule. He seemed to embody a new naturalness and truth in playing Shakespeare: within months of his celebrated first appearance at Drury Lane in January 1814, he was being associated with 'nature', in contrast to Kemble's 'art'. On 13 April 1814 Joseph Farington recorded and interpreted Sir George Beaumont's account of his reactions to Kean as follows: 'Others who remembered *Garrick* spoke highly of Him, and Sir George seemed to mean that those who felt *nature* strongly approved Kean, while those who were devoted to the art of the Kemble School disapproved Him' (Farington 1978–84, xiii. 4488). Ten days later the idea was developed more fully: 'Beaumont was decidedly of opinion that no actor since Garrick exhibited so much genuine *feeling of nature*. At times, sd. He, He appears to be Richard himself. He never, said He, can have dignity or grace, His person is too diminutive, but He is a true natural actor, and wholly free from the measured and artificial practise of the Kemble school' (xiii. 4495).

It might be seen as testimony to Kean's success that there appears not to have been any immediate response in caricature to his acting style. A more cynical view would be that this was because his style was marked by such excesses that caricature was not needed: thus, a seriously meant engraving of his Shylock (pl. 3) looks distinctly like a caricature: could the eyes really have been that bright, the brow that furrowed, the knife—not to mention the head—that large? Hazlitt at once praised Kean's uniqueness and criticized his tendency to the melodramatic when he wrote 'the only person who ever caricatures Mr Kean well, or from whose exaggerations he has any thing to fear, is himself' (HW xviii. 300).

There is a problem here, arising from the relativity of taste: one person's melodrama is the next's 'naturalness' or 'truth to Shakespeare'. Among reviewers, Hazlitt was for a time alone in praising Kean. He singled out the death scene as the 'most brilliant' part of the new actor's Richard III ('He fought like one drunk with wounds' —HW v. 182). This response was subsequently shared by Thomas Barnes, the second reviewer to praise Kean to the skies:

We have felt our eyes gush on reading a passage of exquisite poetry, we have been ready to leap at sight of a noble picture, but we never felt stronger emotion, more overpowering sensations, than were kindled by the novel sublimity of this catastrophe. In matters of mere taste, there will be a difference of opinion, but here there was no room to doubt,—no reason could be impudent enough to hesitate. Every heart beat an echo responsive to this call of elevated nature, and yearned with fondness towards the man who, while he excited admiration for himself, made also his admirers glow with a warmth of conscious superiority, because they were able to appreciate such an exalted degree of excellence. (Barnes 1814, p. 139)

But a more objective, descriptive account makes it easy to see how Kean's performance could be seen as a caricature of passion:

fights furiously back and forth—in turning looses balance, falls on his knee, and fights up—in turning, receives Richmond's thrust—lunges at him feebly after it—clenches—is shoved from him—staggers—drops the sword—grasps blindly at him—staggers backward and falls—*head* to R. H. turns upon right side—writhes—rests on his hands—gnashes his teeth at him (L. H.)—as he utters his last words—blinks—and expires rolling on his back. (Hackett 1959, p. 98)

To us, this sounds crude and melodramatic in the extreme, an impression which belies Barnes's certainty that no one could dissent from the general approbation of Kean. It is not merely a question of the different taste of different ages: although most subsequent accounts of Kean's Richard followed Hazlitt's in being highly favourable, there were dissenting voices—John Finlay (1835, p. 211) said that as Richard he 'waddle[d] like a duck'.

There is no surviving caricature that portrays Kean as a duck. When the satirists did get to work on him, the emphasis tended to be more economic than aesthetic. George Cruikshank's *The Theatrical Atlas* (BMC 12325), published by Hannah Humphrey on 7 May 1814, shows the new star bearing the financially ailing Drury Lane on his shoulders. Another print of May 1814, *The Rival Richards or Sheakspear in Danger* (BMC 12326) by William Heath, an engraver who worked from about 1809 to 1834, depicts Shakespeare as the victim of a tug of war between Kean and C. M. Young, one of the 'Kemble school', who had been brought forward to try to draw audiences back to Covent Garden. A frightened and bewildered Shakespeare cries 'Murder Murder': Heath implies that the Bard will be torn apart by being made merely the means to a commercial end.

Fores published a more complicated *Rival Richards!!!* (pl. 6, BMC 12918) in 1817, when rivalry between Kean and Junius Brutus Booth was at its height. Booth had been brought forward as another Kean; Hazlitt argued influentially that an imitator might have succeeded in capturing Kemble's art, but the attempt to follow in the wake of Kean was by its very nature doomed to failure: 'A Kemble school we can understand: a Kean school is, we suspect, a contradiction in terms. Art may be taught, because it is learnt: Nature can neither be taught nor learnt. The secrets of Art may be said to have a common or *pass* key to unlock them; the secrets of Nature have but one master-key— the heart' (HW v. 355). Hazlitt criticized Booth's Richard III for being 'an exact copy or parody of Mr Kean's manner of doing the same part' (HW v. 354). The *Rival Richards!!!* engraving makes a similar point, in that it shows Booth as a pale shadow of Kean, mirroring his posture at the celebrated moment in the latter's performance when, in the scene set on the eve of Bosworth Field, he stood rapt in contemplation with the tip of his sword touching the ground. But the engraver goes further than Hazlitt and dismisses as commercially inspired imposture the whole business of putting forward rival Richards. Shakespeare's texts, piled up to create a temple of Fame, have been pushed to one side—the opposite side from the theatres. 'Puffs', a 'Patent Clapping Machine', and the 'Box Office' occupy the foreground; the scale on which Booth and Kean are weighed is inscribed 'Folly' and is held by a fool mounted on an ass who directs a stream of urine inscribed 'Damnation' at three other Richards underfoot. Meanwhile, Kemble and his imitator Young flee to the 'Shade of Oblivion'.

There was some opposition from Kean supporters when Booth played Richard at Covent Garden on 12 February 1817. The latter then quarrelled over his salary with the manager, Henry Harris, and went to Drury Lane for a performance in which he played Iago to Kean's Othello. Hazlitt thought that Junius Brutus did as well as could be expected—'the two rival actors hunt very well in couple'— but did not give anything more than 'a very close and spirited repetition' of Kean's own manner of acting Iago; he could not match up to his great original, whose own performance was 'beyond all praise'. 'Any one who has not seen him in the third act of Othello (and seen him near) cannot have an idea of perfect tragic acting', Hazlitt concludes his review (HW v. 356–7).

Booth then returned to Covent Garden, only to be hounded from the stage in a riot when he attempted to play Richard on 25 February. It was rumoured that the Wolves Club, the tavern society over which heavy-drinking Kean presided, had been responsible for this. George Cruikshank's *Richard Harris'd or the Wolves too Keen!!!* (pl. 7, BMC 12919), thick with apposite Shakespearean quotations and other allusions, plays on this event. 'Junius's Letters' are among the papers in the foreground, providing a punning attack on the name *Junius* Brutus Booth. But the allusion to the original Junius is not merely a punning incidental stroke, for the presence of 'Junius's Letters' inevitably summons up the political controversies of the period around 1770—the eye that registers them goes with the mind that will make an association with 'Wilkes and Liberty'. Together with the fact that the 'Wolves' have 'Opposition!' inscribed on their jackets, this invocation of the strongest pre-1789 manifestation of English 'radicalism'[10] suggests that theatrical dissension is being read as a microcosm of political upheaval.

'Harris'd' in Cruikshank's title puns on 'harass' and Harris: the proprietor Harris was in fact a more significant force than the Kean harassers. Hazlitt argued that the real issue at stake as Booth moved from theatre to theatre was the power which managers held over actors:

at this rate, any Manager, by once entering into an agreement with an actor, may keep him dangling on his good pleasure for a year certain, may prevent his getting any other engagement, by saying that they are still in a progress of arrangement, though all arrangement is broken off, may deprive an ingenious and industrious man of his bread, and the public of the advantage of his talents, till the Managers, at the expiration of this probationary year of non-performance, once more grant him his *Habeas Corpus*. (HW v. 357)

This article appeared on 2 March 1817. During the previous months there had been riots over bread prices; as Hazlitt wrote, the suspension of habeas corpus was being debated in Parliament—the Suspension Act passed into law the next day. The allusions to habeas corpus and to being deprived of bread are thus decisive in linking theatrical

---

[10] In April 1820 Lord Byron remarked in a letter to John Cam Hobhouse that '*radical* is a new word since my time—it was not in the political vocabulary in 1816—when I left England—and I don't know what it means—is it uprooting?' (Byron 1973–82, vii. 81). Strictly, the term 'radicalism' should only be applied to the post-Waterloo period, but since radicals at that time proclaimed as their precursors earlier 'friends to liberty', such as the activists of the 1790s and to a lesser extent Wilkes, I have allowed myself some latitude in the use of the term.

and political repression, the proprietors of the theatre and the governors of the land. It is no coincidence that Kean, whom Hazlitt called a 'radical' actor, was at the height of his success during the years of political turmoil and radical activity between Waterloo and Peterloo.

Hazlitt began his article, 'This Theatre was a scene of the greatest confusion and uproar we ever witnessed (not having been present at the O. P. rows)' (HW v. 357). The parenthesis is well judged, for prior to the rivalry between Kean and Booth the theatrical event precipitating most controversy—and most caricature—had been the 'Old Price' riots of 1809. They afford another prime example of caricaturists participating in an argument which began in the theatre but had wider economic and social implications. Covent Garden burned down in 1808; it was rebuilt in a year, but just before it reopened the management announced that to cover some of the cost of rebuilding the price of admission would have to be raised—for boxes from 6s. to 7s., for the pit from 3s. 6d. to 4s. On the first night Kemble came out, wearing a splendid new Scottish Macbeth costume, to deliver an opening speech. He was greeted by abuse, catcalls, and cries of 'Old Prices'. Demonstrations and interruptions persisted at Covent Garden performances for three months, until the management capitulated. J. W. Donohue, citing the *Covent Garden Journal*, describes the end of the affair:

Finally, on 14 December, a large party of [the rioters] dined at the Crown and Anchor Tavern for the purpose of accepting conciliation from Kemble, spokesman for the now desperate management. At this 'O. P. Banquet' the terms proposed were that the private boxes were to be reduced to the scale prevailing in 1802; admission prices for the pit were to revert to the former 3s. 6d., the boxes remaining at 7s.; in addition, an apology would be made to the public, an offensive box-keeper dismissed, and all legal proceedings against the rioters discontinued. The terms were immediately accepted. (Donohue 1975, p. 54)

This was clearly a triumph for the people. It is significant that the higher price was retained in the boxes, where the privileged sat, and reduced in the pit, arena of the volatile representatives of the expanding urban middle and lower-middle classes. Even more significant is the reduction in the number of boxes, for one of the rioters' principal complaints had been that the new theatre had increased the number and incorporated one whole tier of exclusively 'private' boxes, complete with private staircase, so that the aristocracy could avoid all contact with the rest of the audience. Leigh Hunt complained in the *Examiner* that it was against British principles of democracy and social mobility to remove an entire tier from 'lovers of the Theatre' and 'make privacies for the luxurious great' (Hunt 1949, p. 33). James Boaden, friend and biographer of Kemble, acknowledged that the riots were not really so much about the extra sixpence as about the 'absolute seclusion of a *privileged order* from all *vulgar contact*' (Boaden 1825, ii. 492). Along with the cry 'Old Prices' went that of 'No imposition'—it was the imposition of the aristocracy on the space of the people that motivated the battle.

Given Shakespeare's centrality to the repertory (Kemble's *Macbeth* costume is symptomatic), the OP riots may be seen as a battle for the possession of Shakespeare. To remove cheap gallery seats and replace them with secluded boxes was to make Shakespeare less widely available, more exclusive—to appropriate him for the élite. A conjunction of Shakespeare and the cash nexus is apparent in two strong caricatures on the riots, Isaac Cruikshank's *Is This A Rattle Which I See Before Me?* (pl. 8, BMC 11422) and Charles Williams's *A Parody on Macbeth's Soliloquy at Covent Garden Theatre. Boxes 7/-* (pl. 9, BMC 11423). In each case, the inscription is more revealing than the illustration: the figure of Kemble, kilted for Scottish authenticity, draws the reader into the caricature and then the political point is made in the text. Both Cruikshank and Williams parody the extremely well-known dagger soliloquy. In Cruikshank, Kemble–Macbeth recoils from an air-drawn watchman's rattle, one of the rioters' noisiest weapons; in the adaptation of the soliloquy, Kemble's wealth and his family's domination of the theatre world are alluded to in the lines 'oh then I must | forego my Schem[e]s of Power, of Rule, and Tyranny; | give up the Princely income which my Family | have long enjoyed'. The vocabulary—'Power', 'Rule', 'Tyranny'—at once presses home the comparison between Kemble and Macbeth, and carries a contemporary political resonance in that the oppression of the theatre audience is synecdochic for the oppression of the people. 'Princely income' may glance at the Prince of Wales, whose extravagant life-style was a persistent cause for complaint.

The title and the visual composition of Williams's caricature emphasize the increased box-price (this time a 'seven shilling piece' is substituted for the dagger), but it too has radical overtones in its parodic inscription, for the cry of 'Old Prices' is described as 'a forc'd creation | Proceeding from the hard oppressed people'. On the surface, this may seem to be no more than a neat twist on Macbeth's 'heat-oppressed brain', but since the riots were widely perceived as symbolic of larger divisions in society, the reference to the oppression of the people could not but have a disturbing social and political *frisson*. Williams's text is particularly strong because it remains close to Macbeth's original words; while Cruikshank merely uses the soliloquy as a starting-point, Williams follows it throughout (save for a single allusion to *Richard III*), giving new meanings to the old words and occasionally introducing new ones. Precisely because they are at once contemporary in relevance and close to their originals, such alterations as 'hard oppressed people' for 'heat-oppressed brain' make their point and stick in the memory.

Further evidence that Shakespeare was used as a weapon in the OP war may be gleaned from a poem on the affair by Thomas Tegg, himself a print-seller and publisher. His fifth poetic epistle describes some placards held up in the Covent Garden auditorium:

> Kemble and Harris were pourtray'd—
> Macbeth the former, and the latter
> Poor Banquo weighing well the matter:
> Macbeth then, starting with surprise,
> '*Thou can'st not say I did it*,' cries
> Whereupon Banquo makes reply—
> 'A lie! upon my soul a lie!'
>
> (Tegg 1810, pp. 29–30)

Tegg obviously feels that self-conscious allusion to Shakespeare is a telling satirical weapon. Not only does he compare Kemble with Macbeth, he also remarks on an identification of the actor-manager with another tyrant, Richard III: with regard to a drawing of Kemble in the pillory, he writes

> This motto on the top I noted—
> 'To guilty minds' (from Shakspeare quoted)
> 'A terrible example.'
>
> (Tegg 1810, p. 114)

It is characteristic of the volatile sense of Shakespeare's identity which resulted from the prevalence of acting versions that in fact the lines are not 'from Shakspeare quoted' but from Cibber quoted: they come from the address of Henry VI's ghost to Richard in that most popular of stage adaptations (Cibber 1700, V. iv).

Outside the theatre and such theatre-related activities as the Jubilee, probably the two most talked-about Shakespearean events of the period were the opening of Boydell's Gallery and the Ireland family forgeries. Like the OP riots, both had economic, as well as Bardolatrous, motivations. Together with the Jubilee, they offer prime examples of the process whereby in the latter part of the eighteenth century Shakespeare became commercialized and was made into a commodity, an object of material consumption. Inevitably such appropriations encountered resistance, from both those who wished to keep their Shakespeare pure and those who saw through the avaricious self-interest of the entrepreneurs. Gillray was prominent among critics of the Shakespearean ventures of the 1790s; Boydell's Gallery provoked possibly the richest of all his caricatures.

Alderman John Boydell, entrepreneur, print-seller, and patron of the arts, opened his Shakespeare Gallery in Pall Mall in May 1789, with the avowed intention of establishing an English School of History Painting. It was a project he had been planning since 1786, when he had published a prospectus and invited subscribers to a massive undertaking—the commissioning of paintings on Shakespearean subjects by the leading artists of the day, the construction of a special gallery in Pall Mall to exhibit them, and the publication of both a folio of engravings taken from them and a new edition of the plays illustrated with smaller engravings. He attracted over a thousand subscribers. In his celebrated *Discourses* to the students of the Royal Academy, Sir Joshua Reynolds had argued the traditional case that history painting was the highest of the artistic genres, the visual equivalent of epic. Boydell sought to create instantaneously an English version of a kind of painting that had developed over the course of centuries on the continent. What better subject for a new English school than the works of England's National Poet?

One mark of the rise in Shakespeare's cultural status in the mid-eighteenth century had been the growth of illustration. From the 1740s onwards Bardolatry took a variety of visual manifestations.[11]

---

[11] Ronald Paulson would argue for a slightly earlier date: he attaches great significance to Hogarth's *Falstaff Examining his Recruits* of the late 1720s, and goes so far as to claim that Hogarth 'was the first English artist to show that Shakespeare's plays and in particular those dealing with English history could be used as the basis for an English version of history painting—and was thus the original inspirer of Boydell's Shakespeare Gallery, as he was of Boydell's successful dissemination of prints' (Paulson

These ranged from Francis Hayman's inclusion of four Shakespearean subjects in his decorations for the Prince's Pavilion in Vauxhall Gardens, to isolated paintings and drawings of scenes from the plays (Fuseli was especially prolific in this area), to engravings in editions. Most influential of all were portraits of actors and actresses in their most famous roles: Hogarth's *Garrick as Richard III* of 1745 was seminal here, Zoffany's *Garrick and Mrs Pritchard in Macbeth* was particularly admired, and Reynolds's 1784 *Mrs Siddons as the Tragic Muse* furnished a kind of culmination of the tradition in that it translated the actress out of any particular role and into the embodiment of the Muse which Shakespeare himself personified.[12] A volume of plates by Stothard and Smirke published in 1783 under the title *Picturesque Beauties of Shakespear* perhaps gave Boydell the idea of commissioning his large folio, but the conception of a gallery of works by major artists devoted specifically to Shakespearean illustration and divorced from theatrical portraiture was completely new. In a very real sense, the Shakespeare Gallery was the first National Gallery. A mark of its impact was that rival galleries were quickly established, the most notable being Thomas Macklin's Poets Gallery and J. H. Fuseli's Milton Gallery.

The desire both to improve the artistic taste of the nation and to expand further the already buoyant print market earned Boydell the nickname 'the commercial Maecenas'. He made his patriotic and commercial motives clear in the preface to the Gallery catalogue, dated 1 May 1789:

I flatter myself that the present undertaking . . . will essentially serve this country. The more objects of attraction and amusement held out to Foreigners, that may induce them to visit this Metropolis, the more are our manufactures promoted; for every one, on his return, carries with him some specimen of them: and I believe it will be readily granted, that the manufactures of this country need only be seen and compared, to be preferred to those of any other.—The great number of Foreigners who have of late visited this country, may in some degree be attributed to the very flourishing state of our com-

---

1982, p. 37). The problem with this argument is that *Falstaff Examining his Recruits* was not engraved and therefore not widely disseminated.

12 For Shakespearean illustration prior to Boydell, see Boase 1947 and Merchant 1959. For Garrick as probably the most painted Englishman of the eighteenth century, see Bertelsen 1977–8. The genre of stage illustration offered an important alternative tradition to history painting, which was essentially text-based. Stage encroaches on book with, for example, the illustrations in Charles Jennens's cheap 1770–4 edn., where the influence of Garrick's productions of *Othello* and *Lear* is discernible.

merce; and accounts for that great demand for English manufactures, which at present so universally prevails all over the Continent. (repr. Boydell 1805, preface)

It was unfortunate for Boydell that just over two months later the Bastille was stormed and commerce with the Continent began to go into decline. He writes of a flourishing economy; by the turn of the century, there would be a war economy and he would be approaching bankruptcy. His massive investment—he paid major artists like Sir Joshua Reynolds up to a thousand guineas per painting—proved disastrous.

The Gallery lasted for just over a decade, opening with thirty-four paintings and expanding to one hundred and seventy. Initially, it met with a broadly favourable response in the Press. *The Times* published three laudatory articles in the first week after its opening; the *Public Advertiser* of 6 May 1789 praised the paintings for avoiding the 'extravaganza of attitude' that was necessary at the playhouse (see further, Friedman 1976, pp. 73–5). The Gallery became something of a fashionable centre: there is a drawing of 1790 by Francis Wheatley (now in the Victoria and Albert Museum) which shows Boydell receiving the Dukes of York and Clarence, together with Sir Joshua Reynolds; the Duchess of Devonshire is there with R. B. Sheridan, and Lady Jersey is scrutinizing the paintings. But Boydell's artistic aspirations were not fulfilled so well as his social ones. He himself acknowledged in the 1789 catalogue preface that it was difficult to do justice to Shakespeare on canvas, especially to those parts of the plays which gave 'creative imagination' the loose and went 'beyond nature'. But it was the imaginative and the magical which many took to be the unique mark of Shakespeare's genius (see Bate 1986, *passim*), and partly for this reason reviews became increasingly critical.

More generally, intelligent Shakespeare-lovers felt that the Gallery paintings fixed what should be fluid, and imposed on their favourite scenes a heavy style that impaired the imagination. The case for the prosecution was stated vigorously by Charles Lamb some years later in a letter to Samuel Rogers:

What injury (short of the theatres) did not Boydell's Shakspeare Gallery do me with Shakspeare? to have Opie's Shakspeare, Northcote's Shakspeare, light-headed Fuseli's Shakspeare, heavy-headed Romney's Shakspeare, wooden-headed West's Shakspeare (tho' he did the best in Lear), deaf-headed Reynolds's Shakspeare, instead of my, and every body's Shakspeare.

To be tied down to an authentic face of Juliet! To have Imogen's portrait! to confine the illimitable! (Lamb 1935, iii. 394)

The phrase 'short of the theatres' is interesting in view of the feeling in the Gallery's early days that its heroic paintings provided an alternative tradition to that of the stage. Lamb, however, criticizes both painting and the stage for confining the individual imagination. In his essay 'On the Tragedies of Shakspeare', he uses a very similar argument to that applied to the Boydell Gallery. After praising Kemble and Siddons for embodying and realizing on stage 'conceptions which had hitherto assumed no distinct shape', he backtracks: 'But dearly do we pay all our life after for this juvenile pleasure, this sense of distinctness. When the novelty is past, we find to our cost that instead of realizing an idea, we have only materialized and brought down a fine vision to the standard of flesh and blood. We have let go a dream, in quest of an unattainable substance' (Lamb 1912, i. 114–15).

Lamb's essay on the problems of 'realizing' Shakespeare will be discussed further in Part II; as far as the failure of the Shakespeare Gallery is concerned, in the end commercial considerations were more significant than aesthetic ones. Boydell's project collapsed early in the new century for a variety of reasons: changing public taste (the vast canvases rapidly grew to seem cumbersome and outdated), the poor quality of many of the engravings made from the paintings (subscribers to the *Collection of Prints*, which constituted the financial underpinning of the whole venture, began to withdraw), the collapse of the international print market owing to the wars with France. The last factor was probably the most important, for Boydell was first and foremost a print-dealer who relied on the export market.

Since the Gallery must be seen as both a commercial and an artistic venture, Gillray's *Shakespeare-Sacrificed;—or—The Offering to Avarice* is possibly the most powerful questioning of its worth that we have, for it constitutes a two-pronged attack: the title and the foreground image —Boydell sacrificing the plays for the sake of money-bags—condemn the exploitation of Shakespeare for commercial ends, while the surrounding figures provide a sophisticated critique of some major paintings in the collection.

Gillray's treatment of Boydell was quite unmerciful, not least because Boydell had turned down his offer to do an engraving of one of the Northcote paintings in the Gallery. Presumably, Boydell did

not want any association with a man who had made his name in the
low form of caricature, but he may have come to regret his refusal.
When some pictures at the Gallery were slashed in 1791, Gillray
swiftly added fuel to the malicious rumour that Boydell himself had
been responsible, in an attempt to gain public sympathy for his
project (the number of visitors to the Gallery was already diminish-
ing). *The Monster broke loose—or—a peep into the Shakespeare Gallery*
(pl. 10, BMC 7976) not merely shows Boydell with knife in hand, but
identifies him with Renwick Williams, the 'Monster' who had been
arrested in June 1790 after having slashed many women on the
London streets. The inscription propagates the idea that Boydell will
do anything for commercial gain:

There! There! There's a nice gash!—there! oh, this will be a glorious subject
for to make a fuss about in the News-papers;—a hundred Guineas reward
will make a fine sound:—there! there!—O, there will be fine talking about
the Gallery; and it will bring in a rare sight of Shillings for seeing of the *cut*
Pictures . . . these *Small* pictures won't cost a great deal of money replacing;
indeed one would not like to cut a large one to pieces for the sake of making it
look as if People envied us; no! that would cost rather too much, and my
pocket begins—but mum!—that's nothing to nobody—well, none can blame
me for going the cheapest way to work; to keep up the reputation of the
Gallery—there! there! there!—there! there!

Several other Gillray engravings strike at Boydell (BMC 8013,
8121, 9085), but *Shakespeare-Sacrificed* stands alone in its complexity
and sheer subversive brilliance (pl. 12, BMC 7584).[13] It was widely
admired, even by the artists it lampooned: 'When this bold effort of
the inventive powers of Gillray first appeared, it was received by the
general acclamation of the painters and engravers, as the masterpiece
of allegorical burlesque' (Gillray 1830, p. 11). Its enduring popularity
is apparent from a letter which Sneyd sent to Gillray in October 1800,
suggesting that now the print was 'more familiar' he should produce
some coloured impressions of it (Bagot 1909, i. 171). Boydell himself
was not amused. A letter in the *Somerset House Gazette* of 18 September
1824 tells how he called unexpectedly on an Academy artist who had

---

[13] Dorothy George's account of *Shakespeare-Sacrificed* in BMC is not up to her
customary high standard: several of the figures are wrongly identified and others are
not recognized as lampooning Gallery paintings. This is the only instance in which I
have found BMC severely deficient. To compound the problem, George's errors are
taken over by later scholars (e.g. Boase 1947 and Friedman 1976—though the latter is
informative on the Gallery itself).

the print pinned up in his studio; fortunately for the latter, Boydell sat down on a full palette as soon as he came in, and was thus preoccupied while a servant hid the caricature.

Boydell is the largest figure in the aquatint; he is wearing his Alderman's gown, which he was in the habit of ceremoniously putting on when he entered the Gallery. The fire, into which Shakespeare's works have been thrown, blots out the Bard, whose figure is recognizably that of the Westminster Abbey monument, with its cross-legged posture and lines from *The Tempest*. It is a characteristic stroke that, in the context of the print, the text is given new significance: Shakespeare's lines on transience are, as it were, enacted by Boydell's obliteration of Shakespeare. The figure of Avarice, to whom the burnt offering is dedicated, sits on a large 'List of Subscribers to the Sacrifice'. The plays are reduced to tattered papers in the fire, while the book that dominates is a handsome, lapidary volume which we are to imagine contains the names of Boydell's thirteen hundred subscribers: the 'book' of Shakespeare has been replaced by a text for which the sole *raison d'être* is economic ostentation or social prestige. The Greek inscription on the ground—'Let none but Men of Taste enter here'—is taken from the door of the Academy Exhibition Room; it therefore shows that the magic circle in which Boydell stands is the Academy, the established art world. A boy representing painting pushes a boy with an engraver's tool from the circle; Gillray and others were angry that engravers were excluded from the Academy. Fame blows from her trumpet bubbles marked 'Puff, Puff, Puffs'—an accusation that Boydell was putting the newspapers up to their eulogies of his project—and 'Mecaenas! Leo! Alexander! Psha!', a jibe at the Alderman's nickname. The figures in the top half are calculated to debunk the Gallery's major artists and to question the 'Taste' of the whole venture.

The way in which the figures seem to emerge from the smoke of the sacrificial fire suggests that there is a compositional model for the print, which Gillray's original audience would have recognized. One of the best-known portraits of Garrick was that by Robert Edge Pine[14] of the actor reciting his Jubilee ode (pl. 11); it was exhibited at the Royal Academy in 1780 and engraved a number of times. One engraving of it, by Caroline Watson, was published by Boydell in

[14] Pine was a portrait painter, especially of actors and actresses; in 1782 he held an exhibition of a series of his paintings on Shakespearean subjects, a small-scale precursor to Boydell's Gallery.

5. Anonymous caricature of Garrick's Jubilee (1769)

6. Anonymous caricature of Kean and Booth as Rival Richard IIIs (1817)

7. George Cruikshank, Booth hounded by Kean supporters (1817)

IS THIS A RATTLE WHICH I SEE BEFORE ME?

Is this a Rattle which I see before me?
It's Deafning sound portends the din of war
and warns me that my only
Safty is in flight —
Me thinks I hear a voice say, Assignations. Stews.
Bawd rooms, & scenes of such Debauchery. but Ill
become a Theatre. oh then I must
forego my Schems of Power, of Rule, & Tyranny;
give up the Princely income which my Family
have long enjoyed against the claims of much superior
Merit: or suffer this continual Rattle in
mine Ears: I will be off.

London Published October 30th 1809 by S W Fores No 50 Piccadilly

8. Isaac Cruikshank, Kemble confronting the OP Riots (1809)

9. Charles Williams, Kemble confronting the OP Riots (1809)

1784. Pine's painting shows Garrick declaiming in front of the West-minster Abbey statue, a copy of which had been furnished for the Stratford Jubilee, with rays of light streaming down to denote genius or divinity, and clouds of inspiration swirling around. Shakespeare's characters have been conjured from these clouds and brought to life; Lear and a bare-breasted, dead Cordelia are especially prominent. The correspondence of formal properties between this painting and the Gillray print—the declamatory foreground figure, the statue, the clouds, the Shakespearean characters—can hardly be coincidental. The 'magic circle' in *Shakespeare-Sacrificed* may also have been inspired by the prominent circular base of Pine's rendering of the statue. Gillray has substituted Boydell for Garrick and clouds of smoke for clouds of inspiration; he has obscured the statue, turned the Shake-spearean figures into grotesque parodies, and introduced the eco-nomic motif. By travestying Pine's painting of Garrick reading his 1769 ode, Gillray furnishes an oblique attack on the Jubilee as well as an overt one on Boydell's Gallery. Each event, it is implied, does a disservice to Shakespeare and serves only for the self-aggrandizement of the entrepreneur. Boydell's imposture is worse than Garrick's because, as *The Monster broke loose* stresses, the motivations for it are so blatantly commercial.

The idea of a compositional model raises the possibility that the very act of travestying the Gallery paintings draws attention to their own status as travesties. Like so many eighteenth-century paintings in the grand style, a considerable number of the Shakespeare Gallery canvases owe their disposition to Continental masters: Reynolds's *Death of Cardinal Beaufort* is modelled on Nicolas Poussin's *Death of Germanicus*, Northcote's *Burial of the Princes in the Tower* on Caravaggio's *The Entombment of Christ*, Barry's *King Lear Weeping over the Dead Cordelia* on Annibale Carracci's *Pietà*. There was a lively debate in the eighteenth century about whether such borrowing of attitudes con-stituted creative imitation or downright plagiarism,[15] and it may be that Gillray's parodic borrowings from the Gallery paintings are intended to reflect ironically on the way that they themselves depend on borrowing. His implication is that the paintings commissioned by Boydell are plagiarisms rather than creative imitations; *Shakespeare-Sacrificed* is a parodic history painting which argues that the Shake-speare Gallery is a parody of true history painting.

[15] For introductions to this large and complicated subject, see Gombrich 1966, Rosenblum 1967, Paulson 1975.

There is no doubt that Gillray's figures in *Shakespeare-Sacrificed* would have been familiar to anyone who had visited the Gallery. The most striking and easily recognizable characters are Sir Joshua Reynolds's Cardinal Beaufort and Fuseli's Bottom (pls. 13 and 14, Boydell 1805, i. 20, ii. 17). One feature that needs explanation is the demon on Beaufort's pillow, which is absent in the Reynolds painting today, as well as both the large and small engravings of it.[16] *The Times* of 8 May 1789 provides an explanation: the painting was originally exhibited with a demon on the pillow, illustrating the lines 'O, beat away the busy meddling fiend, | That lays strong siege unto this wretch's soul' (*2 Henry VI*, III. iii. 21). But, in the words of *The Times* critic, 'we rather apprehend that some fiend has been laying siege to Sir Joshua's taste, when he determined to literalize the idea. The licence of poetry is very different from that of painting.' The article then goes on to suggest that Boydell should instruct his engravers to omit the demon from the prints based on the painting. This is what has happened in the published versions, though there is an early impression of Caroline Watson's large print which includes the figure and shows that Gillray's version is accurate, if enlarged in size for ironic emphasis.

In response to adverse criticism from many quarters, Reynolds duly painted over the fiend. A critic in the *Gentleman's Magazine* implied that it might have been appropriate in the work of Fuseli, but was out of place in that of Reynolds—'Belzebub is of the race of Fuseli, the father of ghosts and spectres, and we leave him to his parent' (1790, 60: 1089); the *Analytical Review* argued that what is a powerful effect in the imagination is a mere distraction when made visual—'its ludicrous meanness destroys that terror which is the soul of the scene' (1790, 6: 331). Thomas Holcroft's diary, as published by Hazlitt, tells of how one Sir William Beechey 'repeated a conversation at which he was present, when Burke endeavoured to persuade Sir Joshua Reynolds to alter his picture of the dying Cardinal, by taking away the devil, which Burke said was an absurd and ridiculous incident, and a disgrace to the artist' (HW iii. 180). But one suspects that Gillray's visual demonstration of the figure's ludicrous impropriety was as telling as Burke's authoritative pronouncement. The way in which it is given an emphatic position at the apex of the main triangle of composition of the design, and exagger-

---

[16] See further, Roe 1971. The painting, much deteriorated, is now at Petworth.

ated in both its size and the brightness of its eyes, is an even more eloquent criticism than that in the *Analytical Review*. Gillray made much of this devil: three years later he parodied *The Death of Cardinal Beaufort* more covertly in *Tom Paine's Nightly Pest* (BMC 8137), which shows Paine in bed in the posture of Beaufort—out of the window behind him slips a mischievous dark-bodied and bright-eyed figure. Gillray's role in forcing Reynolds's overpainting is a strong example of caricature's capacity to enter into a dialogue with high art and to contest its assumptions about representation, in this instance of a Shakespearean metaphor.

In *Shakespeare-Sacrificed*, Gillray also exaggerates the already thick arm and hand of Reynolds's dying Cardinal; he turns his anguished expression into a grotesque grin and has him clutch at the clouds of smoke rising from the Shakespearean conflagration below. The grin is another literal rendering of a Shakespearean metaphor, Warwick's 'See how the pangs of death do make him grin!' (III. iii. 24). Gillray's visual critique of it is analogous to Hazlitt's verbal one: 'the expression of the Cardinal himself is too much one of physical horror, a canine gnashing of the teeth, like a man strangled' (HW xviii. 59). Hazlitt also provides a context for the coarseness of the Cardinal's arm in Gillray's version: he records a conversation in which the painter James Northcote complained that Reynolds sometimes made 'his heroes look like beggars' and remarked that 'Grandi, the Italian colour-grinder, sat to him for King Henry VI in the *Death of Cardinal Beaufort*, and he looks not much better than a train-bearer or one in a low and mean station' (HW xi. 257). In fact, Reynolds's paint-mixer sat for Warwick, not the King, but that does not matter: the point is that Reynolds was perceived as introducing indecorously low figures into an heroic painting, which is what Gillray is getting at by portraying the Cardinal with the rolled-up sleeve and the formidable biceps of a workman.

The dying Cardinal's gesture down to the fire gives the impression that his anguish is caused by Boydell's sacrifice. Similarly, the principal change in the figure of Fuseli's Bottom is that, instead of holding a miniature naked Robin Goodfellow in his hand, he is gesturing down to Boydell; since he points to his ass's head with his other forefinger, the clear interpretation is that Boydell is an ass. The fire is fanned by a pair of bellows held by a crouching figure wearing a jester's cap. This is none other than the Fool from Benjamin West's admired painting of Lear in the storm (pl. 15, Boydell 1805, ii. 39);

again, we are led to believe that Boydell is a fool—or the mad monarch of Pall Mall.

The other groups in the print do not stand in direct relation to the figure of Boydell, but some of them do to each other. Thus, the fact that in the Shakespeare Gallery painting of the rose scene in *1 Henry VI* (pl. 16, Boydell 1805, ii. 14) Warwick is looking in the opposite direction from the bud he is about to pluck is highlighted by the way that Gillray introduces Fuseli's witches (pl. 17, Boydell 1805, i. 37) immediately above, about to grab the rose from his unsuspecting hand. The technique, then, is to alight on incongruous details in the Gallery paintings. A grotesque disembodied head peeps out beside Fuseli's witches, exactly as in the original; the stylized streak of lightning at the edge of Fuseli's painting is also reproduced and exaggerated.

The rose-plucking tableau is the only travesty of a painting by a second-rank Gallery artist. But since that artist was Josiah Boydell, the Alderman's nephew and partner, it is hardly a surprising choice. Gillray did not burlesque the work of the somewhat lesser-known artists who tended to be commissioned to paint scenes from the comedies. In not parodying the comic subjects, he is perhaps acknowledging that these are the least objectionable Gallery paintings because they are the least pretentious. Looking through the engravings of the paintings today, the artist who comes out with his reputation positively enhanced is Robert Smirke, who is especially successful in his illustrations to *The Merry Wives of Windsor* and his series of socially incisive depictions of Jaques's 'Seven Ages'.

Smirke's are genre scenes, whereas the butts of Gillray's satire are the full-scale history paintings. In the top left corner, Northcote's rendering of the final scene of the *Henry VI* trilogy is parodied (Boydell 1805, ii. 21). Gillray picks on the clumsiness with which the Queen, young Prince, and female attendants are disposed, giving particular attention to the baby's vertical right leg. He also senses an element of prurience in the Queen's low neckline, and consequently gives her bare breasts; he does the same, even more justifiably, with the dead Cordelia in his version of Barry's *Lear*.[17] Immediately above the

---

[17] It seems that, in order to attract audiences, theatre managers contrived to expose as much as they dared of their leading actresses' breasts: this appears to be the point of *The Rival Queens of Covent Garden and Drury Lane Theatre, at a Gymnastic Rehearsal!* (BMC 6126), a caricature of 1782, which shows a bare-breasted Mrs Siddons engaged in a pugilistic encounter with a rival.

group from *3 Henry VI*, Northcote's Richard III (Boydell 1805, ii. 22) is converted into a portrait of the artist himself, with distinctly satyr-like features. His open-handed gesture takes the eye down to the subjects below, which are perhaps the cleverest travesties in the print, the two King Lears.

Fuseli's treatment of the renunciation of Cordelia (pl. 18, Boydell 1805, ii. 38) is mocked in three ways. First, Lear's staff, already out of proportion, is elongated and thickened into a huge club with a bulging end; secondly, his Gothic throne becomes the gable end of a house with two smoking chimneys. This is a wonderful touch, for Fuseli's throne is reproduced almost exactly; all Gillray does is introduce the smoke, and what was previously unremarkable in the original painting becomes absurd. And finally, Lear points not to Cordelia but to a tiny figure in a spider's web. Gillray's purpose may be to prick the grand style of Fuseli's overbearing canvas, but it is also to make a connection between subjects: the figure in the web relates to a detail in that other Fuseli painting, *Bottom*. Act IV scene i of *A Midsummer Night's Dream* was a favourite with Fuseli—he painted several versions of it[18]—because it allowed him to visualize all sorts of grotesque elfin creatures. Near the bottom left corner of his Gallery painting he offers a literalization of Bottom's lines, 'Mounsieur Cobweb, good monsieur, get you your weapon in your hand, and kill me a red-hipped humble-bee on the top of a thistle' (IV. i. 10–12). It is this, greatly enlarged and with the cobweb emphasized, that Lear is pointing to. The trapping of the figure in the cobweb serves to make the same point as the Reynolds devil: it can only be incongruous to include in a painting a literal version of what is a metaphor in Shakespeare.

Fuseli's paintings are singled out for special scorn in *Shakespeare-Sacrificed*, perhaps because he had a reputation as an especially Shakespearean artist: the *Public Advertiser*, for example, said that 'it was the privilege of Shakespeare to create; it is the praise of Mr Fuseli to embody and give form to these creations' (quoted, Friedman 1976, p. 205). Fuseli himself bolstered this reputation by contributing to the *Analytical Review* a series of unsigned essays on the Shakespeare Gallery which paid particular attention to his own paintings.

---

[18] There were two versions of *Dream* IV. i among the first 34 Gallery paintings, a mark of the popularity of this 'supernatural' scene; the second one was by Francis Wheatley, but was not engraved—the 1805 folio included instead a second version by Fuseli.

Gillray accordingly worked especially hard to advance the contrary view that Fuseli's paintings were appalling travesties of Shakespeare. In addition to the connected parodies of Fuseli's Bottom and Lear, as well as the *Macbeth* witches and ghost of Old Hamlet in the top corner, Gillray included in *Shakespeare-Sacrificed* a further allusion to the *Midsummer Night's Dream* painting. Near the centre of the plate an ugly child wearing peacock's feathers, symbol of vanity, squats on the shoulder of 'Avarice' and mockingly blows the bubble of immortality: this figure is based on the grotesque elf on Bottom's shoulder in Fuseli's representation of the line 'Scratch my head, Peaseblossom' (IV. i. 7). Fuseli's literalization of Peaseblossom is parodied by Gillray's brilliant transformation of headgear from *pease* to *pea*cock's feathers.[19]

Adjacent to Fuseli's Lear is James Barry's, with the dying Cordelia in his arms (pl. 19, Boydell 1805, ii. 40). Again, Gillray picks on an incongruous detail we might otherwise have missed: Barry's Lear holds his left hand to his head and wears an aggrieved expression, as if he has received a physical rather than an emotional blow. Gillray therefore converts Lear's billowing white hair into a heavy-looking sack that has landed square on his head; the soldier behind him has his hand to his beard in horror at the king's discomfiture, not Cordelia's death—we are thus alerted to the fact that in Barry's painting the two men are not even looking at her.

Gillray makes us see the Shakespeare Gallery paintings with new eyes. After an examination of his ghost of Old Hamlet, to the right, we return to Fuseli's original (pl. 20, Boydell 1805, ii. 44) and realize that, striking as the posture may be, its halo and trailing cloak do bear sharp resemblance to a devil's horns and tail. Compositionally, the ghost's position mirrors that of the parody of Fuseli's Lear—the figures are on the same level on either side, and each points down and outwards at an angle of 45 degrees—so again a link is made between subjects by the same artist, as the eye is drawn across from one to the other. From his dominating position, the ghost points down to the flames of hell, as if to damn the whole Boydell venture. But Fuseli's painting is also damned: after reading the caricature, we can no longer view the original with the naïve enthusiasm of the *Public*

---

[19] Gillray sustained his attack on Fuseli over many years: *Wierd-Sisters* is discussed below, and in addition he parodied several of his Miltonic subjects, most notably *Sin, Death, and the Devil* (June 1792, BMC 8105), in which the Queen (Sin) holds apart Pitt (Death) and Satan (Thurlow).

Advertiser critic who claimed that Fuseli had 'caught the Spirit of the Poet, and given to his Ghost all that martial sublimity, and awful grandeur, with which this high-wrought character is so wonderfully marked in the pages of Shakespeare' (16 July 1789, quoted, Friedman 1976, p. 206).

Gillray unerringly isolates potentially ridiculous details in his originals. From John Opie's *Infant Perdita* (pl. 21, Boydell 1805, i. 33) he takes three simple properties. The disembodied arm and helmet intruding from the top edge of Gillray's print open our eyes to the wild absurdity of Opie's foreshortened soldier's helmet and arm pointing at the baby. That arm is especially suggestive. Coming from off-stage centre top, it seems to be pointing to the whole print, not just the section from Opie's *Winter's Tale* scene. Like those pointing hands in the margin drawing our attention to key passages in *Clarissa* and *Tristram Shandy*, it is a form of authorial comment.

A sophisticated form at that, for it is self-performing: it is a finger pointed not only at Boydell's Gallery but also at all the finger-pointing that goes on in the Gallery paintings. If there is one common factor in that disparate collection of initially thirty-four, and eventually one hundred and seventy, paintings, it is the predominance of the index finger. All limbs have to manifest the heroic energy of the 'Historical' style; exaggerated gesticulation seems to be the only method of making them do so. Except to a limited extent in the cases of Fuseli's paintings and West's *Lear*, which have a certain vitality, the result is stiff, stilted posturing. Gillray has understood this perfectly; the composition of his individual travesties is such that the whole is a travesty of the entire Gallery. Everybody is pointing to everybody else: my diagram (pl. 12*a*) is an attempt to map the dazzling array of forces. The only figure not drawing our eye to other figures is the skeletal grave-digger, bottom right. He seems to be the only character who does not come from one of the Gallery paintings. Perhaps he should be seen as representative of Gillray himself: he is the only person who is *working*, he is conspicuously outside the circle of 'high' art, and he is a comic figure. By association, he might bring to mind the skull he digs up, that of Yorick, who, since Sterne, had been an emblem of the comic anatomist. So it is that he grins at the audience and points to his head in summary judgement of the Boydell Gallery—the whole venture is mad. Just over a decade later, the grave was filled: Boydell was brought close to bankruptcy, and the paintings were sold in a lottery, then fell under the auctioneer's hammer.

The war was the main reason for the Gallery's decline, but by the middle of the 1790s there were other distractions. Late in 1794 William Henry Ireland began producing his Shakespeare forgeries, starting with short documents and graduating to complete plays.[20] With Boydell's Gallery no longer a novelty, Samuel Ireland's Norfolk Street home became London's Shakespearean Mecca in 1795; a wide range of people were taken in by the forgeries—James Boswell, Mrs Jordan the actress, and Poet Laureate Henry Pye, to name but three. Boswell seems to have been especially susceptible to the more extreme forms of Bardolatry: having appeared at the Garrick Jubilee in the costume of a Corsican chief, now in Ireland's front room he knelt before the sacred relics and pronounced the Nunc Dimittis. The Ireland imposture was fully exposed only with the publication on 31 March 1796 of Malone's massive *Inquiry into the Authenticity of Certain Miscellaneous Papers and Legal Instruments*, and the performance of 'Shakespeare's lost play' *Vortigern and Rowena* two days later (1 April had originally been suggested), which ended in uproar.

The Ireland affair exhibits a number of now familiar characteristics. Initial enthusiasm from a Shakespeare-obsessed public, manifested by many column inches in the periodicals, was mingled with scepticism and outright scorn, especially apparent in caricature. The manufacture of objects was the central activity, one which capitalized on an interest in Shakespearean relics that may be dated back to the Garrick Jubilee. The motivation was primarily commercial. Here, however, one needs to make a distinction: the Boydell venture combined the profit motive of the print collection with the cultural motive of the desire to improve public taste and national prestige in the fine arts, whereas the Ireland project combined money-making with a desire to please, rather than to educate, the public. The two sides may be seen in the different activities of father and son: the son, industrious but simple-minded William Henry, produced an ever-increasing number of forgeries because that was what his father and the public wanted; the father, entrepreneurial engraver Samuel, publicized and marketed the productions for his own gain—he asked four guineas a copy for the lavish folio *Miscellaneous Papers and Legal Instruments under the Hand and Seal of William Shakespeare: Including the Tragedy of King Lear and a Small Fragment of Hamlet, from the Original*

[20] The best account of the Ireland affair is in Schoenbaum 1970, pp. 189–235. Schoenbaum's book is the definitive study of that strand of Bardolatry which emphasizes the life rather than the works.

MSS. in the Possession of Samuel Ireland, of Norfolk Street. William Henry would do anything to please, while his father would do anything to make money.

Gillray's assault on Samuel Ireland depends, like *Shakespeare-Sacrificed*, on a prior, seriously intended work. Ireland's pose in *Notorious Characters No. 1* (pl. 22, BMC 9064) is identical to that in H. D. Hamilton's portrait of him, as engraved by the sitter himself. The only differences are that in the Gillray he holds a copy of 'Ireland Shakspe' as well as the fold of his robe, and that he is old, balding and smiling slyly, instead of young and well groomed. Gillray's inscription beneath the title asks his audience to get out their copies of Bromley's *Catalogue of Engraved British Portraits* (London, 1793). The Seventh Class, where Ireland has been 'erroneously' placed, is 'Literary Persons'; if we turn, as instructed, to page 449, we find the title of the Tenth Class: 'Phaenomena, Convicts, and Persons otherwise remarkable'. In short, Ireland's appropriation of Shakespeare is dismissed as a criminal misappropriation. The lines below the figure of Ireland, beginning 'Four Forgers, born in one prolific age', attributed to William Mason though probably by George Steevens, parody Dryden's 'Lines on Milton', replacing the 'fourth poet' with the 'fourth forger'. The point made is a telling one. William Lauder's sacred poems, James Macpherson's Ossian, and especially Chatterton's Rowley, were highly accomplished forgeries, significant manifestations of the taste for the medieval and the Gothic, as opposed to the classical, in the later eighteenth century; but to forge Shakespeare was mere 'impudence'.

In the British Museum collection, there are two further caricatures attacking Ireland, though both are of inferior draughtsmanship. Silvester Harding's *The Spirit of Shakspere appearing to his Detractors* (pl. 23, BMC 8883) adopts the strategy, familiar from several theatrical prints, of making Shakespeare into a radiant figure returning from the dead. The tattered documents on the ground allude to Ireland's colourful attempts at Elizabethan spelling ('Tributary lines to Ireland Irelande or Irlaunde for I could not spell his name W Shakspere') and to the performance of 'Vortigern condemned by a most Disintrested Audience April 2 1796'. There is a further allusion to *Vortigern* in the lines accompanying the print. Among the couplets after the biting quotation from *Lear*—'. . . Undivulged crimes, | Unwhipp'd of justice' (III. ii. 51–3)—is the line 'But now this Solemn mock'ry's o'er'. It had been Kemble's repetition of the unfortunate line 'And when this solemn mockery is ended' that had brought the house down in the final act of *Vortigern* on its first and only night at Drury Lane.

A number of details are also worth observing in John Nixon's *The Oaken Chest or the Gold Mines of Ireland a Farce* (pl. 24, BMC 8884), which shows the Ireland family engaged in forging documents and artefacts, such as a six-foot long 'Lock of my Dear Williams Hair'. Loutish William Henry sits on the floor reading a children's book, while in front of him lie 'Fifteen Plays by Shakespeare which will be brought forward'. Among the papers littering the floor in the bottom left corner is 'Bacons history of Henry VII. 1622 notes by Shakspeare': Malone's *Inquiry* showed that accurate facts and dates were not the Irelands' strong points. Even the portraits on the wall are made to do their work: 'Anna Hatherrewaye' is another jibe at neo-Elizabethan spelling, while 'My Own Portrait Drawn by my own Hand from that rare Print by M Droeshout' is directed at the Irelands' use of readily available, far from unique material. The woman admiring the 'lock of hair' is Mrs Freeman, housekeeper and amanuensis; her presence is a further insult, because it seems to have been fairly well known that she was in fact Ireland's mistress and the mother of his children.[21]

The Oaken Chest is one of many caricatures that carry a Shakespearean epigraph. The dramatist himself is turned against the Irelands through the application to their forgeries of Banquo's lines on the witches, 'the Earth hath Bubbles as the Water has and these are of them'. The wit of such a quotation depends on the audience's recognition of it. Given the popularity of the plays on stage and page, the public interest in such fashions as the Jubilee and the forgeries, and the way in which Shakespeare had assumed the status of National Poet, such recognition could be readily assumed. Furthermore, the voracious public appetite for Shakespeare in the later eighteenth century was such that a fullness of allusion to him could be deployed in all kinds of caricature, not merely those that had a direct bearing on the representation and appropriation of the plays. The technique of castigating a contemporary person or tendency by means of epigraphic or epigrammatic Shakespearean quotation was used in a great variety of contexts. It is to one particular context, that of political life, that I now wish to turn.

[21] See e.g., Joseph Farington's diary for 13 Jan. 1796.

3

Politics

BECAUSE the theatre is a public institution it is a political institution. The Elizabethan court knew this, and that is why there was a Master of the Revels to read and censor all new plays. It was politics that kept *Sir Thomas More* off the stage and the deposition scene out of the early quartos of *Richard II*; prosecutions over the 'seditious' *Isle of Dogs* in 1597 and the Essex faction's commissioning of a performance of *Richard II* on the eve of their rebellion in 1601 are only the most graphic of the many examples of the application of Elizabethan drama to contemporary affairs. That Richard II could be compared to Elizabeth I, not least by the Queen herself, demonstrates that a play about the past could be applied to the present. By the same principle, a play *from* the past could be applied to the present: Shakespeare's political influence thus extended beyond his death. The enduring popularity of the plays was both a cause and an effect of their being applied to the public affairs of later ages.

Indeed, the history of the rewriting of Shakespeare for the theatre during the Restoration and the eighteenth century was a history not only of regulation—the submission of the plays to neo-classical canons —but also of politicization. In *The History of King Lear*, Nahum Tate sought to polish and string the disordered 'Heap of Jewels' (Tate 1681, Epistle Dedicatory) that constituted Shakespeare's original, but he also gave the play contemporary political relevance. Tate's prologue ends with a reference to the Popish Plot, and the first performance of his *Lear* was contemporaneous with the trial in London of Oliver Plunket, Archbishop of Armagh and Primate of Ireland, on trumped-up charges of conspiring to land a French army. Tate may have introduced a love affair between Cordelia and Edgar because the Restoration theatre demanded a romantic interest, but in doing so he was also altering the play's political complexion: it had been difficult enough for Shakespeare to place the cause of right in the hands of a French king invading England—in 1680-1 such a course would have been impossible. The exclusion of the King of France was as important for Tate as the romanticizing of Edgar.

Lear was not Tate's only Shakespearean adaptation in this period. He produced a *Richard II* in 1680, but ran into the old problem of the deposition scene; in order to remove the embarrassing contemporary relevance, he renamed the play *The Sicilian Usurper* and gave it an Italian setting. But it was still banned by the Lord Chamberlain after two performances. Then the following year, he adapted *Coriolanus* as an anti-Whig tract called *The Ingratitude of a Common-Wealth*, designed to let 'the People see what Miseries *Common-Wealths* have been involv'd in, by a blind Compliance with their popular Misleaders' and to 'Recommend Submission and Adherence to Establisht Lawful Power, which in a word, is *Loyalty*' (Tate 1682, Epistle Dedicatory, 'Loyalty' in bold type). John Crowne's rewriting of *2 Henry VI* with the unequivocal title *The Misery of Civil-War* also belongs to this period.

Many eighteenth-century adaptations also had a direct political thrust. John Dennis's 1719 version of *Coriolanus*, entitled *The Invader of His Country*, was characteristic in combining an artistic impulse to confer order upon the 'wild Confusion' of Shakespeare and a political impulse to draw an analogy with the Pretender who 'Combin'd with Foreign Foes t'invade the State' (Dennis 1720, prologue). That most popular of adaptations, Cibber's *Richard III*, had its tribulations when first written in 1700: Cibber incorporated into his first act material from *3 Henry VI*, only to have it banned on the grounds that the deposed Henry VI 'wou'd put the Audience in mind of the late *King James*' (Cibber 1700, preface). Contemporary applications of this sort can easily be multiplied. Unlikely as it sounds, *The Taming of the Shrew* furnished material for an anti-Jacobite farce performed at Drury Lane shortly after the 'fifteen: adapted by Charles Johnson from the Christopher Sly material, it was entitled *The Cobbler of Preston*, in allusion to the capture of the Jacobite rebels on Preston Heath. A further spate of adaptations playing on fears of a Jacobite uprising appeared a few years later: 'The whole cluster of adaptations of Shakespearean tragedies from 1720 to 1723 indeed point the single moral. Each one deals with faction and uprising: Dennis's *Invader of His Country*, Theophilus Cibber's *Henry VI*, Lewis Theobald's *Richard II*, Buckingham's *Julius Caesar* and *Marcus Brutus*, Hill's *Henry V*, and Ambrose Philips' *Humfrey Duke of Gloucester*' (Branam 1956, pp. 62–3). Cibber's adaptation *Papal Tyranny in the Reign of King*

John finally reached the stage in the year of the 'forty-five;[1] Garrick launched a new production of *Henry VIII* in 1761 specifically to celebrate the coronation of George III and his marriage to Charlotte of Mecklenburg; and the version of *Cymbeline* performed at Covent Garden during the Seven Years War was designed to show 'what Britons ought to be' in 'these restless days of war's alarm' (Hawkins 1759, prologue).

At the end of the century, John Philip Kemble showed strong political motivation in his choice of plays. To have mounted a production of *Henry V* in, of all years, 1789 must have been a political act, especially since the play was adapted to favour English prowess and subtitled 'The Conquest of France'. An ardent monarchist and a defender of 'rank and station' (Boaden 1825, i. 119), Kemble launched his *Henry V* in October 1789: a year before Burke published his *Reflections*, the actor-adapter was sounding a warning-note, raising patriotic fervour and dampening the enthusiasm with which the fall of the Bastille had initially been greeted in England. Kemble played the role of Henry sixteen times between 1789 and 1792, then revived his production in 1803, the year in which war was renewed after the fragile peace of Amiens; the performance of 25 November that year was given '*for the Benefit of the PATRIOTIC FUND*' and furnished with a concluding 'Occasional Address to the Volunteers'.[2] Kemble had a way of placing emphasis on the nobility of dying in the king's company while at war with France, and for this he was rewarded with much applause.

Kemble's politics were not confined to surface allusions of this sort; they also lay behind the style of many of his productions. He 'always spent as much time at rehearsal, in marshalling and disciplining the corps dramatique, as in any other occupation' (Finlay 1835, p. 244). 'Marshalling and disciplining' are the key words here: the managing of large numbers was Kemble's particular speciality. John Finlay singled out for praise the mob in his *Julius Caesar* of 1815, but most celebrated of all was the triumphal 'Ovation' in his production of *Coriolanus*, a procession in which one hundred and sixty-four people

---

[1] The play had been written nearly 20 years earlier, and gone into rehearsal 8 years earlier, when new Shakespearean plays were being demanded by the Ladies Club, but had not been performed for fear of being damned by an anti-Cibber faction led by law students (see Avery 1938).

[2] Reported, *Gentleman's Magazine* 1803, 73: 1160. For Kemble's patriotic productions, see further Rostron 1972.

passed across the stage.[3] Crowd scenes were irresistible in a theatre that adored spectacle; but, more than this, to marshall such huge numbers on stage was to make a point about ceremony, decorum, and public order. From 1789 onwards any 'mob' would have had overtones of the revolutionary crowd; Kemble's firm handling of them in the Roman plays served as an image of control, a proclamation that London would not go the way of Paris.

It is constantly true, then, that Shakespeare in the theatre is political. What was new from the 1730s onwards was the political appropriation of Shakespeare outside the theatre. The increasing popularity of the plays on stage and the multiplication of printed editions meant that Shakespeare had become sufficiently well known, especially in educated and hence politically conscious circles in London, for allusions to his words to be recognizable and to exercise the kind of authorizing function previously reserved for classical tags. Shakespearean allusion thus became an available resource in political discourse. The *Craftsman* was the best opposition journal of the age, not least because of its powerful range of literary and historical allusions, its comparisons of Walpole with such figures as Sejanus and Cardinal Wolsey. And it was with the *Craftsman* that the politicization of Shakespeare took on a new force.

The first hint of allusion occurs in the tenth issue, dated 6 January 1726,[4] which takes the form of a letter to the editor, 'Caleb D'Anvers' (the pseudonym of Nicholas Amhurst, the *Craftsman*'s founder and chief contributor), from one 'Timothy Shallow'. It is presumably with Master Shallow, the foolish Justice of *2 Henry IV*, in mind that Caleb's introduction begins, 'I shall always have the greatest Respect for the Family of the SHALLOWS, whom I have Reason to look upon as *rising Men*, several of them having already distinguished themselves as the greatest *Ornaments* and *Supports* of their Country, both in *Church* and *State*.' An allusion to Shallow fulfils a number of functions: the name is suggestive in itself but also carries the implication that England is as corrupt as in the time of Henry IV and that the 'rising Men' in Church and State are foolish men. The *Craftsman* was an organ of the Tory opposition associated with Bolingbroke, and thus

---

[3] See *Coriolanus; or, The Roman Matron. . . . Printed Conformable to the Representation at the Theatre Royal, Drury Lane* (1789), 27–9. In the 1811 production, the number of people in the procession had—with judicious use of doubling—increased to 240 (see Shattuck 1974, app. to vol. ii).

[4] i.e. 1726 old style, 1727 new style; all subsequent dates will be given in new style.

represented an interest which especially despised the whiggish parvenus who had attained supremacy with the establishment of the Hanoverian dynasty.

Some six months later, in the fifty-sixth *Craftsman*, dated 29 July 1727, more sustained use was made of *Henry IV*. This paper takes the form of a letter attacking favourites in positions of power—which is to say, attacking Robert Walpole—and carrying the signature 'Philo Panegyricus'. It begins,

Sir, I have just been reading ROBIN's *Panegyrick* on HIMSELF and his FRIENDS at *Westminster*, etc. advertised in your last Paper; which puts me in Mind of a Scene in *Shakespeare*, where the famous Sir *John Falstaff* applauds himself in the same *modest* Manner; Part of which is so delicate and finely touch'd, that I desire you to publish it in your next Journal, as a Pattern to all Self-Panegyrists.

There is then a substantial quotation from the great tavern scene in *1 Henry IV*, with its climactic 'banish plump Jack, and banish all the world'. This issue of the *Craftsman* was published in the brief period between the death of George I and the accession of George II: allusion to *Henry IV* was especially resonant at a time when questions about the future king's conduct were at the centre of the political stage. The polemical thrust of the quotation is that Walpole is a Falstaff—corrupt, fat, womanizing (Moll Skerrett as Doll Tearsheet?)—who will have to be banished by the new king as soon as he accedes. 'Philo Panegyricus' is one of the first to use a Shakespearean speech or scene as a 'Pattern' for the reading of contemporary politics.

The Walpole–Falstaff correspondence did not really take hold, as the Fox–Falstaff identification would later in the century, presumably because there did not exist a state of affairs whereby the politician could be branded as the corrupter of the heir apparent. A better analogue for Walpole was Cardinal Wolsey. The *Craftsman* first made this connection in February 1727 (No. 23), but did not initially mention Shakespeare. That October, however, *Henry VIII* was revived at Drury Lane, with Cibber in the role of Wolsey. The production was a great success; on 7 November it was performed 'By Their Majesties' Command' in the presence of the King, Queen, Princess Royal, and Princess Carolina; on 13 November, the *Daily Post* wrote, 'We hear King Henry the Eighth, with the magnificent Coronation of Queen Anne Bullen, and the Christening of Queen Elizabeth, still continues to draw numerous Audiences, which is

owing to the Excellency of the Performance, and the extraordinary
Grandeur of the Decorations.' The principal reason for the command
performance and the length of the run was that the coronation scene
was staged as a re-enactment of the recent coronation of George II.
But the *Craftsman* put a different construction on the play. The issue
of 18 November took the form of an unsigned letter, probably by
Nicholas Amhurst himself, in which the author says that he has been
to see *Henry VIII* and found that the character who stood out was 'the
great *Minister*'. He means Wolsey, but with the word 'great' signals
that he means Walpole too. 'There you see an ambitious, proud, bad
Man of Parts, in the possession of a wise and brave Prince, amassing
Wealth, taxing the griev'd Commons, and abusing his Trust and
Power to support his Vanity and Luxury.' Wolsey's character in the
play is thus read in accordance with Walpole's misdemeanours on the
political stage. The correspondent then adduces a series of quotations
from the play which are relevant to contemporary events, and ends
with Wolsey's fall—thus predicting or demanding Walpole's fall. He
signs off, 'Thus, Sir, I have thrown together some of the Out-lines,
by which the Character of this ambitious, wealthy, bad *Minister* is
described in the very Words of *Shakespeare*. Reflecting People may
observe from this Picture how like human Nature is in her Workings
at all Times.' The terms of reference here are telling: the stress on
'the very Words of *Shakespeare*' both gives authority to the portrait of
Walpole and detaches it from the writer, a useful defence should there
be an accusation of libel; 'Reflecting People' serves to suggest that
anyone who is both literate and politically conscious will begin to
think through correspondences between the past, as portrayed by
Shakespeare's history plays, and the present. There is one emphasis
that would have been different had the passage been written at the
end of the century: then, Shakespeare's cultural status having been
elevated immeasurably, it would have closed not with a remark about
the constancy of human nature but with a panegyric on the permanence and prophetic power of Shakespeare.

On 8 March 1729 the *Craftsman* ironically suggested that, in order
to avoid the subversive application of old plays to current events, an
Index expurgatorius of objectionable passages should be compiled. The
Poet Laureate could supervise the censorship. One subversive passage
was put forward in the issue of 13 January 1733, when a correspondent calling himself 'Phileleutherus' recommended to the 'serious
Consideration' of the editor a passage concerning 'the Grievances of

the Nation': John of Gaunt's 'This England' speech from *Richard II*. Typography pressed home the point: 'this dear dear Land . . . Is now *leased out* . . . That England, that was wont to conquer others, | Hath made a shameful Conquest of ITSELF'. Nicholas Paxton, the Treasury solicitor, marked the quotation, and sent it to Charles Delafaye, Under-Secretary of State, together with a memorandum noting that it was libellous and recommending it to the Secretary for prosecution. The matter went no further on this occasion, but when the offence was compounded some years later, in the wake of the new Theatre Licensing Act, governmental action was taken.

In the *Craftsman* of 2 July 1737 a letter signed '*C.C.*P.L.'—'Colley Cibber Poet Laureate'—offered the new licenser assistance in the identification of the 'Multitude of Passages in Plays now in Being, which will be proper to be left out in all future Representations of them'. 'For Method's Sake I have put them under several Heads, as they regards [*sic*] *Politicks, Divinity*, or *Bawdry*. The *first* of these shall be chiefly my Province', continues '*C.C.*P.L.'. Fifteen passages are cited, the first eight of them from Shakespeare. The first four are from *King John*, of which Cibber's alteration had recently gone into rehearsal, but not reached the stage, for fear of a hostile reception (as '*C.C.*P.L.' puts it, 'the Town was so unreasonably prejudiced against Me, that They almost unanimously combined against its Representation').[5] All four passages are dangerous, says '*C.C.*P.L.', because of the way they might be applied to contemporary politics. He claims that for this reason he has omitted them from his version of the play.[6] The first, 'When *Law* can do no Right . . .' (*King John*, III. i. 185–90), is described as 'a downright Assertion that *England* was then under a *Parliamentary Tyranny*, or *legal Slavery*'; '*C.C.*P.L.' says he has cut it because 'you Malcontents are charged with hinting at something of the same Nature at present'. The second, 'If but a dozen *French* | Were there in Arms . . .' (III. iv. 173–80), is an encouragement to the Dauphin to invade England, the king 'having intirely lost the Affections of his People'. As for the third and fourth—'It is the curse of *Kings* . . .' (IV. ii. 208–13) and 'Our discontented Counties do revolt . . .' (V. i. 8–16)—'*C.C.*P.L.' leaves it to the editor and 'the Reader'

---

[5] See further, n. 1, above.

[6] The author of the 'Cibber' letter was astute in his choice of passages: when Cibber's play was performed and published, it omitted three of the passages cited. It may, however, have been that Cibber excised them *after* the publication of the *Craftsman* letter, even in response to it.

to decide how they 'may be apply'd'. But the context leaves no doubt that rebellion against a corrupt government is the application.

'*C.C.P.L.*' then turns his attention to *Richard II*, a play 'which hath not been acted within my Memory, and I think never ought, without considerable Castrations and Amendments; for it not only represents an *obstinate, misguided Prince* deposed by his *People*, which is agreeable enough to the Principles of the *Revolution*; but likewise contains several Passages, which the *disaffected* may turn to their Account'. Three such passages are cited, including John of Gaunt's lines on the leasing out and shameful self-conquest of England. 'INKY BLOTS' and 'ROTTEN PARCHMENT BONDS' are capitalized to emphasize the attack on 'the whole Mystery of *Treaty-making*'—an allusion to Walpole's tendency, so aggravating to the Patriot opposition, always to favour a compromise and a treaty when there was a dispute with another European power. The final Shakespearean passage cited is from *2 Henry IV*, 'The Commonwealth is sick of *their own Choice*; | Their *over-greedy Love* hath surfeited' (I. iii. 87–8): 'The *Jacobites* may take Occasion from hence to suggest, I dare not say what. . . . Let this Passage therefore be expunged, as well as several others in both *Parts of the same Play*, which I have mark'd down in my *Index expurgatorius*.' Seven passages from other plays, such as Jonson's *Sejanus* and Dryden's *All for Love*, are then submitted to similar treatment.

The government quickly established that Cibber had not, of course, written the letter: Hardwicke, Lord Chancellor and one of the architects of the Licensing Act, wrote to the Duke of Newcastle, saying that Nicholas Amhurst should be arrested as the author, since the printer's copy was in his handwriting.[7] On Newcastle's warrant, Amhurst was arrested, together with his printer, Henry Haines. Haines was indicted and convicted for printing seditious libel; the indictment, interestingly enough, cited the eight Shakespearean passages and not the seven other ones. On 15 May 1738 Haines was sentenced to twelve months in prison and a fine of £200. He was unable to pay the fine, and seems to have spent the rest of his life in prison. It was from there that he wrote *Treachery, Baseness, and Cruelty Display'd to the Full; in the Hardships and Sufferings of Mr Henry Haines* (1740), an account of his involvement with the *Craftsman* and his prosecution.

It is testimony to Shakespeare's potency as a political weapon that a

---

[7] BL Add. MS 32690, fos. 303–4, cited, Liesenfeld 1984, p. 234. My account of these events is indebted to Liesenfeld, pp. 153–4, and Avery 1939.

man should have rotted in gaol for having printed some quotations from his plays. The printer is usually the person who suffers in cases of this sort, but the fact that Amhurst was not indicted is especially suggestive: presumably it was because the prosecution realized that they would have been unable to secure a conviction since he would have claimed, with perfect justification, that he had not written the treasonable passages in question. Who had written them? Shakespeare, who could hardly have been hauled into the dock. Amhurst could also have made a defence like that published in the *Craftsman* of 6 August 1737:

I appeal to any Man of common Sense and Candour, whether the natural and obvious Design of that Paper was not to shew that several *old Plays* are capable of as bad Applications as any *new ones* can be. For this Purpose, several Passages are quoted out of old Plays, with Relation to *Kings, Queens, Ministers of State*, which it is said *malicious People* may apply in a bad Sense; but the *Author of that Paper* makes no Application of them himself, and only recommended them to the Care of the *Licenser*, or his *Deputy*. I hope, for the Honour of our Country, which hath long boasted of its *Freedom*, that a few Quotations out of *old Plays*, in order to illustrate this Point, cannot be deemed criminal in Law.

This is a neat argument: Shakespeare is not being seditiously applied to contemporary affairs; rather, a public service has been done through the pointing out of his plays' *potential* for 'bad Applications'. But the fact remains that, in the case of Haines, 'a few Quotations out of *old Plays*' *were* 'deemed criminal in Law'. That Haines the artisan suffered for Shakespeare's treasonable language gives a new twist to Walter Benjamin's claim that oppression of the anonymous toilers is implicit in the production of cultural treasures.

Victor Liesenfeld writes:

The *Craftsman* for 2 July, which was intended as part of a series on the new law restricting the liberty of the stage, sparked a debate in the newspapers over the freedom—or licentiousness—of the press that lasted into the winter. The prosecution of Haines quickly became a *cause célèbre*. It was frequently cited by the Opposition press as evidence that the government was, as it had warned, bent on suppressing all criticism and dissent, and was cited by the government to show that attacks on the king had become intolerable. (Liesenfeld 1984, p. 154)

I would contend that the affair also marked a watershed in the political appropriation of Shakespeare. The *Craftsman* of 2 July 1737

showed how extraordinarily potent the language of the plays could
be: the quotation of the now authoritative definition of true Englishness from *Richard II*, with an emphasis on that part of the passage
which castigates those in power for abnegating their responsibilities to
England, had become sufficiently dangerous for the government to
risk the adverse publicity caused by a prosecution. Accordingly, from
the 1740s onwards, Shakespeare was cited more and more frequently
in political discourse, whether verbal or visual.

I have not discovered any political caricatures prior to 1740 which
use Shakespearean quotation. Despite the *Craftsman* of 18 November
1727, an engraving of March 1733 entitled *A Satire on Sir Robert
Walpole, Comparing him with Cardinal Wolsey* (BMC 1925) does *not*
allude to the fall of Wolsey in Shakespeare's *Henry VIII*. Later in the
century a comparison with Wolsey would almost invariably be
accompanied by quotation of 'Farewell, a long farewell, to all my
greatness! . . .' (*Henry VIII*, III. ii. 351 ff.). It was only after the
Licensing Act and the prosecution of Haines that Shakespearean allusion spread from pamphleteering to visual caricature. The
first engraving in the British Museum collection that makes a Shakespearean comparison is George Bickham's ironic comparison of
Walpole to Julius Caesar, *The Stature of a Great Man or the English
Colossus* (March 1740, BMC 2458). The text of this illustration of
Walpole as the Colossus at Rhodes consists of Cassius' 'Why Man,
he doth bestride the narrow World | Like a Colossus', continuing
down to 'The fault, dear P————y, is not in our Stars, | But in our
Selves, that we are Underlings' (*Julius Caesar*, I. ii. 135–41).
'P————y' is William Pulteney, Earl of Bath, a leading figure in the
agitation in favour of war—the engraving is an attack on Walpole's
prevarication over war with Spain. The substitution of him for
Brutus is an early example of the technique of interchanging Shakespearean and contemporary characters, a device that became increasingly popular as the century unfolded—*The Modern Characters
from Shakespear*, for example, a book published in 1778, consisted of
quotations from the plays applied flatteringly to contemporary
figures, beginning with the Royal Family and going through the
aristocracy.[8]

The Stature of a Great Man established a model. Three months later,

---

[8] The BL copy, c.109.bb.17, has MS decodings and additions at one time attributed
to King George III. Another anthology of the same sort, *Shakespeare's History of the
Times*, was also published in 1778.

Julius Caesar was quoted again in *The Cardinal in the Dumps, The Preferment of the Barber's Block With the Head of the Colossus* (BMC 2454), which shows rising from a Wall a Pole (Wal-pole) with the head of the Colossus on it, and Cardinal Fleury, the French first minister, in distress over Admiral Vernon's victory against the Spanish at Porto Bello. The inscription is from later in Cassius' speech: 'Age thou art Sham'd! . . . When could they say, till now, who talk'd of *Rome*, | That her wide Walls encompass'd but *one Man*?' (*Julius Caesar*, I. ii. 150-5). This serves a dual effect, in that it both praises Admiral Vernon as the one man who has saved the honour of the country and damns Walpole for his Caesar-like quest for supreme power.

The *Craftsman* controversy and this pair of caricatures initiated a tradition of making political capital out of Shakespeare in the latter years of the Robinocracy. Despite this, quotation from the plays remained relatively scarce in political caricatures through the 1740s and 1750s. Captions more frequently consisted of invented couplets or allusions to satirical texts such as *The Dunciad, Hudibras*, and *The Beggar's Opera*. It is symptomatic that *The Junto* (BMC 2846), a 1746 satire on tavern politics, quotes from *The Merchant of Venice* but then adds 'Vide Shakespear's Shylock'—later in the century, caricaturists would not consider it necessary to indicate their Shakespearean sources so explicitly, assuming instead that the provenance of their quotations would be familiar to all readers.

It was when caricature became more central to political debate soon after the accession of George III that Shakespearean allusion became more central to caricature. Equalling the number of caricatures which depict Bute as a boot are those that call him 'Sawney', a derisive allusion to his Scots origin. The idea of a Scottish nobleman making a bid for supreme power led to the identification of Bute with Macbeth. Thus, *The Magical Installation or Macbeth Invested* (pl. 25, BMC 3896), published in London and Edinburgh on 22 September 1762, an engraved broadside with a design and verses, shows a sceptre in the air with Bute approaching to grasp it, saying 'Is it a Scepter that I see before Me? | The handle towards my Hand—Come, let me clutch thee!' Three witches encounter him. The first says 'Henceforth be Knight—the first that ever graced the Scottish Annals', a reference to Bute's having assumed, or conferred upon himself, as his critics saw it, the Order of the Garter; the second says 'All hail Macbeth—thou shalt be King hereafter', and the third, 'All hail Macbeth thou shalt be more than King'. The verses beneath, with rebuses, explicitly make the comparison with Macbeth's traitorous mounting of the throne.

The startling news of Bute's resignation the following April provoked another broadside, *Macbeth and the Doctor; or, Sawney in a Fever*, which included the exchange 'Can'st thou not minister to a Mind diseased[?] | Therein the Patient must minister to himself.' This engraving appears in an interesting collection of 'Antibutonian' material gathered and published two years later in 1765 by John Pridden under the title *The Scots Scourge: or, Pridden's Supplement to the British Antidote to Caledonian Poison*. Pridden also included a sustained verbal caricature of 1763 that plays on the identification of Bute with Macbeth. Entitled 'The Three Conjurors. A Political Interlude. Stolen from Shakespear. As it was performed at sundry places in Westminster', it features 'Macboote' and three conjurors or witches, named Gremonte, Haxy, and Veville—these represent Lord Egremont, Lord Halifax, and George Grenville, the so-called 'triumvirate' who took power on Bute's retirement. They speak lines like 'Fair is foul, and foul is fair, | To screen *Macboote* is all our care', and repeatedly warn against Wilkes, whose press campaign in the *North Briton* had been a thorn in the ministry's side, in such couplets as 'Macboote, Macboote, Macboote, of W—kes beware, | Avoiding him, nought else is worth thy care' and 'Be bloody, bold, and resolute, laugh to scorn | The pen of W—kes.' It was Halifax who, in his capacity as Secretary of State, issued a general warrant for the arrest of all concerned in the production of the *North Briton*, number 45, published on 23 April 1763, in which Wilkes had written his most stinging attack on the government. The battle between the ministry and the representatives of the electorate is enacted in *The Three Conjurors* version of the *Macbeth* show of kings: it takes the form of a show of Members of Parliament, the last of them being Wilkes with a paper in his hand inscribed 'M-g-a Ch-r-a'. Macboote responds with such cries as 'Thou art like the spirit of impeachment' and 'For W—kes in *M-g-a Ch-r-a* arm'd, grins at me' (the Wilkesian grin was immortalized by Hogarth in his engraving of May 1763). Macboote puts up a final resistance, with the Scottish cry 'Hang those that speak of W—kes, give me some whisky', then resigns and skulks off, leaving the stage to those under the banner of 'LIBERTY, PROPERTY, and NO EXCISE'. This is the earliest example I have found of the verse parody of a Shakespearean scene in terms of contemporary politics—a kind of polemic which is closely related to caricature and which will be discussed in Chapter 4, below.

The comparison of Bute with Macbeth seems to have inspired caricaturists to experiment with other Shakespearean correspond-ences. Almost contemporaneously with *The Magical Installation or Macbeth Invested*, there appeared an etching with the title *The Tempest or Enchanted Island* (BMC 3958). *The Enchanted Island* was the title of Dryden and Davenant's reworking of *The Tempest*. The engraving shows the Princess of Wales (George III's mother) and her 'favourite', Bute, being blown into the air by the discharge of two land-mines; Fox the Elder is thrown down by the blast. The Princess cries 'O when shall we three meet again?' and Fox replies 'When Peace is Sign'd with F[rance] and S[pain]'. The mine or petard that has 'hoist' them is the Press, meaning principally Wilkes's *North Briton*. Here then, the text is again from *Macbeth* but the title expands the Shakespearean frame of reference. *The Tempest*, so often thought of as an apolitical play of pure imagination, served as a frequent point of reference for the next generation of caricaturists. The enclosed 'Enchanted Island', potentially a Utopia but harbouring a rebellious faction consisting of a monster and two upstart drunkards, becomes a favourite image of England or of the realm of high politics. Anti-butonian satires later in the 1760s raided other parts of Shakespeare too: *The Colossus* of 1767 (BMC 4178) reworked the Julius Caesar theme, and an engraving in the *Oxford Magazine* the following year showed Bute as *Claudius pouring Poison into the King's Ear, as he is Sleeping in the Garden* (BMC 4329), a motif repeated at one remove two years later in *The R——l Dupe* (BMC 4442), where George III sleeps in the arms of his mother while Bute steals the sceptre and a picture on the wall shows the poisoning of Old Hamlet. The association between Bute and the Princess translates nicely into an image of Gertrude's supposed complicity with Claudius.

From about 1780 onwards the repertoire of Shakespearean allusion in political caricature expanded in both range and sophistication. A number of circumstances seem to have combined to bring this about. For one thing, two caricaturists of exceptional sophistication, James Sayers and James Gillray, began their careers. Sayers started his series of anti-Fox caricatures. The first of these was *Paradise Lost*, of 17 July 1782 (BMC 6011), which used Miltonic allusion to satirize Fox's exclusion from office. Following Sayers's lead in the deploy-ment of literary allusion in the portrayal of this subject, Gillray

produced his first strongly allusive caricatures: on 22 July 1782
Hannah Humphrey published his *Gloria Mundi, or—The Devil Addressing the Sun* (BMC 6012), in which Fox as Satan quotes from *Paradise
Lost*, IV; then *The Soliloquy* of 12 August 1782 (BMC 6020) shows Fox
locked out of the Treasury, reciting Wolsey's lines from *Henry VIII*,
'Farewell, a long Farewell to all my Greatness . . .'. Gillray's first
caricature on the rivalry between Fox and Pitt, published that
December, picks up on Sayers's use of *Paradise Lost*: it is entitled, in
allusion to Satan, *'Aside he turn'd for envy, yet with jealous leer malign, eyd
them askance'* (BMC 6044). Sayers made glancing use of Shakespearean allusion in the print that Fox said so damaged his career, the
celebrated *Carlo Khan's Triumphal Entry into Leadenhall Street* (BMC
6276): it establishes its atmosphere partly by means of a quotation
from *3 Henry VI*, or rather from a part of *3 Henry VI* that was well
known since Cibber had incorporated it into *Richard III*. Beneath a
crow in the top left corner of the engraving there is an allusion to
Henry's words to Richard of Gloucester, 'The night-crow cry'd, fore-
boding luckless time' (Cibber's *Richard III*, I. ii). Readers of the print
might also have sensed something of the atmosphere of *Macbeth*:
beneath the copy of the print in the British Museum Sayers folio there
is a slip of paper on which is written in an old hand: 'The Ravens
hoarse that croaks the fatal entry of Duncan under our Battlements'.[9]

Gillray returned to the Cardinal Wolsey soliloquy on a number of
occasions: each fall from grace provided him with a chance to replay
it. Thus, when Thurlow was dismissed from the office of Lord Chancellor in May 1792, he produced *The Fall of the Wolsey of the Woolsack*
(BMC 8096), which, in a neat pun, shows 'Wolsey' and the King
engaging in a tug of war with the symbol of office, the Woolsack.
Gillray does not seem to have been the first to apply Wolsey's lines to
Thurlow. There is a print of 22 May, two days before his, called *The
Fall of Wolsey, or Turning a Great Man out of Office* (BM, acquired since
Catalogue), which shows George III turfing Thurlow out of the
window of a privy—the Privy Council?—as Pitt goes out through the
door, doing up his trousers. Thurlow is given Wolsey's 'Oh! how
wretched | Is that poor man, that hangs on princes . . . And when
he falls, he falls as Lucifer | Never to hope again.' The Shakespearean

[9] *Satirical Prints by James Sayers*, Banks Collection II, BM Print Room, 298.d.3.
Comments in the same hand under other prints in the folio give much contemporary
and historical detail, suggesting that the author is a reliable guide.

parallel is by this time a widely available resource, not the preserve of a single satirist.

It was not only that literary-minded caricaturists started work in the early 1780s: Shakespearean allusion also became more prominent because history and, more particularly, the heir apparent, played into the hands of satirists. In December 1779, when he was seventeen years old, Prince George was much struck by Mary Robinson, the actress who played Perdita in Garrick's adaptation of *The Winter's Tale* at Drury Lane. Since she was known as 'Perdita Robinson', because of her success in the role, the Prince signed his admiring letters 'Florizel'. When she became his mistress, the 'low-born lass' and the Prince proved irresistible to satirists; a string of 'Florizel and Perdita' caricatures appeared,[10] together with such pamphlets as a *Poetical Epistle from Florizel to Perdita: with Perdita's Answer. And a Preliminary Discourse upon the Education of Princes.* The Prince soon grew bored with the actress, and the King, embarrassed by the Florizel and Perdita Press campaign, had her paid off with an annuity. Struck with paralysis from the waist downwards, she began a new career as a poetess and in 1795 wrote a neo-Shakespearean blank-verse tragedy called *The Sicilian Lover*, which has a certain poignancy in view of the loss of her own Florizel. The Prince, meanwhile, moved into a new circle of acquaintance, and interest quickly shifted to Shakespeare's fullest exploration of 'the Education of Princes'.

From the mid-1780s onwards George spent a great deal of time with the Opposition group who were consistently criticized for their dissolute life-style: heavy-drinking C. J. Fox, theatrical R. B. Sheridan, and adventurer Colonel Hanger. Gillray was especially well placed to watch their activities, for his lodging at Mrs Humphrey's in St James's was just down the street from Brooks's, the Club where the group most frequently met. Fox was overweight, Sheridan had an alcohol-induced red nose, Hanger was a swaggerer: enter Falstaff, Bardolph, and Pistol to lead the Prince astray. Horace Walpole wrote in his journal in March 1783, 'The Prince of Wales had of late thrown himself into the arms of Charles Fox, and this in the most indecent and undisguised manner. . . . Fox's followers . . . were strangely licentious in their conversations about the King. At Brookes's they proposed wagers on the duration of his reign' (Walpole 1910, ii. 496).

---

[10] BMC 5767, 5865, 6117, 6266, 6318, 6655, 6811.

They almost seem to be self-consciously mimicking the behaviour of Falstaff and his followers at the Boar's Head.

In May 1783 the engraver and water-colourist John Boyne published *Falstaff and his Prince* (BMC 6231), with an Elizabethan Fox and a fashionably dressed Prince. Next came the identification of the whole group as the cast of *Henry IV. A Shaksperean Scene* (pl. 26, August 1786, BMC 6974), by William Dent, an amateur caricaturist active throughout the 1780s, shows the Prince's friends rejoicing at a rumour that the King had been killed when Margaret Nicholson, a madwoman, had attempted to stab him on 2 August 1786. Dent's dramatis personae include not only the major figures, and Mrs Fitzherbert, the Prince's morganatic wife, as Doll Tearsheet, but also several lesser luminaries: Shallow is the Duke of Portland, Silence is Devonshire, the page Lord John Cavendish, and serving-man Davy, Weltje, the Prince's cook and favoured servant. Dent, using a technique at which Hogarth had excelled, reinforces his argument by means of objects on the wall: a placard points to *2 Henry IV*, a crucifix to the fact that not the least disturbing aspect of the Prince's liaison with Mrs Fitzherbert was her Catholicism. Hanger's lines are those of Pistol as he enters with the news that Henry IV is dead; the Prince's, on the other hand, are from Hal's fulsome speech of filial repentance in act IV scene v. Dent's allusion openly asserts that George owes his father a similar humble apology. But there was no reconciliation, despite Fox's attempts to bring one about. The latter was aware of the dangers of a split between the King and the Prince, but the public did not perceive this to be his position and partisan caricaturists would take every opportunity to make him seem more self-interested than he was.

It is always important to remember that it is in the nature of caricature to gloss over political nuance: Fox was not a 'radical' in the sense that Paine was, but caricaturists lumped them together as such. Equally, caricature will, at least on the surface, also gloss over literary nuance. The force of an allusion to *Henry IV* in an anti-Foxite print is dependent on the assumption that Hal is right to reject Falstaff. But any reader or viewer of *Henry IV* will have distinctly mixed feelings about the rejection: Hazlitt speaks for the majority, in both his own time and ours, when he writes 'The truth is, that we never could forgive the Prince's treatment of Falstaff . . . Whatever terror the French in those days might have of Henry V yet, to the readers of poetry at present, Falstaff is the better man of the two. We think of him and quote him oftener' (HW iv. 285). While political discourse, especially when it takes the form of caricature, tends to polarity, literary texts, especially Shakespearean ones, tend to multivalence. The risk, though also the excitement and the potential subversiveness, of Shakespearean allusions in political caricature is that they cannot easily be contained; to 'quote' Falstaff is to give new life to a set of values which governments would generally prefer to restrain.

The political aspirations of the Foxites were given a fillip by the Whig success in the Westminster by-election of July 1788. It was a dirty campaign. One allegation, that the Whig candidate Townshend had tried to seduce the Duchess of Rutland, gave Boyne the opportunity to combine an image of Fox as Falstaff with the quasi-Shakespearean intonation, 'I am thy injured Husband's Ghost. Beware of the foul Deeds done in the Flesh while I was on earth' (*Falstaff and the Merry Wives of Westminster, Canvassing for their Favourite Member Ld T——d* (BMC 7343)). The following day J. Atkins published another print that branded Fox as Townshend's procurer. *Falstaf and the Merry Wives of Westminster Returning from Canvassing for Ld T————* (BMC 7345) shows him wearing the antlers of the final act of *Merry Wives* and escorting two ladies who look as if they are of questionable morals.

Four months later, the King fell into his first serious, incapacitating bout of insanity—insanity in the eyes of the age, that is: historians now speak of porphyria instead. Once again, Hanger could say 'thy tender lambkin now is King'. He does so in Gillray's *King Henry IVth The Last Scene* (pl. 27, BMC 7380), where a huge Falstaff–Fox is given the lines 'The Laws of England are at my commandment. Happy are they which have been my friends; and woe to my Lord Chancr.' The change from 'woe to my Lord Chief Justice' (*2 Henry IV*, V. iii. 138) hints at Fox's opposition to the secret negotiations between the Prince and Thurlow, the Chancellor, on their possible co-operation in the event of the King's death or permanent incapacity. The influence of Gillray's print—or perhaps the force of the Shakespearean parallel *per se*—was such that in the Parliamentary debate of 19 December 1788, James Martin said that Fox's behaviour 'brought to memory a scene in Shakspeare's play of Henry 4, where Falstaff reckoned upon what would be done for him and his associates, when the Prince should come to the crown, which was then daily expected, and was assigning places of dignity and character to the most deserving of his friends' (Hansard 1806–20, xxvii. 793).

Once Dent and Gillray had established the frame of reference, comparisons with Henry IV became common. In May 1792 the Prince of Wales made his first speech in the House of Lords, on the occasion of the debate on the King's Proclamation against Seditious Writings, a response to Paine's *Rights of Man*; he spoke vigorously in defence of the Proclamation, and from that point on broke—at least for a time—with the Foxites. Thus in March 1793 Fores published Isaac Cruikshank's *False Liberty Rejected or Fraternizing and Equalizing Principles Discarded* (pl. 28, BMC 8311), in which the Prince is given a version of Hal's rejection of Falstaff, quoted in prose and slightly altered: 'I know you not, Vain Proffligates. fall to your prayers; how ill White hairs become a fool and jester; I have long Dream'd of such kind of Men, so surfeit swelld. Seditious and Profane; but being awake, I do despise my dream . . . I have turn'd away my former self, so will I those that kept me company . . . the Tutors and the Feeders of my Riots.' This is a good example of Shakespearean quotation being particularly effective because the context is exceptionally resonant and very few words are changed. 'Vain Proffligates' replaces 'old man' and 'Seditious' is substituted for 'old'; 'man', 'tutor', and 'feeder' are made plural: the alterations occur in the key words and are thus emphatic. Cruikshank's public would have alighted on 'Vain Proffligates' and 'Seditious' because these are novel intrusions into an otherwise highly familiar text.

False Liberty Rejected is among Cruikshank's most allusive prints. Contained within the title are the three principles of the French Revolution, *liberté, égalité, fraternité*; this association is picked up in the engraving itself, for Sheridan and Fox are dressed as sansculottes. This is a typical instance of caricature's tendency to elide political difference for the sake of establishing a revolutionary demonology: Fox and Sheridan were not really English Jacobins, let alone sansculottes (what is more, in France at this time, there were major divisions between Jacobin and sansculottes interests). Cruikshank also invokes another comparison for the Prince's relationship with the King. George III's reference to the fatted calf and the Prince's 'I will return to my Father and say unto him . . .' make the print biblical as well as Shakespearean. The Prodigal Son parallel had first been used in a print of January 1787 (BMC 7129), though since it is a significant point of reference in *Henry IV* it may well be that the allusion reaches back to its biblical provenance via the medium of Shakespeare.

A year after *False Liberty Rejected*, Sayers's *Citizen Bardolph Refused*

Admittance at Prince Hal's (BMC 8441) was published by Hannah Humphrey. 'Citizen' grossly exaggerates Sheridan's moderate liberalism by applying to him the appellation with which true radicals like Thelwall addressed each other, in imitation of the French 'citoyen'. The caricature shows Sheridan being turned away from Carlton House and, like Dent's *Shaksperean Scene*, reinforces its point with a playbill on the wall. Dent's bill had been a double thrust, since it had included both *2 Henry IV* and an after-piece entitled *The Mistake*; Sayers's is a triple one, listing Shakespeare's play, George Colman's *The Manager in Distress*, a cut at Sheridan's dual life as politician and manager of Drury Lane, and Otway's *Venice Preserved*, with its ominous subtitle 'a Plot discovered'.[11]

Gillray made another contribution to the field in 1796. *Hint to Modern Sculptors, as an Ornament to a Future Square* (BMC 8800) shows the future George IV, albeit rather portly, splendidly attired on horseback; the inscription is from Vernon's speech on Hal's transformation, 'I saw young Harry with his beaver on . . .' (*1 Henry IV*, IV. i. 104). Gillray changes 'young Harry' to 'him', so that his readers will think 'to whom did this originally refer?' On remembering that it was Hal, they would hope that George was on the way to becoming another Henry V—or, more likely, despair at the contrast between the fat prince and his 'feather'd Mercury' of a forebear.

The Prince was also cast in other roles. His corpulence led to a variation whereby he became Falstaff. As early as 1794 he had been given some of Falstaff's words in Isaac Cruikshank's *John Bull's Hint for a Profitable Alliance* (BMC 8487), but the first time he is actually represented as Sir John is in Williams's print on his infatuation with Lady Hertford, *All for Love* (December 1806, BMC 10625). Curiously enough, despite his allusion to *Merry Wives*, Williams fails to make any overt capital out of the possible pun in 'heart-Ford'. The parallel with Falstaff endured after George had taken the throne. Heath's *Falstaff and his Ragged Crew* (July 1820, BMC 13766) is a satire on the disreputable witnesses he obtained to support his allegations against

---

[11] The identification of Sheridan with Bardolph remained popular (BMC 7528, 7837, 7920, 10606), not least because 'Sherry', as he was also known, shared Bardolph's love of drink. Sheridan–Bardolph is prominent in Gillray's *Homer Singing His Verses to the Greeks* (BMC 9023), aimed specifically at the Opposition's drinking habits—here Fox is given Falstaff's 'come, sing a bawdy song; make me merry' (*1 Henry IV*, III. iii. 13) with 'bawdy' changed to '*Boosey*'. Gillray's attack is strengthened by the context of the line quoted: Falstaff is irresponsibly asking Bardolph for a song at a time when the country is threatened by war.

Queen Caroline. In 1827 Heath again used *King Henry IV* (BMC 15411) in a satire on the King's sexual affairs; this time, Lady Conyngham plays the part of Doll Tearsheet and her husband that of Mistress Quickly. A hanging on the wall depicts the Prodigal Son, an allusion back to that earlier image of George.

Since he was both overweight and a lover of women, the Prince of Wales was also caricatured as Henry VIII. In 1802 there was a masquerade at the Union Club to celebrate the Treaty of Amiens; the Prince seems to have gone as Henry VIII, though some accounts say he was a Sicilian noble.[12] In Williams's *The Union Club Masquerade* (BMC 9871) he is cast as Henry, with Mrs Fitzherbert as Anne Boleyn. Ten years later, in *He Has Put his Foot in it* (BMC 11887), Williams makes the identification again. The engraving is a satire on the Prince's desire to get rid of Lady Hertford, whose political influence was proving embarrassing. There are two portraits on the wall; one is labelled 'Henry Fifth' and the other, immediately above the Prince, 'Henry Eighth'. The head of each portrait is cut off by the top of the print; that of Henry V is badly torn. We may read them as follows: were the heads visible, they would both be the Prince; 'Henry V' is torn because hopes that George would follow Hal in outgrowing his misspent youth were in tatters; he is instead in the shadow of Henry VIII, a monarch well known for his tendency to dispose of women when they were no longer of any use to him and— remembering Mrs Fitzherbert's Catholicism—to be led by marriage into religious controversy.

The most effective prints of George as Henry VIII are those that also cast Princess Caroline as Queen Katherine. The first investigation into the conduct of the prince's wife, a stratagem to see if there were sufficient grounds for divorce proceedings to be initiated, took place in 1813. One of Williams's engravings on the subject, *State Mysteries* (BMC 12028), has Caroline quoting Katherine's plea, 'Sir I desire you do me right and Justice . . .' (from *Henry VIII*, II. iv. 13 ff.). The same speech is used in a print entitled *King Henry VIII. Act II, Scene iv* (BMC 13829) on the occasion of the 1820 Bill of Pains and Penalties to deprive Caroline, by then Queen, of her rights and title. Here George plays Henry again and Castlereagh is Wolsey.

---

[12] According to BMC 9871, the *Annual Register* said that he was Henry, the *London Chronicle*, the Sicilian. I have checked *Observer*, 6 June 1802, and *European Magazine* 1802, 41: 499, which both say that he went as Henry VIII—but *The Times*, 2 June, plumps for the Sicilian.

There are other caricatures of George as Henry VIII which do not allude to the play, just as Byron's squib 'Windsor Poetics' accuses the Regent of being 'Henry to his Wife' but does not refer to Shakespeare. Nevertheless, chiefly because of the opportunity it provided for spectacle, *Henry VIII* was highly popular on the early nineteenth-century stage, so, as with *Henry V*, for much of the public the historical figure would have been inextricable from the Shakespearean representation. Caricature, like theatrical performance and history painting, entrenched the view that Shakespeare's history plays were a prime source from which the English people could learn their own history. Considerable ideological pressure was therefore brought to bear on the way in which Shakespeare's histories were interpreted. As will be shown in Part II, Hazlitt's criticism explored the possibility that *Henry V* and *Henry VIII* offered powerful critiques of those most celebrated kings. To read the plays in this way was to disturb an orthodoxy about the glories of the English monarchy which both court and ministry had the strongest interest in maintaining. Caricaturists producing work in support of the Queen at the time of her trial in 1820 implicitly followed Hazlitt's reading of King Henry VIII—and, by parallelism, King George IV—as vulgar, arrogant, sensual, cruel, hypocritical, without decency and humanity, 'of all the monarchs in our history the most disgusting: for he unites in himself all the vices of barbarism and refinement, without their virtues' (HW iv. 305).

But Hazlitt's vision of the political complexity of *Henry V* was not so obviously shared by the many caricaturists who compared the Regent to Hal. The tendency there was to set up Hal as a positive role model and to use his reformation as either stick or carrot to cajole the Regent. Politicians as well as satirists alluded to the *Henry IV* plays in this way. For instance, during the session of the Court of Common Council on 8 January 1811, Alderman Birch, speaking against a move to give absolute power to the Regent, adverted to the parallel between the youth of the Regent and that of Prince Hal. His words are reported in the *Courier* of 9 January 1811:

He then quoted from the play of Henry IV.

> 'Are you in such haste
> To count my sleep as death? This speech of thine
> Will add to my distemper.'

Birch has adapted the Shakespearean lines to fit the contemporary

context: 'This part of his conjoins with my disease' (*2 Henry IV*, IV.
v. 63) is altered to 'This speech of thine | Will add to my distemper',
so that it refers to the pro-Regent speech to which he is replying, and
a reference to the king's 'disease' is replaced with the milder 'dis-
temper'. The Alderman obviously expects his audience to recognize
the immediate context, the idea of a prematurely taken crown. He
perhaps overlooks the wider context, the facts that Henry IV has
been an ineffectual king and that Hal was not actually stealing the
crown.

After the Regency Act was passed the following month advice to
Prince George came swiftly off the presses. The *Satirist* of that month
carried the first of a series of 'Letters to his Royal Highness the Prince
of Wales'. Some passages are worth quoting because, as Alderman
Birch did, they make explicit the parallel with Shakespeare's Hal.

Shew the world that if you once practised some of Harry Monmouth's indis-
cretions, you also possess the kingly virtues of Henry the Fifth: tell those who
would basely influence you to sacrifice your duty to your father, your king,
and your country, for the gratification of their own avarice or ambition, in the
words of this illustrious monarch:

> 'Presume not that I am the thing I was,
> For Heaven doth know, so shall the world perceive
> That I have turn'd away my former self
> So will I those that kept me company.'

(*Satirist* 1811, 8: 105)

'In the words of this illustrious monarch' provides a strong instance of
the correspondence between Shakespeare's history plays and popular
conceptions of English kings: the words of Shakespeare's Henry V
are treated as if they were those of the monarch himself.

The writer goes on to condemn the opposition members who
seemed to be sorry that the King's health was improving slightly.
They are described as base characters whose enthusiasm in the future
King's favour has brought about a change in their political creed
which

might induce a man, unacquainted with the virtues of your [the Regent's]
heart, to believe that you had exclaimed in the language of Shakespeare:

> 'All your sage counsellors hence!
> And to the English court assemble now
> From every region, imps of idleness . . .'

10. James Gillray, Boydell slashing the Shakespeare Gallery paintings (1791)

11. Robert Edge Pine, Garrick reciting the Jubilee Ode (1780)

James Gillray, Designed & Pub. *Pub.d June 20 1789 by H. Humphrey No 18 Old Bond Street.*

Price 5 s.

SHAKESPEARE - SACRIFICED; or _ *The Offering to Avarice.*

— as _subscriber will be published, price Two Guineas N.o of SHAKESPEARE ILLUSTRATED, with the Text, containing &c. complete : the Engravings to be carried on in emulation of the Alderman's liberal plan — further particulars will shortly be given in all the Public papers —

12. James Gillray, *Shakespeare-Sacrificed* at Boydell's Gallery (1789)

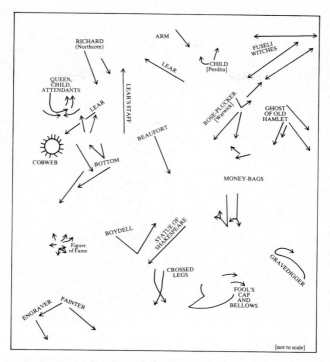

12a. Gillray's *Shakespeare-Sacrificed*: who is pointing to whom?

13. Sir Joshua Reynolds, *The Death of Cardinal Beaufort* (1789)

14. Henry Fuseli, *Titania and Bottom* (1789)

15. Benjamin West, *Lear in the Storm* (1789)

The quotation continues for another seven lines, describing the ruf-
fians, revellers, robbers, and murderers who, says Bolingbroke, will
be given 'office, honour, might' under 'the fifth Harry' (*2 Henry IV*,
IV. v. 120–9). The Shakespearean parallel is the linchpin of the rhetoric
here. It works on two levels. First, there is the power of the language
itself; it is a vision of corruption so telling that the Prince is, one
senses, being forced to come out and say that of course he will no
longer move in bad company. The quotation, along with the phrase
'unacquainted with the virtues of your heart', corners the Prince: he
must prove that he has those virtues by showing that the quotation is
not applicable. At a deeper level, but one altogether comprehensible
in the context of the tradition associating George with Hal, there is
the fact that the Prince's reply has already been written for him; he
must re-enact Hal's 'O, pardon me, my liege . . .' and follow his
forebear in committing himself to his duty as a future king.

The parallel is clinched just before the end of the 'Letter' by an
allusion to the Lord Chief Justice's speech in act V scene ii:

On the assumption of the royal power, I conjure your Royal Highness to
exercise your own understanding, be guided by the genuine impulse of your
own excellent heart:

> 'Question your royal thoughts, make the case yours,
> Be now the father and propose a son.'

In this way, the Regent is exhorted to do as Harry does in this scene
and affirm that he will follow the dictates of justice and a king's
innate nobility, not be swayed by his sometime followers. The frontispiece to the following month's *Satirist* provides a visual 'reply' to the
Letter. Entitled *The Cats Let Out of the Bag or the Rats in Dismay* (pl. 29,
BMC 11714), it portrays Sheridan and other reformers as rats, while
the Prince is given a fine bearing and speaks the crucial lines from the
'rejection' speech in *2 Henry IV* that had been quoted in the Letter
('. . . I have turnd away my former | Self, so will I those that kept me
company'). This engraving also appeared independently and, to
judge from the fact that there are three copies of it in the British
Museum collection, must have been popular.

In this context, it seems to me that for the distinguished legal
historian Alexander Luders to have published in 1813 an essay entitled
The Character of Henry V when Prince of Wales was a political as well as a
scholarly act. Luders uses historical sources to vindicate Hal from the

wantonness and irresponsibility that Shakespeare had thrust upon him; in doing so, he implicitly challenges the current Prince to follow his historical rather than his Shakespearean precursor.

When the Regent eventually took the throne and became George IV, as Hal had become Henry V before him, the reading of Shakespeare in terms of contemporary politics spilled over from graphic satire and polemical prose, and back on to the stage. *2 Henry IV* had not been played in London since 1804; in the summer of 1821 it was revived at Covent Garden with strong emphasis on the spectacular ending: according to the playbill, '4 additional scenes will be introduced displaying the grand Coronation'. The run began on 25 June; on 19 July, 'This being the day of the Coronation, the King commanded the theatre to be opened gratuitously to the public—Henry 4th pt. 2d— with the Coronation'. The play's success, reminiscent of that of *Henry VIII* at the time of George II's coronation, may be judged from the fact that on 7 August, the last night of its run, 'some of the Performers' benefits were bought up—an additional pit door was opened, and orders [complimentary admissions] of every description were refused' (Genest 1832, ix. 113–14). The free performance of *2 Henry IV*, in which Hal was seen to reject Falstaff and his ragged crew, to be crowned in splendour, to become Henry V of glorious memory, was George IV's final rejoinder to the satirical tradition that had plagued him since the 1780s.

Although Shakespeare's English histories were the most obvious and most widely used sources for contemporary political comment, other popular plays were also alluded to and assimilated. I have already quoted one *Courier* article from the difficult period when the Regency Act was being debated; another, published on 25 January 1811 under the title 'Dethroning of the King', alludes powerfully to *Macbeth* in the course of its argument that the King was being deprived of his power prematurely: 'Grievous indeed would it be to the whole country to see the King *thrown aside*; he has "*borne his faculties so meekly*," been "*so clear* in his great office".' On 30 January *Cobbett's Weekly Political Register* took objection to this article, asserting that the *Courier* was an organ 'of the hypocritical enemies upon the Prince, those vile men, who under the garb of affected attachment to the King, are calumniating and insulting his son, by means of the basest insinuations'. Cobbett singles out the quotation in a way that tells us much about how the process of Shakespearean allusion was perceived in the political discourse of the time:

The words, used as the title of the article: 'DETHRONING OF THE KING,' taken in connection with the quotation from SHAKESPEARE, convey a most malignant meaning. MACBETH, when he is about to *murder* king DUNCAN, reasons with himself, and, during the soliloquy, he says, that Duncan, 'has borne his faculties *so meekly*, has been *so clear* in his great office, that his virtues, like angels trumpet-tongued, will cry out against *the deep damnation of his taking off.*' These are the words, as nearly as I can recollect them. Why did not the venal man go on with the quotation? Why did he not quote the *latter part* of the sentence as well as the former, and leave the whole, as he has done a part, to be applied to the King's son, who is to succeed him in the Royal Authority, as Macbeth did Duncan? But, though he took not the words, the context is in every man's mind, and the inference is full as clear as those inferences upon which many a man has been convicted of libel. (*Cobbett's Weekly Political Register* 1811, 19: 231)

This passage provides an object-lesson in the reading of politicized Shakespearean quotation. It demonstrates that commentators and satirists could make the assumption that the context of a Shakespearean quotation would be 'in every man's mind' and that political allusion of this sort works by a sophisticated kind of 'inference' which sometimes depends on a movement from text to context. More specifically, it is an example of one polemicist contesting another's application of Shakespeare: Cobbett shows that the *Courier* article is implicitly reading the Regency Act as a *Macbeth*-like usurpation and the Prince as a potential Macbeth; he then goes on to suggest that this is a misappropriation of *Macbeth*, for there is no contemporary analogy—it is not a case of the sceptre being wrenched from the king's hand, for 'it *fell* from his hand'.

A number of situations during, and at the end of, the Regency years made for comparison with Shakespearean tragedy. Most telling of all was the question of the King's madness: because of its analogy with contemporary reality, *King Lear* was kept off the London stage from 1811 to 1820. Indeed, the parallel between the mad Lear and the mad George was so explosive that it was rarely used in caricature. The only print in the British Museum collection to identify the King with Lear is George Cruikshank's *State Miners* (BMC 11707), published in that crucial month when the Regency Bill was being debated, January 1811. As often, the allusion is in a picture on the wall. Labelled 'King Lear and his Daughter', it shows the King raising his arms in horror at the sight of a woman, obviously Cordelia, lying prostrate on the ground. What Cruikshank is representing here, most cruelly, is the death of George III's cherished youngest daughter, Princess Amelia, which had occurred on 2 November 1810—a death which was generally thought to have been the cause of his final insanity. Considering this close connection between the King's madness and his daughter's death, it is a bold statement on Cruikshank's part, and would probably not have been possible as the main subject of a print; it is surprising that it was not suppressed, even with the distancing effect of confining the image to a picture on the wall.

The paucity of representations that go to the extreme of portraying George III as the mad Lear may perhaps be due to a desire on the part of caricaturists and their publishers not to put at risk the licence they did have. So long as they kept within certain boundaries they could actually represent the king, often in an unflattering light. Gillray often has him stammering 'what!—what!', one of his well-known foibles (see, for example, *A Kick at the Broad-Bottoms!—i.e.— Emancipation of 'All the Talents. etc.'*, March 1807, BMC 10709). Despite this, according to *London und Paris*, the King sent new caricatures about himself express by court messenger to the University library at Göttingen (cited, Hill 1965, p. 118). Caricaturists certainly had no qualms about representing the mad king's son, even after he took the crown. *King Henry VIII*, the satire on his attempt to get rid of his wife, may have been headed 'Principal Characters, King of England by the —— Queen of England by the Q—— Cardinal Wolsey—L—d C————h' (the less high-ranking the personage, the more initials can be used), but there was no doubting the identity of the protagonists in the engraving itself.

The idea of conspiracy to dispose of a member of the royal family was also approached through *Hamlet*. On 1 January 1813 an engraving by Williams appeared in the magazine *Town Talk*. Entitled *The Spirit of the Book—or Anticipation of the Year 1813* (BMC 11990), it showed a ghostly figure brandishing a huge book, causing the Regent to rise in terror and Lady Hertford to fling herself from the throne which she has usurped. The ghost, representing a 'Book' announced for imminent publication which would attack the Regent through his treatment of his wife, says 'I will to the peoples ear a tale unfold, shall make their matted and combined locks to part—and each particular hair to stand on end like quills upon the fretfull porcupine.' The quotation follows the ghost's original in *Hamlet* closely, save for the telling introduction of 'the people'. The Regent replies, ' "Angels and Ministers of Grace", but alas I have no Angels but fallen ones, and my Ministers are not Ministers of Grace.' There is a nice sense here of the interruption of a Shakespearean quotation: the Regent begins with Hamlet's formula, then stops on realizing that it is not applicable. The lines are rewritten, with fallen supporting angels—a cross-allusion to *Paradise Lost?*—and disgraced government ministers. Furthermore, the use of allusion suggests that 'The Book' is not merely the text of the Regent's marital misdemeanours but also the prophetic and admonitory spirit of Shakespeare's text. 'O, my prophetick soul', Hamlet says a little later in his dialogue with the ghost: the prophetic soul of Shakespeare is seen to 'anticipate' the year 1813.

The 1820 Bill of Pains and Penalties provoked another version of the ghost scene. *Ghost as seen in the Hamlet of St Stephens Chapel* (pl. 30, BMC 13825) is a densely allusive unsigned engraving. Set in the House of Lords, it shows the ghost of Queen Caroline's daughter Charlotte, who died after the birth of a stillborn child in 1817, condensing two of Hamlet's speeches accusing his mother (III. iv. 40–5, 91–3). The lines spoken by the four lawyers, the Queen's defendants, Brougham and Denman, and the prosecuting counsel, Gifford and Copley, are all from the ghost scenes in the first act of *Hamlet*. Hamlet's ejaculation, 'Angels and ministers of grace defend us', is quoted in many caricatures. The most effective citations of it are those that give it a new twist: the word 'minister' is the obvious one to turn to political advantage, as in *The Spirit of the Book*; the same twist occurs in *The Ghost of St Stephen's or the Stranger at Home* (BMC 9511), a caricature of 1800 on Fox's return to the Commons, which shows Pitt in the pose of Garrick as Hamlet confronted by the ghost.[13] But in the context of the trial of the Queen, 'defend' is the word that is given strong new overtones. An even more original twist is the application to the notorious Green Bag, symbol of dubious evidence, of some lines from *Macbeth*: 'rather shall this Bag the multitudinous Realm incarnadine making the Green one Red'.

This was not the only allusion to Shakespeare in the context of the spurious evidence put forward by the prosecutors of the Queen.

---

[13] In *London und Paris* 1800 (5: 238–9) there is a copy of this print, with a verbal explanation that makes the link between Pitt's pose and that of Garrick's well-known because frequently engraved stance as Hamlet startled by the ghost. I suspect that there are many other correspondences between postures in theatrical engravings and those in satirical ones. For example, *St Stephen's Mad-house; or, The Inauguration of King William the 4th* (BMC 7495), a satire on William Pitt's supremacy, shows the Prime Minister and his followers as madmen—Pitt wears a crown with fragments of straw on it, an image that must be derived from Garrick's celebrated staging of *Lear*.

Macready's performances as Iachimo at Covent Garden in 1820 attracted particular interest because of the trial, and reviewers were quick to point out parallels: the *Globe* said that Iachimo 'at the present season might be denominated the most prominent of the piece' and that 'It is almost superfluous to observe, that the play abounds with passages most obviously applicable to the circumstances of the great investigation now in progress' (quoted, Jackson 1971, pp. 71, 73). Especially telling was the fact that the central allegation against the Queen was that she had committed adultery with an Italian courier named Bartolommeo Bergami (a.k.a. Pergami)—to the Queen's defendants, he was obviously a Iachimo figure. The play then transcended the stage and became an authoritative point of reference in the trial itself. Denman, the Lord Chief Justice, actually cited Shakespeare's Italian villains when summing up the case for the Queen's defence: 'It was remarkable that in all the numerous scenes described by our great dramatic poet, whenever he had occasion to paint the character of a man anxious to blacken the reputation of an innocent wife, he chose his scene in Italy' (quoted, Fulford 1967, p. 207).

Denman obviously had in mind Iago as well as Iachimo. Another engraving on the allegations against the Queen, *A [Key] to the Investigation or Iago Distanced by Odds* (BMC 12031), by Charles Williams, includes a character holding open a copy of *Othello* and has as epigraph Iago's lines from act III scene iii on filching of 'good name'. It may be noted, then, that *King Lear*, *Hamlet*, *Macbeth*, and *Othello*, the four plays which during the Regency years were being designated in criticism—Coleridge, Hazlitt, and the English translation of Schlegel—as Shakespeare's 'great tragedies' were all absorbed.into relation with the contemporary monarchy. Nearly a hundred years later, in the work of A. C. Bradley, the four plays retained their exalted status, but in *Shakespearean Tragedy* they are drained of contemporaneity.

If one tragedy were to be singled out for its political importance throughout the period from 1760 to 1830, it would have to be *Macbeth*. It is symptomatic that this was the play whose appropriation Cobbett contested with *The Courier*; even more significantly, it was to *Macbeth* that Burke alluded at a key moment in the *Reflections on the Revolution in France*. Perhaps the most famous passage in the *Reflections* is the account of the attack on Versailles, which begins 'History will record, that on the morning of the 6th October, 1789, the King and Queen of France, after a day of confusion, alarm, dismay, and slaughter, lay down, under the pledged security of public faith, to indulge nature in a few hours of respite, and troubled, melancholy repose' (Burke 1790, p. 68). Burke prepares for this image of troubled sleep by alluding a few lines earlier to Macbeth's 'balm of hurt minds' (II. ii. 36), thus sowing in his readers' minds an association between sleeplessness and regicide, which will be invaluable for his subsequent argument. The power of the allusion is such that it is almost as if he is comparing the assassination of Duncan to the execution of Louis XVI even before the latter event has taken place. Wordsworth must at some level have been registering Burke's allusion when he went to the same speech of Macbeth's for the terrifying cry 'sleep no more' in his poetic recollection of the September massacres.[14]

Gillray and other caricaturists followed Burke in turning *Macbeth* to political account. As in the case of *Henry IV*, William Dent seems to have established a model. His *Revolution Anniversary or, Patriotic Incantations* (pl. 31, July 1791, BMC 7890) shows Fox, Sheridan, Priestley, and Dr Joseph Towers, dissenter and member of the Society for Constitutional Information, dancing round a cauldron 'to tune of free-made France', awaiting the day 'when the Hurly-burly's done, | And all Ranks confounded in One'. Sheridan sings 'Bauble! Bauble melt with trouble! Fire burn, and Nation bubble'; 'bauble' serves as a Paine-like term for the Crown, which is being precipitated into the cauldron. One suspects that it was Sheridan's double role as politician and theatre manager that gave Dent the idea for his linking of Shakespeare and politics. The figure of Sheridan holds a book inscribed 'Drury's Prompt Book. Cauldron Scene Macbeth': the scene may thus be imagined as simultaneously representing a production at Drury Lane and the radicals' preparation of an infernal broth to be consumed at their forthcoming dinner in celebration of the second anniversary of the fall of the Bastille.

Rowlandson worked in this tradition with his frontispiece to the *Anti-Jacobin Review* of February 1799, *A Charm for a Democracy, Reviewed, Analysed, and Destroyed* (pl. 32, BMC 9345, also published independently, three copies in the British Museum). This time the incantation consists of a catalogue of rebels, past and present,

> Eye of Straw and Toe of Cade
> Tylers Bow Kosiuskos Blade
> Russels Liver Tongue of Cur
> Norfolks Boldness Foxs Fur . . .

[14] 1805 *Prelude*, x. 77, see further, Bate 1986, p. 114.

Jack Straw, Jack Cade, and Wat Tyler were all figures who had been proclaimed by radicals as their precursors: Cade and Tyler had appeared in pictures on the wall in the Dent engraving; Gillray made the link with the trio in *Copenhagen House*, his attack on Thelwall and the London Corresponding Society; Southey's play *Wat Tyler* was to become notorious. John Russell, later sixth Duke of Bedford, was a well-known radical sympathizer and member of the Society of Friends of the People. Charles Howard, eleventh Duke of Norfolk, had supported Fox in his stance against the American War and remained close to the whig opposition. 'Boldness' alludes to the proverbial phrase in *Richard III*, 'Jocky of Norfolk, be not too bold' (V. iii. 304): it is convenient for anti-Norfolk caricaturists that his family name had been tarnished by association with Richard of Gloucester. Rowlandson's engraving is denser than Dent's; it adapts more lines from the original scene. The Devil says 'Pour in Streams of Regal Blood | Then the Charm is firm and good'; the 'witch' in the foreground, Horne Tooke, chants 'Tis time tis time tis time', and his companions, 'Thrice! and Twice King's Heads have fallen', 'Thrice the Gallic Wolves have bayed'. The point of the two kings' heads is that at both ends of the political spectrum there was a tendency to associate the execution of Louis XVI with that of Charles I. The repeated use of threefold repetition and the word 'thrice' derives not only from the threefold figurations in *Macbeth*, traditional to witchcraft, but also from the fact that threes were central to the iconography of the French revolution, with its tricolour, its '*liberté, égalité, fraternité*', and its triple symbols of liberty cap, liberty tree, and citizen's pike.

Some further associations of the cauldron scene are suggested by the title of Gillray's sally in this area: *A Phantasmagoria* (pl. 33, BMC 9962). Subtitled 'Conjuring-up an Armed-Skeleton', this aquatint shows Addington, Hawkesbury, and Fox as the three witches. The skeleton is Britannia. The British lion's tail and paw are already in the pot; in the foreground a crowing Gallic cock, with liberty cap, stands triumphantly on the lion's head. Addington is ladling in guineas 'To make Gruel Thick and Slab'. The caricature is dated January 1803, and is an attack on the 'Francophiles' who promoted the Peace of Amiens. It owes its title, its central image of a skeleton, and its shape, an oval superimposed on a dark brick wall, to Philipsthal's 'phantasmagoria', a magic-lantern device first shown at the Lyceum in 1802, which made shadowy spectral apparitions appear, move backwards and forwards, change in size, and disappear. Gillray does not merely elide the Shakespearean and the popular supernatural: he works within the tradition that associates the evils of *Macbeth* with the French Revolution, and reinforces it by implicitly reminding his audience that Philipsthal's phantasmagoria came from over the Channel and could therefore be seen as a dangerous French innovation.

Such associations, together with the casting of specific public figures as the three witches, make this the most effective of the satires which evoke the cauldron scene; verbal and visual allusions reinforce each other to create a fully rounded and politically potent 'Shakespeare Travestie'. The latter term is taken from *The Cauldron—or Shakespeare Travestie* (BMC 13787), an engraving of August 1820 that is strongly influenced by Gillray's *Phantasmagoria*. It is one of many caricatures published in support of the Queen during the new King's action against her. Here the witches are Liverpool, Sidmouth, and Castlereagh. The King, as Macbeth, asks 'Tell me ye d—n'd infernal Hags of Night, shall Fr———k reign?', an allusion to the fact that if he could not get a divorce and remarry, his brother Frederick, Duke of York, would succeed. The best touch in this print is the labelling of the items going into the cauldron: Liverpool casts in 'the Divorce' and Castlereagh, 'Britain's shame'. The witches afford ideal material for caricaturists because as a trio they enable politicians to be grouped together and demonized in an undifferentiated fashion: thus Heath's *The Last Recorce or Supernatural Committee Employ'd* (May 1810, BMC 11555) has for its Macbeth Prime Minister Perceval, faced with the troublesome reforming Member for Westminster Sir Francis Burdett, going as a last resort to the unlikely sisters, Pitt, Fox, and Burke.

Other caricatures make more incidental use of the witches: Dent calls undercover diplomats 'secret, black and Midnight Things' (BMC 7653), and for Sayers Westminster Hall during the trial of Warren Hastings resembles the witches' cave (BMC 8647). Others still look elsewhere in the play. Gillray's *Nightly Visitors, At St Ann's Hill* (September 1798, BMC 9244) shows the ghost of Lord Edward Fitzgerald, the United Irishman who had died as the result of a struggle with Pitt's agents, appearing to Fox, his cousin. Gillray wants to convey the idea of guilt, of Fox's hands being stained with his kinsman's blood. He therefore gives him Macbeth's exclamation on seeing the ghost of Banquo, 'Why do'st thou shake thy Goary Locks at me? . . . Thou can'st not say, I did it!' But in addition to the idea of guilt, the ghost of Banquo also brings to mind hired assassins. This presents a problem for a reading of the print in terms of a more general correspondence between Fox and Macbeth as traitors to their country. It had been *Pitt* who had hired the assassins, so there is a sense in which *he* is the Macbeth figure. It may be that this caricature is an example of Gillray at his most Janus-like: by 1798 he was in the pay of the government, and would therefore have been expected to attack Fox, but the Shakespearean allusion subtly raises the obverse possibility that Pitt is a Macbeth-like tyrant.

Gillray thus modifies the identification of Fox as Macbeth which Williams had established earlier in 1798 with his *The Resignation* (BMC 9175), a satire on the dismissal of Norfolk for sedition after he had toasted 'Our Sovereign—the Majesty of the People' at a dinner celebrating Fox's birthday. Williams's engraving has Pitt saying to Norfolk 'How did you dare, | To trade and traffic with Macbeth | In Riddles and affairs of death'. Even here, one wonders whether the engraving can be unequivocally pro-government: Pitt is speaking from a protected position behind the king's chair, and one cannot but detect a sneaking admiration for the contrasting *boldness* of 'Jockey of Norfolk' as he stands square on, discomposing the king. Similarly, Isaac Cruikshank's *A Recent Escape* (December 1795, BMC 8705) had used the same quotation as Gillray from the banquet scene, but adapted it in such a way as to rebound against Pitt–Banquo: Fox–Macbeth says to a mud-spattered Pitt, 'Why dost thou shake thy Dirty Locks at me? | Thou canst not say I did it—*Muddy Banquo!*'. The point is that Pitt has been blaming Fox for the political, military, and social problems of 1795, which were really his own responsibility.

It is interesting that a sequence of caricatures published between 1795 and 1798 made such complex use of the banquet scene in *Macbeth*, for it was a scene which had created great interest in 1794, when Kemble had played it without a ghost on stage, in order to show that the image of Banquo was a figment of Macbeth's guilty imagination. Kemble's controversial production made the scene a ready point of reference among the theatre-going classes. Those same classes formed much of the audience who read—as opposed to merely looked at—political caricatures; once Kemble had activated a context and it had become associated with controversies of interpretation, caricaturists could intervene and impose their own preoccupations upon it, opening up new controversies of interpretation. There was an assumption that the public would have certain images of Macbeth and Banquo; caricaturists were interested in the effect of superimposing contemporary politicians upon such prototypes. The effect was to create an active interplay between the interpretation of Shakespeare and the ways in which public affairs were presented to the public.

The richest of all *Macbeth* allusions in political caricature is Gillray's *Wierd-Sisters; Ministers of Darkness; Minions of the Moon* (pl. 34, BMC 7937), published in December 1791 and described by *The Morning Chronicle* of 3 January 1792 as Gillray's 'Chef d'Œuvre', a work of 'more genius and skill than any jeu d'esprit of the kind . . . unfortunately for the country there is Biting truth in it'. *Wierd-Sisters* combines all the resources of Shakespearean allusion that are used more selectively in other prints: it turns on an especially well-known scene, the apparition of the witches in *Macbeth*, it makes telling character identifications, and it uses a complex web of quotations.

It also relates to the handling of Shakespeare by a contemporary artist. The inscription, with its dedication, 'To H: Fuzelli Esqr.', proclaims the print to be a parody of another of Fuseli's well-known paintings, *The Three Witches*, which had been exhibited at the Royal Academy in 1783 (pl. 35). Gillray succeeds in hitting at Fuseli's wild, bombastic renderings of the 'sublime' Shakespearean supernatural in the course of a satire on an altogether different theme. Fuseli's reputation stemmed largely from the way that he responded to, and partly shaped, the age's interest in energy, the Gothic, the supernatural, and the terrible. A description of his studio gives a strong sense of how he was perceived by the public: 'Galvanized devils— malicious witches brewing their incantations,—Satan bridging Chaos, and springing upwards like a pyramid of fire—Lady Macbeth . . . humour, pathos, terror, blood, and murder, met one at every look!' (Haydon 1853, i. 25). These are precisely the elements which were also favoured by caricaturists when they based engravings on the supernatural parts of Shakespeare that were so popular in the period. The caricaturist could assume that a broad audience would recognize and relish his portrayals of politicians as 'malicious witches brewing their incantations'; but at the same time he could mock 'high' artists, such as Fuseli, who responded in more pretentious fashion to the contemporary taste for the sublime. As one early reviewer put it, Gillray 'shows us that the ludicrous is not divided by a step from the sublime, but blended with it and twined around it' (*London and Westminster Review* 1837, 6: 261). *A Phantasmagoria:— Scene—Conjuring-up an Armed-Skeleton* offers a characteristic juxtaposition, in that its main title summons up Philipsthal's popular 'low' theatrical spectacle and its subtitle alludes to one of Fuseli's many sublime paintings of the Shakespearean supernatural, *Macbeth and the Armed Head*.

The extraordinary power of Gillray lies in his capacity to enter battle on the aesthetic and the political fronts at one and the same time. *Wierd-Sisters* describes itself as an 'attempt in the Caricatura-Sublime'. Gillray may be implying through this coinage that the project to elevate English history painting by means of sublime Shakespearean canvases is misguided and self-indulgent. He offers instead a form of Shakespearean painting that alludes to *contemporary* history. Thus, as in *A Phantasmagoria*, his attack on Fuseli becomes bound up with a satire on politicians.

The specific occasion of *Wierd-Sisters* was ministerial confusion during the Regency crisis. The witches are Dundas, Pitt, and Thurlow, uncertain at how to respond to the Queen's ascendancy. The King symbolically slumbers on the dark side of the moon (the moon being associated with madness). The ministers lay their choppy fingers to their not so skinny lips, but more in the manner of perplexed schoolchildren than imperious figures demanding silence, as in the Fuseli original being parodied. The three-pronged title lashes hard: they are 'Wierd-Sisters', 'Ministers of Darkness' (another punning twist on Hamlet's 'ministers of grace'), 'Minions' of Queen Charlotte. 'Minions of the moon' carries a set of associations from outside *Macbeth*, for the phrase is Falstaff's:

Marry, then, sweet wag, when thou art king, let not us, that are squires of the night's body, be called thieves of the day's beauty; let us be—Diana's foresters, gentlemen of the shade, minions of the moon: And let men say, we be men of good government; being governed as the sea is, by our noble and chaste mistress the moon, under whose countenance we—steal. (*1 Henry IV*, I. ii. 23)

The single phrase summons up the whole speech: the imagery of night and day relates to the dark and light sides of the moon; Pitt and his colleagues are branded as thieves, men of bad government who steal under the licence of their 'noble and chaste mistress' Queen Charlotte. There could be no better example of the way in which Gillray alludes suggestively yet subtly. The economy of his art depends on the reader of the print putting the brief quotation back in its context and working through the implications from there. There is one final stroke, an example of the device crucial to caricature whereby inscription and design feed off each other. Under the title,

Gillray adapts a line of Banquo's, 'They should be Women!—and yet their beards forbid us to interpret,—that they are so.' Our interpretation depends on the drawing: Pitt, Thurlow, and Dundas are beardless. They *are* women.

The popularity of the *Macbeth* witches testifies to the centrality of the Shakespearean supernatural in the period. Unpromising as it might seem and infrequently as it was performed, *The Tempest* was also a source of many caricatures. The anti-Butonian *The Tempest or Enchanted Island* provided an early example, but, as with *Henry IV* and *Macbeth*, Dent was the first to render a scene in detail. In April 1784 he engraved *Reynard's Hope, A Scene in the Tempest between Trinculo, Stephano and Caliban* (BMC 6535). Like *A Shaksperean Scene*, this is a satire on the Prince's collusion with the Foxites. The Prince is Trinculo, bottle of wine in hand, saying to Stephano–Fox, 'give me dear woman—and give me good wine—and you may govern all things else as thine.' Fox's presumptuous reply keeps close to Stephano's original (*Tempest*, III. ii. 108): 'when the Island's ours—my brave Boy—I—I'll be King—and you shall be Viceroy'. The part of Caliban is played by a fawning Lord North; the wrecked ship is pointedly called 'Royal George', an allusion to a man-of-war, the pride of the fleet, which had gone down when being repaired off Spithead in 1782. Dent makes the sinking ship into a metonymic representation of the sinking King.

Caricatures alluding to *The Tempest* show up the range of uses to which Shakespeare was put in the period. For Romantic poets, Prospero was a magician—a Shakespeare—ruling his kingdom of the imagination, but for caricaturists he was simply the man ruling the isle. Thus, *Prospero on the Enchanted Island* (pl. 36, Autumn 1798, BM, acquired since catalogue) shows the King as Prospero on a cliff-top marked Albion, standing on a torn tricolour. Prospero's 'rack' becomes the 'Wreck' of the French fleet at the Battle of the Nile. Caricaturists do not concern themselves with a magical new found land; they make their own sceptred isle into an enchanted, invulnerable—if beleaguered—kingdom.

Two prints by Isaac Cruikshank on the 'Enchanted Island' theme appeared on 6 December 1798 (BMC 9275–6). In each, the island is Britain. In one, Prospero is played by Pitt; in the other, the Prime Minister is Ariel, flying off with the words 'This will I tell my Master'—George III is thus made into Prospero again. The identification of a Prime Minister with Prospero occurs as late as 1827,

when a pro-government engraving, *The Tempest or Prospero Triumphant*
(BMC 15384), has an imposing Canning as Prospero standing fast on
the 'Rock of Integrity'. To us, these patriotic and political appropriations of *The Tempest* seem odd, but they are as important a part of the
play's presence in the period as those allusive effects which incorporate Prospero's 'so potent art' into theories of poetic vision in the way
that I demonstrated in *Shakespeare and the English Romantic Imagination*.
They also pave the way for a critical reading of the play itself in
political, instead of airily imaginative, terms, a reading first adum-
brated in Coleridge and Hazlitt. When Coleridge called Caliban 'an
original and caricature of Jacobinism', he was following in the foot-
steps of Isaac Cruikshank's caricature in which Caliban–Fox was
portrayed as a hairy, ragged figure wearing a tricolour scarf, and of
Prospero on the Enchanted Island, with its squat black figure representing
Jacobin France as a cross between the devil and Caliban claiming
'These Lands are mine | By Sycorax my mother.'

We should pause for a moment on the politics of Isaac Cruikshank.
The version of *The Tempest* that he engraved in 1795, *Shakespeare's
Prophecy, the Last Act but one in the Tempest* (pl. 37, BMC 8618), appears
on the surface to be one of many satires on Fox and the opposition.
Thurlow, Fox, and Sheridan as Caliban, Trinculo, and Stephano are
driven off by ministerial hounds set on by Ariel (Pitt) and Prospero
(the King). But a closer inspection reveals that Prospero's words are
marked by stammering repetitions—a parody of the King's conversational manner—and that amidst the dogs of Pitt ('Hey, Mountain,
hey! Silver!') there is one 'Tyrant'. That Prospero relies on a spirit
transformed into a dog named Tyrant may tell us something about
his way of ruling the isle in *The Tempest*; that Pitt cries, 'there Tyrant,
there!' may suggest that Cruikshank is as alert to the dangers of absolutism as he is to those of democracy. In 1793 Gillray had portrayed
a noble Pitt at the helm in *Britannia between Scylla and Charybdis.
Or—The Vessel of the Constitution steered clear of the Rock of Democracy, and
the Whirlpool of Arbitrary-Power* (BMC 8320). By 1795 'Arbitrary-
Power' had reared its head. Through such allusions as 'there
Tyrant', Cruikshank is able, whilst working within an essentially
anti-radical idiom, to offer a veiled critique of Pitt's repressive
measures.

This idea of a double critique can be further exemplified, but first it
needs to be pointed out how widespread the manipulation of Shakespearean language was in the political caricature of the age—it was

not confined to those prints which set up an elaborate parallel between a contemporary situation and a scene or character. Scores of engravings, by Gillray pre-eminently, but also by others, make glancing allusion to the plays in all kinds of contexts. One has always been aware that ever since the eighteenth century the English have had a way of quoting Shakespeare in all sorts of surprising contexts, but it is truly astonishing just how deeply the plays penetrated the art of graphic satire in its golden age, and must therefore have penetrated the culture of the time more generally. Incidental Shakespearean quotations are all too easy for us to overlook: George (or Robert?) Cruikshank's *Massacre at St Peter's or 'Britons Strike Home'!!!*[15] has become perhaps the most famous caricature of the period—but how many people today notice that the Manchester Yeomanry mowing down the crowd on St Peter's Field are pointedly associated with two of Shakespeare's bloodiest despots? Their banner reads 'Loyal Manchester Yeomanry—"Be Bloody, bold and Resolute"—"Spur your proud Horses and Ride hard in blood" '. Readers and theatregoers among Cruikshank's public would have picked up the allusions to *Macbeth* (IV. i. 79) and *Richard III* (V. iii. 340) and, in their case, indignation would have been spurred. Shakespeare was thus made into a weapon which could be put into the hands of the trampled people.

In view of Falstaff's popularity and the behaviour of the Prince of Wales, it is not surprising that *1 Henry IV* was the play from which Gillray quoted most frequently. Second and third for frequency of incidental allusions were *Hamlet* and *Macbeth*, a position which accords with their centrality to the sensibility of the age; next was *Richard III*, illustrative of violent political activity and always popular, in Cibber's revision, on stage.[16] Gillray did, however,

---

[15] August 1819, BMC 13258. The phrase 'Britons Strike Home' first occurs in a chorus in an adaptation of Beaumont and Fletcher's play about Boadicea, *Bonduca*, set to music by Purcell in 1695: 'Britons, strike home, Revenge, revenge your country's wrongs . . .'. It frequently appeared in patriotic caricatures and broadsheets. The strength of Cruikshank's use of it is the inversion: Britons have struck home against Britons, struck against home instead of in defence of home; the country's wrongs that must be revenged have been inflicted by the authorities at home, not by foreigners or invaders.

[16] The 7 plays most frequently performed in the London patent theatres between 1751 and 1800 were, in order of popularity, *Romeo and Juliet*, *Hamlet*, *Richard III* (Cibber's text), *Macbeth*, *The Merchant of Venice*, *The Taming of the Shrew* (as an afterpiece by Garrick entitled *Catharine and Petruchio*), and *King Lear* (in versions of Tate, Garrick, Colman the Elder, Kemble). Those not performed at all were *Henry VI*, *Love's Labour's Lost* (the only play unperformed throughout the century), *Pericles*, *Richard II*, *Titus*

occasionally make use of rarely performed plays or ones that were not
performed at all in the period, such as *Troilus and Cressida* (quoted in
BMC 7531); he clearly expected at least some of his audience to have
a thorough *reading* knowledge of Shakespeare.

Caricaturists value Shakespeare because so much of what he writes
appears self-contained or aphoristic, and can therefore be wrenched
from its context without compunction. The lines 'get thee glass
Eyes | And like a scurvy Politician, seem | To see the things thou dost
not' (epigraph to BMC 9049) were as valid in 1797—and presumably
will be as valid in 1997—as they were when *King Lear* was written and
when it was set. A modern literary critic might complain that this
kind of appropriation does Shakespeare a disservice, for the lines are
not so self-contained as they seem, in that 'eyes', whether of glass or
jelly, run as a leitmotif throughout *King Lear*. To us, it appears
difficult to make compatible an intrinsic reading of Shakespeare that
is appreciative of the organic quality of his images and an extrinsic
reading that brings those images to bear on contemporary life. But
this did not seem to be a problem in the age of Gillray and Hazlitt,
which was able to embrace many Shakespeares. It was an age in
which the achievements of Malone, Gillray, Coleridge, and Keats
stood side by side; an age large enough for painstaking historical
scholarship, the application of extracts to contemporary 'scurvy
Politicians', 'organic' practical criticism of the plays, and the en-
thronement of Shakespeare as 'presider' over the creativity of subsequent poets. As I hope to show, Hazlitt is a vital figure because he
moves easily between intrinsic and extrinsic readings of the plays.

The 'scurvy Politician' quotation reveals how easily Shakespearean
language can be used as a stick with which to beat those in power.
Particular interest attaches to quotations from *Lear* during the later
years of George III's reign, given its peculiar power in relation to the
King's madness. Gillray steered clear of overt references to insanity,

---

Andronicus, and *Troilus and Cressida* (see Hogan 1952–7, ii. 716–19). Both the *London
Stage* and Hogan's *Shakespeare in the Theatre* extend as far as 1800; for the period 1801 to
1825 I have drawn up a list of most frequently performed plays from the information
recorded in Genest 1832. During these years the most popular 7 were *Hamlet*, *Macbeth*,
Richard III, *Romeo and Juliet*, *Othello*, *1 Henry IV*, and *The Merchant of Venice*. *Othello* and
1 Henry IV thus return to the position of popularity they had occupied in the first half
of the eighteenth century. The number of revivals of *1 Henry IV*, which played at
Covent Garden nearly every season, is especially interesting in view of the identification of Hal with the Regent. *Lear*, meanwhile, drops down the list because of the
embargo on performances during the years of the king's madness. *Love's Labour's Lost*,
Pericles, *Titus Andronicus*, and *Troilus and Cressida* remained unperformed.

but did quote from the scenes where Lear is at his most politically incisive. A characteristic example is the use of 'crimes which are left as yet unwhipt of Justice' in *Guy Vaux* [i.e. Fox] *Discovered in his Attempt to Destroy the King and the House of Lords* (BMC 7862, May 1791). I think that what might be termed the radical potential of *King Lear* sometimes gets the better of Gillray's overtly pro-government stance. *The Noble Sans-Culotte* (pl. 38, May 1794, BMC 8448) is a satire on Charles Stanhope, staunchest of radical aristocrats, who had styled himself 'a Sans Culotte Citizen in the House of Lords'. But above the engraving are Lear's words, '—off, off, ye lendings'. Is it so very reprehensible for Stanhope to cast off the robes of aristocratic privilege? Does not the quotation from *Lear* summon up a number of related passages—'take physick, pomp; | Expose thyself to feel what wretches feel'; 'Robes, and furr'd gowns, hide all'—which might more justifiably be appropriated in the name of *égalité*? Or, to look at it another way: Stanhope is portrayed as a fool (note the ass's head on the *égalité* banner and the bell on the liberty cap), but the allusion to *Lear* brings to mind Lear's fool who is no fool, who is indeed the character who sees most clearly the corruption and hypocrisy of the aristocratic regime.

The Rights of Man (May 1791, BMC 7867) is one of Gillray's many satires on Tom Paine. The first lines spoken by the figure of Paine are 'Fathom and a half! Fathom and a half! Poor Tom!' The words are printed prominently, in a type twice as large as the lines that follow; the Shakespearean allusion draws the reader into the body of the engraving, a single stroke having equated Tom Paine with the Mad Tom of *King Lear*. The identification stuck, for it was soon used by other caricaturists, who no longer needed to quote directly from *Lear*; in September 1791 W. Locke published *'Hannibal Scratch''s Mad Tom, or the Man of Rights* (BMC 7900), and the following May saw the appearance of Isaac Cruikshank's *Mad Tom's First Political Essay on the Rights of Man* (BMC 8087). Again, however, the complexity of Shakespeare's play works against any simplistic reading of the allusion: once it is recalled that Poor Tom is in fact Edgar, a very different complexion is put on the parallel, and one begins to call into question the appeals to 'nature' of *Edmund* Burke.

Other of Gillray's caricatures are open to a similar kind of analysis. For instance, *Copenhagen House* (November 1795, BMC 8685) shows a mob at a mass meeting of Thelwall's London Corresponding Society; the text beneath it reads 'I tell you, Citizens, we mean to new-dress the Constitution and turn it, and set a new Nap upon it', an adaptation of 'I tell thee, Jack Cade the clothier means to dress the commonwealth, and turn it, and set a new nap upon it' (*2 Henry VI*, IV. ii. 4–6). The slight changes are enough to equate Thelwall with Jack Cade the rabble-rouser, and to emphasize the way in which radical demands in this period were most frequently made with regard to the Constitution. But the matter is complicated by the principle that a quotation may summon up its context: in the play, the reply to this line is 'So he had need, for 'tis threadbare'; a few lines later we are reminded that 'the king's council are no good workmen'. Cade's own ambitions may be implicitly condemned by the play, but his rebellion is the symptom of an *ancien régime* in terminal decay.

The use of Shakespearean allusion in such contexts throws light on the difficult and much-debated question of Gillray's political allegiances.[17] The traditional view is that he followed the common pattern of being initially well disposed to the French Revolution, but then turned against it because of the execution of Louis XVI and Marie-Antoinette, the Terror, and, decisively, the war. He is seen as above all else a patriot, an apologist for John Bull, the ordinary Englishman who may have his pocket picked by Pitt as well as his nation threatened by Napoleon. But then Gillray's attitude to the court is not exactly patriotic—and his portly, gluttonous John Bull is hardly a paragon (physiognomically he often bears a striking resemblance to the fat Hanoverian king). One also has to take into account the fact that Gillray was brought before a Bow Street magistrate in January 1796, on the publication of his print *The Presentation—or—The Wise Men's Offering* (BMC 8779, a supposedly blasphemous biblical allusion). The case seems never to have gone to trial, but it was soon after this that Gillray was taken into the pay of Canning and the government: according to John Landseer, writing many years later in the *Athenaeum*, the caricaturist

had unluckily got himself into the Ecclesiastical Court for producing a politico-scriptural caricature, which he had entitled 'The Wise Men's Offering;' and while threatened on the one hand with pains and penalties, he was bribed by the Pitt party on the other with the offer of a pension, to be accompanied by absolution and remission of sins both political and religious, and by the cessation of the pending prosecution. Thus situated, he found, or fancied himself obliged to capitulate. (Landseer 1831, p.667)

17 For a general discussion of this subject, see Paulson 1983, pp. 183–211.

Landseer believed that Gillray was only 'a reluctant ally of the tory faction', that 'his heart was always on the side of whiggism and liberty'. He recalled Gillray, *after* he had 'transferred his nominal allegiance to the Pitt party', toasting the Jacobin Jacques-Louis David as 'the first painter and patriot in Europe' (ibid.).

The private political feelings of the caricaturist are less important than the effect of his work. Evidently Gillray's anti-Jacobin prints were read as propaganda—and were thought to be sufficiently effective propaganda for him to be worth a sizeable State pension (£200 a year, according to Cobbett). But, at the same time, his works seem remarkably open to a kind of double reading. One of his favourite techniques was to draw a line down the middle of his plate and juxtapose two contrasting images—*French Liberty. British Slavery.* (BMC 8145) is a strong example. Where we would expect a positive, patriotic image to be juxtaposed to a negative, xenophobic one, in fact, as Paulson observes, the print 'pushes Tory England as far to one extreme as it pushes revolutionary France to the other, and England becomes a sleekly-fat, suspiciously Hanoverian-looking lout, complaining about taxes and a government that will make slaves of us all' (Paulson 1983, p. 185). Allusion may serve to create similar, though more muted, ambivalence. Text may subvert image.

A superficial glance at a Gillray anti-Jacobin print will confirm a crude audience's anti-Gallic prejudices. But closer inspection, and in particular examination of the text, may suggest an alternative reading. Once the context of a Shakespearean quotation is brought into play, the multiplicity of possible interpretations of Shakespeare opens the caricature to a similar multiplicity of possible interpretations. If Gillray quotes Shakespeare, he must expect some of his readers to know and have thought about Shakespeare. Any reader who has thought about *King Lear* and then sees 'Off, off, ye Lendings' prominently displayed above *The Noble Sans-Culotte* must either view Citizen Stanhope more favourably than the engraving first appears to, or be implicated in the value-system of the court—of Goneril and Regan—which Lear is rejecting.

Such ambivalences are of a piece with Hazlitt's recognition that studying *Coriolanus* was like reading both Burke and Paine; they demonstrate that Shakespeare could not be confined to a single camp in the debate on the French Revolution. Sayers's *Thoughts on a Regicide Peace* (BMC 8825) endorses Burke's patriotism by quoting John of Gaunt's 'sceptred Isle' prophecy in *Richard II*, but the *Craftsman* had shown long ago that this quotation can never be uncomplicatedly chauvinistic, since to a reader of any sophistication it always evokes not only the glory but also the degradation, the leasing out, of England.

The 'golden age' of English caricature came to an end in the course of the 1820s. Graphic satire occupied a central place in political discourse for the last time during the radical activity of 1819 and 1820, the heyday of Thomas Wooler's *Black Dwarf* and Richard Carlile's *Republican*. George Cruikshank was the key figure here. Both his skilled draughtsmanship and his political deployment of an intimate knowledge of Shakespeare mark him out as the true successor not only to his father, Isaac, but also to Gillray. So too does his political ambivalence: both in his own time and today there are conflicting views over whether he simply produced caricatures on behalf of whichever faction would pay him most, or whether he did have some genuine allegiance and, if so, on which side of the question he came down. He was quite capable of producing within the space of a few months equally strong anti-government and anti-radical images. One moment he would portray 'Radical Reform' as an infernal rapist, as in *Death or Liberty! or Britannia and the Virtues of the Constitution in danger of Violation from the great Political Libertine, Radical Reform* (BMC 13279), the next he would illustrate William Hone's radical pamphlets, such as *The Right Divine of Kings to Govern Wrong!*, for which he furnished a tailpiece consisting of a startling image of royalty in the form of Spenser's Iron Man trampling on the bodies of the people, including a child, as he approaches the tree of liberty with a sword in one hand and a firebrand in the other, while the Cato Street conspirators are hanged in the background (pl. 39, BMC 14134). The caption to this cut is a composite Shakespearean quotation, evoking rulers who ravage their own country and such speeches as the Bastard's tirade against Monarchy in act II scene i of *King John*. Its climax is a powerful pun, drawn from *3 Henry VI* (II. ii. 139), on 'English g[u]ilt'.

Some of George Cruikshank's caricatures are profoundly ambivalent. *Coriolanus Addressing the Plebeians* (see frontispiece, February 1820, BMC 13677) is a beautifully executed engraving that at first seems to praise the new king and exhort him to be a Coriolanus standing firm in the face of Carlile, Cobbett, Hunt, Wooler, and the rest—the plebeians are all recognizable radical activists, including, for example, Wooler the 'Black Dwarf'. But a closer inspection would have to attend to the two figures at the extreme right who occupy a prominent position among the motley crew of plebeians whom 'Coriolanus' denounces, and who are closest to the viewer. They are William Hone, holding two clubs, one marked 'PARODY' and the other 'MAN in the MOON—HOUSE that JACK BUILT', and George Cruikshank, holding a folio marked 'Caricature'. It is exceptional for a caricaturist to include a self-portrait of this sort. The clear implication is that 'PARODY' and 'Caricature' are important weapons in the hands of the representatives of the people.

The *British Museum Catalogue* description of this engraving does not raise the possibility of ambivalence. Coriolanus has a noble bearing, the plebeians cower and quake, the inscription is a searing denunciation of the agitators ('What would you have ye Curs that like nor Peace, nor War? . . .'): the print is therefore taken to be unequivocally pro-government. I do not think that such a reading can be justified. Immediately above the figure of Cruikshank is a plebeians' banner, topped with a cap of liberty, inscribed 'LIBERTY of the PRESS': the caricaturist's profession necessitates his allegiance to this most fundamental of liberties. And is Coriolanus' bearing noble? Might it not be smug? Alternatively, might an audience familiar with the tradition that portrays George as the wayward Hal take the identification with Coriolanus to be ironic? The portrayal is as likely to suggest *un*likeness as likeness. Most interestingly of all, for our purposes, does not the reading of the engraving as simple anti-radical propaganda depend on an over-simplified reading of *Coriolanus*? The plebeians do have a case, for they gather in the first scene of the play because of food shortages and to make demands on the specific matter of corn prices—concerns that were very familiar in the years 1815 to 1820. Coriolanus' peremptory response to their demands, of which Cruikshank's caption reminds the reader, suggests that he is not precisely a model statesman. Readers of Cruikshank's engraving had available to them Hazlitt's recent account of the play, which had demonstrated that, although Shakespeare may seem to have had 'a leaning to the arbitrary side of the question', there were two sides to the question. I think that both publicly and privately Hazlitt presides over this engraving. Some months before the appearance of the caricature, he had begun a friendship with Hone and Cruikshank; in August 1819 Hone had published his *Political Essays*—indeed, Hazlitt had collected them at Hone's behest. Furthermore, Hazlitt's reading of *Coriolanus* was in the public eye at this time, since, as will be seen in

Part II, it had been at the centre of his acrimonious dispute with
William Gifford.

Once Hazlitt had demonstrated the political complexity of *Coriolanus*
an allusion to the play could no longer be simple. It was also Hazlitt
who recognized that a quotation from John of Gaunt's 'This England'
speech can never be unequivocal: 'We should perhaps hardly be disposed to feed the pampered egotism of our countrymen by quoting
this description, were it not that the conclusion of it (which looks
prophetic) may qualify any improper degree of exultation' (HW iv.
275). Hazlitt's insights enable the formulation of a general principle:
the overt function of caricature is often to reinforce prejudice and
political bigotry, but the covert effect of Shakespearean allusion in
caricature may be to undo prejudice and force an acknowledgement
of political plurality.

4

Parody

'CARICATURE is parody' wrote William Hone.[1] Cruikshank the caricaturist and Hone the parodist made a formidable team. Hone's pamphlets, consisting of satirical verses together with cuts by Cruikshank, circulated cheaply in huge numbers. Beginning with *The Political House that Jack Built* (1819), they were very influential, provoking many ripostes. They played a major role in fomenting unrest in 1819 and 1820; ironically, the success of this new hybrid form also played a significant part in the decline of the independently published satirical engraving. *The Political House that Jack Built* included mottoes from Cowper's *Task* beneath Cruikshank's woodcuts; the pro-government reply, *The Real or Constitutional House that Jack Built* had mottoes from Cowper, Shakespeare, and Young. Subsequent pamphlets on both sides used Shakespearean mottoes, as if contesting the political sympathies of the National Poet. In addition, Shakespeare was sometimes introduced as an authority in Hone's verses:

> Shakspeare says, in King John, it's a curse most abhorrent,
> That '*Slaves* take the humours of Kings for a warrant.'
> A more *useful* truth never fell from his pen,
> If Kings would apply it like sober-bred men.[2]

The work of Hone and Cruikshank provides an especially strong instance of the close relationship between visual and verbal parody, and between the art of allusive inscription in caricature and that of self-proclaimed poetic parody. But this interplay was active throughout the period. For instance, when in 1803 there was a threat that Napoleon might invade, a popular parody entitled 'Buonaparte's Soliloquy at Calais'

---

[1] BL, Add. MS 40108, fo. 325ᵛ—this is a note by Hone among the manuscript materials for a history of parody which he began putting together when collecting evidence for his trial, discussed below.

[2] *The Queen's Matrimonial Ladder* (1820), repr. in Rickword 1971, p. 183.

(To go, or not to go? that is the question;
—Whether 'tis better for my views to suffer
The ease and quiet of yon hated rival,
Or to take arms against the haughty people,
And by invading end them? . . .)

was published both in its own right and as the inscription to a caricature of Napoleon by George Woodward.[3]

The invasion fears of 1803 provoked a flurry of nationalistic appropriation. A patriotic adaptation of *King John* by Richard Valpy,
headmaster, was performed at Reading School in aid of 'the subscrip-
tion to the naval pillar, to be erected in honour of the naval victories
of the war', then transferred in May to Covent Garden, where 'some
speeches introduced into it made so strong an impression on the
feelings of an English audience, on the renewal of the War, that the
Play was acted in almost every Town in Great Britain and Ireland'
(Nichols 1812–15, ix. 758). *Shakespeare's Ghost!*, a single-sheet broadside consisting of a cento of patriotic speeches from *King John* and
Henry V, was also popular at this time. It carries the explanation:

SHAKESPEARE often delights us on the Stage in the hour of Amusement,—let
him now in the HOUR OF PERIL inspire us with that PATRIOTISM and
COURAGE which animated our Forefathers to those DEEDS OF GLORY which
he describes.—SHAKSPEARE now speaks in the Character of A TRUE ENGLISH-
MAN and A STURDY JOHN BULL, indignant that a FRENCH ARMY should WAGE
WAR IN OUR ISLE . . .[4]

Gillray mockingly reproduced broadsheets of this sort in his caricature *John Bull and the Alarmist* (BMC 10088): it is typical of him at once
to participate in and parody the alarmism that stirred up the feelings
of Englishmen by means of red-blooded Shakespearean quotation.

Shakespearean allusion in caricature must, then, be seen as part of
a wider tendency to quotation, which embraced such forms as verse
parody and theatrical travesty.[5] The golden age of caricature was also

[3] It appeared in several magazines, including *London und Paris*, 1803, 12: 80–1. The
Woodward caricature is BMC 10104.

[4] Klingberg and Hustvedt 1944, p. 125; also printed in *Gentleman's Magazine*, 1803,
73: 664.

[5] Full-scale theatrical travesty in the non-patent theatres was a genre initiated by
John Poole's popular and much imitated *Hamlet Travestie* (1810)—see Wells 1977–8,
esp. vol. i—but incidental comic quotation was common in the theatre before this.
There is a character-type in comedy and afterpiece whose trademark is obsessive
Shakespearean quotation. Examples include Dick Wingate and his fellow-members of
the 'Spouting-Club' in Arthur Murphy's *The Apprentice* (1756), Rover in John

the golden age of English parody, high points being marked by Canning's *Anti-Jacobin* of 1797 to 1798 and Horace and James Smith's 1812 *Rejected Addresses*. There are two distinct types of parody. In Coleridge's words, 'Parodies on new poems are read as satires; on old ones (the soliloquy of Hamlet for instances) as compliments' (Southey and Coleridge 1969, No. 105). Both the *Rejected Addresses* and Canning and Frere's assaults on the likes of Southey and Erasmus Darwin imitate contemporary poets in order to attack their style and sentiments. Shakespearean parodies of the period, on the other hand, are never designed as attacks on Shakespeare; instead, his language—because it has the authority of genius and of his status as National Poet—is used as a weapon, turned against the follies of a later age. One such folly may be the imitation of Shakespearean blank verse in heroic drama, but the parodies of Elizabethan fustian in, say, Sheridan's *The Critic* are directed against the neo-Shakespearean tragedy that proliferated in the eighteenth century, not the thing itself.

Modern studies of parody have concentrated on the first type ('satires') at the expense of the second ('compliments').[6] This is probably because, from Shakespeare himself—Ancient Pistol's Marlovian bombast—to Beerbohm and beyond, it has produced some superb comic literature. We are naturally more suspicious of the hack writer who exploits a work of genius for his own satiric ends. Yet, in the charged political climate of the early nineteenth century, the second form was much discussed.

It was especially prominent in 1817: in December that year William Hone was tried three times for blasphemous libel on account of his having published three parodies of religious texts, 'The Late John Wilkes's Catechism', 'The Political Litany', and 'The Sinecurists' Creed'. He was acquitted each time, in what was widely seen as a triumph for the freedom of the Press, the independence of jurymen, and the radical cause.[7] Hone conducted his own defence, and based it on the critical distinction between the two types of parody:

O'Keefe's highly successful *Wild Oats* (1791), and Dr Pangloss in George Colman the Younger's *The Heir at Law* (1797). From the 1820s onward, Planché's extravaganzas are packed with Shakespearean quotation and travesty (see Wells 1963).

[6] See e.g., Highet 1962, Jump 1972.

[7] Smith 1984, ch. 5, discusses Hone's trials in terms of 'vernacular language', and Bunyan in particular; my emphasis here is different, but I share her sense of the trials' importance for the freedom of the Press.

'There are two kinds of parodies; one in which a man might convey ludicrous or ridiculous ideas relative to some other subject; the other, where it was meant to ridicule the thing parodied. The latter was not the case here, and therefore he had not brought religion into contempt' (Hone 1818, p. 23). It is a rare thing for a case in a court-room to be based on what is essentially a piece of literary criticism. Hone goes further, and supports his critical principle with a mass of evidence from literary history. He demonstrates that there is a venerable tradition of parodies of this sort—he quotes a biblical one by none other than Martin Luther. He cites a ministerial (Canningite) parody of the 'Te Deum' dedicated to Wellington: 'Oh, Emperor of France! we curse thee. | We acknowledge thee to be a Tyrant.' He asks why this is not blasphemous and why Gillray was not prosecuted over his caricature *The Apotheosis of Hoche* (BMC 9156—an attack on General Lazare Hoche, Jacobin bugaboo), which parodied the first commandment by applying 'Thou shalt have no other God but me' to 'Equality'. Mr Justice Abbott had to acknowledge that the Gillray was 'a wicked publication'. 'It was on the right side—that made all the difference', replies Hone, devastatingly (Hone 1818, p. 58).

Further evidence was brought forward in the second trial:

Gentlemen of the jury, with a view still further to show that an article may be humorously parodied, in order to excite ridicule, without either the humour or the ridicule being directed towards the article parodied, I shall read a parody on Hamlet's Soliloquy, which appeared in the *Morning Herald*, in 1808.

> 'To stand, or not to stand—that is the question.
> Whether 'tis nobler for us to lose th' Election,
> And all the honours that attend upon it,
> Or to demand a poll, and risk th' expense, etc. etc.'

(Hone 1818, pp. 109–10)

The judge claimed at this point that Shakespeare was not relevant, but for the purposes of the argument he is: his canonical status enables him to be the means rather than the object of parody. After Hone's triumph, there could be no more appropriate response than a 'Parody on Hamlet's Soliloquy, Supposed to be spoken by a certain Law Lord, after some recent Trial', which asks

> Whether 'twas better in the end, to suffer
> The future insolence of vulgar mobs,

Or to take umbrage at their grins and jeers,
And, by resigning, end them?[8]

The Hone trials give a wonderful sense of the issues involved in the parodying of classic writings for political purposes. In thinking more specifically about how Shakespearean parody functions, further help is provided by John Poole's discussion of dramatic burlesque in the preface to his influential *Hamlet Travestie* of 1810:

From the force of its sentiments, the beauty of its imagery, and, above all, the solemnity of its conduct, there is, perhaps, no tragedy in the English language better adapted to receive a burlesque than 'HAMLET'; and from its being so frequently before the public, so very generally read, and so continually quoted, it is, more than any other, calculated to give to burlesque its full effect, and which can only be produced by a facility of contrast with its subject work. For it is obvious that in a work of this nature . . . many parts must appear ridiculous and even contemptible, when considered independently of the passage or passages to which they allude. For a reader, therefore, to derive entertainment from a burlesque, but more particularly to be enabled to decide whether it be ill or well executed, a familiar acquaintance with the original is indispensable. (p. 6, repr. in Wells 1977–8, vol. i)

This analysis applies equally well to magazine parodies of specific passages. The first prerequisite of a parody is that the original should be well known. Since the language of Shakespeare, of Hamlet in particular, ran in the bloodstream of the age, it was a time especially propitious for Shakespearean parodies. A reader's enjoyment of them, and his or her value-judgements as to their success or failure, will depend on their relationship with the passages to which they allude, for there can be no doubt that when read in isolation many of them must, in Poole's words, 'appear ridiculous and even contemptible'.

The most sustained series of Shakespearean parodies in the period appeared in the *Gentleman's Magazine* between 1792 and 1805. Occasional parodies are, however, to be found from the mid-eighteenth century onwards. As with caricature and incidental quotation for political purposes, the 1730s furnish an early example: *Iago Display'd*, a pamphlet published in about 1731, cast Walpole as the villain, the Earl of Bath as Cassio, and Baron Hervey as Roderigo.

[8] Clipping from an unidentified magazine in Hone's manuscript *History of Parody*, BL Add. MS 40108, fo. 336ᵛ.

This satire on intrigue in the War Office is, however, Shakespearean only in its names. Early imitations or travesties of specific passages seem to have been restricted to variations on the soliloquy singled out by Coleridge, as their titles indicate: 'The Batchelor's Soliloquy. In imitation of a celebrated speech of Hamlet' (*Scots Magazine*, April 1744); 'The Soliloquy To be, or not to be?- in Hamlet, Travestied' (*General Advertiser*, 24 September 1747); 'Hamlet's Soliloquy imitated' ('To print, or not to print' by Richard Jago in Dodsley's 1758 *Collection of Poems by Several Hands*). 'To wed, or not to wed' is not particularly effective, but the *General Advertiser* piece, 'To *drink*, or not to *drink*', establishes the technique of keeping as close as possible to the original and marking departures with italics.

Early in the reign of George III, Shakespearean parody broadened in range. To these years belong the first major political examples and the first parodies of complete scenes as opposed to individual speeches. First there was the anti-Butonian 'Three Conjurors', then in about 1770 there appeared a broadside attacking Wilkes, *The Rout; or, The Despairing Candidate. A Parody on Shakespeare's King Richard III, Act Vth*. The same scene was appropriated by the pro-Wilkes, pro-America, anti-tyranny cause in No. 6 of the *Crisis*, a weekly twopence-halfpenny pamphlet that ran during 1775 and 1776. The *Crisis* is charged with vigorous rhetoric: there are references to Lord North being 'engendered in the Womb of Hell' by 'SATANIC Parents', headings such as 'A Bloody Court, A Bloody Ministry, and A Bloody Parliament' and 'The present Necessary DEFENSIVE War on the Part of AMERICA, justified by the Laws of God, Nature, Reason, State, and Nations; and therefore no TREASON or REBELLION', and a stream of capitalized keywords (No. 4 alone has DESPOTISM, PUBLIC LIBERTY, MASSACRE, BUTCHERED, ENSLAVED, TYRANNY, LAWLESS POWER on the one hand, and REASON, JUSTICE, TRUTH, LIBERTY on the other). No. 6 is headed, in bold type, 'Is there not some hidden CURSE in the Stores of HEAVEN, Red with uncommon Wrath, to BLAST the Man who Owes his GREATNESS to his COUNTRY'S RUIN?' and ends with 'A Parody, for your Lordship's Perusal, on the 3d Scene of the 5th Act of Richard the 3d'. Here, North is roused and castigated by 'the Ghost of Britannia' and 'the Ghosts of those barbarously Murdered at Brentford, Boston, and in St George's Fields, in the merciful Reign of the present King'. A later issue (No. 60, 9 March 1776) has a further Shakespearean parody, headed 'A PROPHESY' and based on the 'Jockey of Norfolk' passage, also from *Richard III*, that became popular in caricature: 'Good Georgy of Brunswick, Oh be not so bold; | For Britain thy Kingdom is bought, and is sold! . . .'

The parody of the ghosts appearing to Richard has an interesting afterlife in that a copy of it dropped through William Hone's letter-box when he was preparing his defence in 1817. It was transcribed in a letter signed 'Veritas', together with a full reference, explaining that it had been 'extracted from the Crisis Nr. 6. Saturday Febry 25. 1775'. 'Veritas' also expressed admiration for T. J. Wooler through an allusion to *Hamlet*: 'the Black Dwarf is admirable, upon your case. Take *him* for all in all, I ne'er shall look upon his like again' (BL Add. MS 40117, fos. 66ʳ–68ʳ).

'Veritas', whoever he may have been, perhaps drew the *Crisis* to Hone's attention because it afforded a rare early example of a Shake-spearean parody that was radical in its sympathies. Generally speaking, between 1760 and 1790 the form remained genteel and often frivol-ous. Symptomatically, when a journal made a regular, rather than a merely occasional, feature of Shakespearean parody, it was the Revd Charles Stanhope's *New Lady's Magazine*. Its parodies, further variations on Hamlet's soliloquy, steer well clear of politics: they consist of a different version of 'To wed, or not to wed', two attempts at 'To write—or not to write', one of which expresses the vain desire 'To be a second Shakespear', and 'The Young Student's Soliloquy', 'To learn, or not to learn'.[9] The *Gentleman's Magazine* soon followed the *New Lady's*. It had already published some parodies of Hamlet's soliloquy, including the original 'To wed, or not to wed' in 1744.[10] Another bachelor's soliloquy was contributed by one 'Philomeides' of Cambridge in March 1792; this led a correspondent to submit '*To* ride, *or not to* ride', 'written in 1758, and approved of by Mr. Shen-stone, to whom it was shewn, though never yet printed'. This was published in June. One may assume that the interest of which it was symptomatic, together with the example of Stanhope, led to the idea of publishing a whole series of parodies.

So it was that from October 1792 to December 1805 Shakespeare was pressed into the service of conservatism by a series of approxim-ately one hundred and fifty brief 'Parodies' which appeared under the name first of 'Mowbraensis', then from the end of 1792, of 'Master Shallow'. The technique was simple: to take a well-known passage and adapt it to a pressing social or political issue. At least, that is the

---

[9] *New Lady's Magazine*, 1786, 1: 101, 549; 1788, 3: 491; 1790, 5: 477.
[10] See *Gentleman's Magazine*, 1744, 14: 218; also 1752, 22: 87; 1788, 58: 691.

case with the more ambitious 'Parodies'—some of them are merely improvisations on the coming of spring or the charms of the country-side. Genteel parodies akin to those published by Stanhope's *New Lady's Magazine* were thus juxtaposed with sharper, more public ones.

'Master Shallow' was the Revd Thomas Ford, who for most of his life was vicar of Melton Mowbray (hence his original pseudonym). According to his nineteenth-century biographer, he was popular locally and known for his witty conversation—and for spicing his sermons with quotations from the English poets, cited with all the weight of biblical texts (see Wing 1864). He had previously published two of his sermons, *Compassion to the Poor Recommended* (1782) and *The Gospel Message Illustrated, and the Duties of Christian Ministers Enforced* (1775). His parodies give a fascinating sense of the preoccupations of 'gentlemen' in this turbulent decade; they are also another guide to the comparative popularity and appropriability of different parts of Shakespeare.

The term 'gentleman' needs to be defined with some care, especially since the *Gentleman's Magazine* played an important role in the shaping of that class's consciousness of itself. Edward Cave started the magazine in 1731, using the editorial pseudonym 'Sylvanus Urban', which indicated that he was attempting to reach both city and country audiences. Partly because the magazine pioneered parliamentary reporting, a circulation of ten thousand was soon reached; the greatest years were those when Dr Johnson was associated with it, but by the 1790s the *Gentleman's Magazine* had an old-fashioned feel to it. Even so, it remained, in the words of its editor, John Nichols, a leading voice of 'true Protestantism and true Patriotism' (preface of 1791, quoted, Nichols 1821, p. lxviii).

The readership of the magazine can be established with much more precision than can the audience for independently published carica-tures. First and foremost, there was the traditional 'gentry': owners who did not personally have to work their land, who dominated their local communities and the back-benches of Parliament, many of whom developed commercial interests in the later part of the century. But when Burke spoke in his *Reflections on the Revolution in France* of 'the spirit of a gentleman' (Burke 1790, p. 76), he did not merely have the landed gentry in mind. Johnson said that 'An English tradesman is a new species of gentleman', Guy Miège that 'the title of gentleman is commonly given in England to all that distinguish them-selves from the common sort of people by a good garb, genteel air or

good education, wealth or learning' (quoted, Porter 1982, p. 65). By
the end of the eighteenth century, then, gentlemanliness was circumscribed less by breeding than by education, wealth, and leisure. A
gentleman was the kind of man who had the money to buy, the time
to read, and the wit to understand the *Gentleman's Magazine* and the
host of other periodicals that had grown up in the second half of the
century. More specifically, in the context of my argument, he was
the kind of man who was sufficiently at ease with Shakespeare to
enjoy the nuances of the 'Parodies'.

A sense of the readership may be gained from the identity of people
who announced births, marriages, and deaths in the columns of the
magazine. They came from a wide social and geographical spread. In
October 1792, the issue that included the first of Ford's parodies,
announcements were placed not only by Lords, Earls, gentlemen at
their country seats, and Members of Parliament, but also by rectors,
middle-ranking military men, surgeons and tradesmen (an auctioneer, a linen-draper, a bookseller, a binder, hosiers, printers, and
bankers). The readership embraced both a 'Manchester warehouse-
man' and one George Dixon, 'a very considerable farmer under Lord
Mulcaster'—not to mention a 'wafer-maker, of St John's-Lane,
Clerkenwell' (*Gentleman's Magazine* 1792, 62: 959–61).

In 1819 *Blackwood's* described the gentleman as 'to a very great
extent the guide of society' (Perkin 1969, p. 275). Thirty years earlier,
the *Gentleman's Magazine* provided an invaluable guide to the taste of
society. The success of the 'Parodies' tells of a taste for Shakespearean
appropriation among a wide cross-section of the literate community
that one suspects is the kind of thing that Wordsworth had in mind
when he expostulated in his 1802 preface to *Lyrical Ballads* about those
'who talk of Poetry as of a matter of amusement and idle pleasure;
who will converse about a *taste* for Poetry, as they express it, as if it
were a thing as indifferent as a taste for Rope-dancing, or Frontiniac
or Sherry' (Wordsworth 1974, p. 79). Yet with this taste went a
pressing need to make Shakespeare into 'A TRUE ENGLISHMAN and
A STURDY JOHN BULL'. And, once the well-to-do took possession of
Shakespeare in this way, radical culture inevitably staked its counter-
claim.

The Revd Ford's choice of passages for his parodies provides
evidence of the common reader's choice in Shakespeare. Predictably
enough, *Hamlet* is the most popular source, being used twenty-two
times; it is nearly always Hamlet's soliloquies that are plundered,

especially 'To be or not to be', which is adapted thirteen times. The other favourite set pieces are Romeo's 'I do remember an apothecary' (thirteen out of fifteen *Romeo and Juliet* parodies) and Jaques's Seven Ages (eleven out of thirteen from *As You Like It*). A wider range of passages is employed in the eleven parodies based on *Henry V*, which was particularly important for patriotic reasons, and the nine from *Macbeth*. The tragedies provide more material than the comedies: *Othello*, *Lear*, and *Julius Caesar* each furnish Master Shallow with six pieces, while the most popular comedy—if we discount Jaques's oration—*A Midsummer Night's Dream*, is the basis of only four. The second most frequent history is *King John*; this suggests that there is some correlation with the stage, for the play was popular throughout the decade after Kemble restored it to the repertory in 1791, and doubly so after Valpy's patriotic version of 1803. As late as 1811 Jane Austen wrote of 'a very unlucky change of the play for this very night—Hamlet instead of King John' (Austen 1955, p. 113). Austen does not elaborate as to why she would have rather seen *King John* than *Hamlet*, but it is beyond question that in the two decades of war against France many people cherished the lesser-known play for nationalistic reasons.

Ford used thirty plays in all. Those that he ignored were, on the whole, the ones which were least frequently talked about and staged during the period: *All's Well*, *The Comedy of Errors*, *Merry Wives*, *Much Ado*, *Pericles*, and *The Taming of the Shrew*. The surprising exception is *Coriolanus*, which was overlooked despite its political potential and the fact that it was Kemble's *tour de force*. Hazlitt remarked that a reading of *Coriolanus* would save anyone the trouble of reading 'the Debates in both Houses of Parliament since the French Revolution or our own' (HW iv. 214): had Master Shallow parodied the play, the readers of the *Gentleman's Magazine* would have had the chance to make the comparison with the Proceedings of the National Convention in Paris, because in many numbers the parodies were printed on the page facing the Minutes of those Proceedings. That he does not make use of this opportunity is symptomatic of Ford's provinciality.

Ford's first attempts, published in October and November 1792, are slight; it is as if the genre is being tried out on the magazine's readers before it is put to serious use. Only in December are the 'Parodies' applied to the all-consuming question of sedition. 1792 had been the year of two crucial events in the history of English radicalism, the publication of the second part of Paine's *Rights of Man* and

16. Josiah Boydell, *The Rose-scene* from *1 Henry VI* (1789)

17. Henry Fuseli, *Macbeth, Banquo, and the Three Witches* (1789)

18. Henry Fuseli, *The Renunciation of Cordelia* (1789)

19. James Barry, *King Lear Weeping over the Dead Body of Cordelia* (1789)

20. Henry Fuseli, *Hamlet and the Ghost* (1789)

21. John Opie, *The Infant Perdita* (1789)

Inscription under a Picture of the Editor of SHAKSPEARE's Manuscripts, 1796.
by the Rev.ᵈ William Mason , Author of Elfrida & Caractacus.

" Four Forgers born in one prolific age,
" Much critical acumen did engage.
" The First was soon by doughty Douglas scar'd,
" Tho' Johnson would have screen'd him, had he dar'd; *
" The Next had all the cunning of a Scot; ‡
" The Third, invention, genius, — nay, what not ? ♡
" FRAUD , now exhausted, only could dispense
" To her Fourth Son, their three-fold impudence.

22. James Gillray, Samuel Ireland caricatured (1797)

the founding of the London Corresponding Society. Against this background, we gain a sense of the urgency of the three December parodies. 'So work their mischief rebels . . .' inverts Henry V's image of the bees as a metaphor for order in the State, applying it to seditionists and disorder; *Henry V*, act I scene ii, is especially significant in this context because it turns on the relationship between rebellion at home and possible war with France. The second parody is 'Let us praise Heaven we can each one sit | And tell glad stories of the fall of traitors . . .'; this is a good example of the way in which the poems depend upon a knowledge of their originals, for the gentleman reader would have been delighted by the transformation of Richard II's 'sad stories of the death of kings'. The French monarchy had been formally abolished by the Convention of 21 September 1792; Paine's tract had presaged the fall of kings in England—'glad stories of the fall of traitors' were much needed to reassure the Establishment. The third parody pushes the point home, beginning 'O beware, my lord, of conspiracy! | It is a squint-eyed monster' and ending 'Good Heaven, the souls of all my tribe preserve | From a Republick!' (62: 1132). This is a less sophisticated piece in that it neglects the context of the original: if any thought were given to the fact that it is spoken by Iago, the irony would backfire.

One begins to see that, in the hands of an amateur, Shakespearean quotation can be a two-edged sword. Ford's parodies were sufficiently well regarded for John Nichols to think it worth publishing in 1794 *Confusion's Master-Piece: or, Paine's Labour's Lost. Being a Specimen of some well-known Scenes in Shakespeare's Macbeth. Revived and improved; as enacted by some of his Majesty's Servants before the pit of Acheron. By the Writer of the Parodies in the Gentleman's Magazine.* This pamphlet, about ten pages in length, is Ford's most sustained attack on radicalism. Parts of it have some verve: three citizens playing the role of the witches, 'I come, *Roberspierre*!', '*Danton* calls', 'Right is wrong, and wrong is right', 'Where hast thou been, brother? | Dropping handbills', 'Double, double, strife and trouble; | Faction, blaze! and, treason, bubble!', an apparition of Wat Tyler (Southey's infamous play also belongs to 1794):

> Britain shall ne'er new-model'd be, until,
> From Dunkirk, *Sans Culottes*, in complete garb,
> Shall come against it.

The 'Scenes' end with a descent of Britannia and a proclamation of loyalty to king and country, but all the vitality has belonged to the language of the radicals whom Ford is attempting to condemn. Ironically, they are the ones who seem to be truly Shakespearean—rather as in the play itself we are much more interested in the regicide Macbeth than the restorer of order, Malcolm.

Perhaps because political parodies are dangerous and can take on a life of their own in this way, Ford confined many of his attacks to slothful undergraduates, professionally irresponsible doctors and lawyers, damaging gossips, and ambitious country vicars ('Bishops! and ministers of state prefer *me!*'—*Gentleman's Magazine* 1793, 63: 1135). There is something self-satisfied about him: he remains in a world where the most positive values seem to be good hunting, shooting and fishing, fine food, and post-prandial cards or dice. The high-minded moralism of 'Look here upon this picture, and on this' (*Hamlet*, III. iv. 53 ff., turned to praise a wife and damn a mistress) is somehow undercut by the indulgent tone of 'Cry—Talleho! England! and Fox-hunting' or 'If Lobsters be the sauce for Turbot, heap on | Give me another plate—that so the appetite | May gourmandize before the season's out' (March, November, July 1794, 64: 262, 1073, 654). Class attitudes are revealed as the gentleman parodist derides those whom we would now call petty bourgeois ('The Tailor, the Barber, and the Innkeeper, | Are of deception all compact'— March 1795, 65: 239) and patronizingly extols the industry of men who work the land: 'A Summer's day divides | The strength of labourers in divers functions . . .' (June 1795, 65: 512), another telling use of that crucial speech in *Henry V*, act I scene ii, on 'Obedience' and 'The act of order'.

Ford also returned to political themes in 1795, as one would expect in the year when Pitt introduced the Seditious Meetings and Treasonable Practices Acts as a response to increasing unrest. 'See in their treatment of confinèd pris'ners | The contrary spirit of two opposing nations . . .' (March, 65: 239, based on Hamlet's contrast between his father and Claudius) begins with a comparison of respective prison conditions in England and France, then develops a general attack on French 'Anarchy' and 'Atheism'. A parody recommending that a traitor should be hanged without mercy appropriately uses a speech on the sanctity of social bonds from a play about treachery, 'He was in double trust . . .' (August, 65: 688, from *Macbeth*, I. vii. 12 ff.). Perhaps the most vigorously felt piece of this type is a parody of February 1796, which revivifies Claudius on the divine right of kings:

> But such divinity doth hedge a King,
> That Treason can but peep to what it would.
> God and his angels guard the sacred throne . . .

> (66: 152, adapting *Hamlet*, IV. v. 124 ff.)

This is another extract used regardless of context; there is no implied parallel between Claudius and the voice speaking the parody. By this criterion, a more effective parody is one on the opening of *Richard III*, 'Now is the winter of our discontent | Made glorious summer by this son of Chatham' (July 1797, 67: 598), which is written as if spoken by a radical Member of Parliament. His resolution to 'fawn upon the people's majesty' and his subversive activities—he intends to persuade 'the king's valiant troops to mutiny'—are made all the more shocking by the constant implication that he is another Richard of Gloucester.

As has been suggested, the other factor determining the strength of a parody is how close it can keep to its original. If the parodist's point can be made by a few telling changes of words and phrases rather than a full-scale departure from the original, the result is far more effective. In terms of both contextual relevance—fear of civil war— and adherence to the original text save for a number of purposeful substitutions and inversions, the piece published with 'Now is the winter of our discontent' is unusually successful:

> O heaven! that one might read the book of fate;
> And see the revolution of the times
> Make mountains level, and the continent
> (Weary of solid firmness,) melt itself
> Into the sea! . . .

> (*2 Henry IV*, III. i. 45 ff.)

is adapted into

> Heaven! that one might read the end of faction,
> And see the revolution of old times
> Make murmur hush, and the deluded country,
> Weary of inward wars, restore itself
> To solid firmness! . . .

> (July 1797, 67: 599)

But when Shakespeare's and Master Shallow's respective subjects are inappropriately matched, the effect is ludicrous. The masque in *The Tempest* and the Battle of St Vincent just do not have enough in common to give any weight to 'Our battles now are ended: these our Sailors, | As I foretold you, were all heroes . . .' (November 1797, 67: 967).

There is no parody celebrating the Battle of the Nile the following year, only a patriotic version of 'Now all the youth of England are on fire' by the Laureate Henry James Pye, written as a 'Prologue to Henry the Fourth (Part 1) lately performed by the young Gentlemen of Reading School for the Benefit of the Widows and Orphans of the gallant Seamen and Marines who fell on the glorious First of August'.[11] Master Shallow's concerns that year were more mundane. His three offerings for December were 'To hunt, or not to hunt?', 'Is this a mitre that I see before me' (preferment seems to have been an issue close to the Revd Ford's heart), and 'I have almost forgot the taste of Oysters' (68: 1065).

But within a couple of months the Irish question loomed sufficiently large to draw him from his hunting and his oysters. It was in 1799 that Pitt's policy of Union came into the open; a vehicle for Ford's treatment of this theme was provided by the peace between England and France sealed by King Harry's marriage at the end of *Henry V* (V. ii. 349 ff.):

> —Let the opposed kingdoms,
> England and Ireland, whose very shores reach out
> T'embrace and form each other's happiness,
> Cease from dissention; let sacred Union
> Establish freedom, loyalty, and strength . . .
> . . .Pitt, this act be thine.

(February 1799, 69: 152)

The first of the August 1799 parodies is an example of full-scale departure from the original text. Macbeth's 'Now o'er the one half world | Nature seems dead . . . witchcraft celebrates | Pale Hecat's off'rings' (II. i. 49 ff.) is transformed into

> Now holds throughout this happy land
> Justice her circuit, and equal right dispenses
> To all aggriev'd; each county celebrates
> Its own charter'd assize . . .   (69: 693)

One cannot help feeling that Macbeth's lines on 'wither'd Murder'

---

[11] Oct. 1798, 68: 880; the Reading connection was Richard Valpy, mentioned above, p. 106.

are hardly the most fortunate analogue for an encomium on the English courts.

The 'Parodies' are surprisingly varied in quality and tone. Turning the page from 'Now holds throughout this happy land', we find the most vigorous of Ford's many improvisations on Romeo's 'I do remember an Apothecary':

> I do remember a poor Negro,
> Under the torrid sun by parching thirst
> Oppress'd; with sweat-bestreamed brow he slaved,
> Planting of sugar-canes; fierce were his looks,
> Curs'd Tyranny had almost made him mad;
> And on his goary back a blanket hung,
> To hide his fester'd sores, and torn-up back
> By deep-indented lashes; within the huts
> Air-piercing shrieks are heard, and dismal groans;
> Wire-platted whips, fetters, and massy chains,
> Remnants of cords, and old spikes of iron,
> Were scatter'd here and there, to make up terror.
> Noting these cruelties, I cried aloud,
> If Heaven hath store of right-aim'd thunder-bolts,
> Scourges for guilt, and pains for damned men,
> Here are unfeeling traders, that grow rich,
> And fatten on the blood of human victims.
> Oh! this same thought doth harrow up the soul,
> Knock at the heart, and bid soft Pity weep!
> No holiday allow'd, the sufferer drops,
> And enters into rest.

(August 1799, 69: 694)

I have quoted this parody in its entirety because it seems to me exceptional. Its tone is anything but self-satisfied, its impassioned vocabulary anything but trivial or indulgent. It is the only piece in which Ford's vocation outweighs his respect for things as they are, his only serious questioning of the position of the government and the editorial policies of the *Gentleman's Magazine*—in *The Rise and Progress*, Nichols says that the magazine sought to resist the instant abolition of slavery. Here Ford strikes out on his own, whereas elsewhere his work accords with the other editorial policies mentioned by Nichols, namely condemnation of both the French Revolution and civil unrest at home.

Ford is in good company alluding to Shakespeare in the context of the slavery issue. In 1795 Coleridge had adopted the same strategy in two of his important Bristol lectures. In the sixth lecture of his course 'On Revealed Religion', he quoted *Macbeth* while speaking of British slaves: 'I hang my head when I think of them, they leave an indelible stain on our national character—all the waters of the Ocean cannot purify, all the perfumes of Araby cannot sweeten it.' Then in his lecture 'On the Slave-Trade' he referred to abolition as 'a consummation most devoutly to be wished' (Coleridge 1971, pp. 226, 246). The allusion to *Macbeth* is by far the more effective of these two instances because references to the ocean and the perfumes of Arabia take on a new resonance in a discussion of trade, whereas the phrase from *Hamlet* is merely used proverbially with no contextual pressure.

'I do remember a poor Negro' has a certain crude power in its own right; it is not merely dependent on its original (*Romeo*, V. i. 37 ff.). Structurally and rhythmically it is close to the apothecary monologue ('And in his needy shop'—'And on his goary back'; 'Noting this penury'—'Noting these cruelties'), while its variations of vocabulary are sometimes quite subtle: 'slaved' is introduced as a verb rather than the more obvious noun; we would expect the negro to have 'meagre' looks like the apothecary, but in fact they are 'fierce' with justifiable anger and near madness; 'Curs'd Tyranny' apportions blame in a way that Romeo's 'Sharp misery' does not. The catalogue of torture instruments moves far from the items in the apothecary's shop, but then the conclusion returns to Shakespeare, combining 'O, this same thought' with an allusion to *Hamlet* (I. v. 15) which strengthens the impression that this is indeed a tale 'whose lightest word | Would harrow up thy soul, freeze thy young blood'. Here Ford has succeeded in writing a parody which stands on its own yet also summons up a variety of evocative earlier texts.

After this *tour de force* there is a falling-off in the 'Parodies'. They tend, after the turn of the century, to dwell on such slight, if interesting, matters as the decline of classical education ('How many gentlemen in this knowing age | Can construe Greek?', 70: 163) and the potential of the lottery as a means of ending one's debts ('To buy, or not to buy?', 75: 1148). There are some characteristic patriotic pieces and, in February 1801, a final tribute to Pitt,

> This noble *Son of Chatham*
> Hath shewn his faculties so bright, hath been
> So clear in his high office, that his virtues,

Like his great Father's, ever fam'd, will cause,
At this his resignation, deep regret . . .

(71: 162, from *Macbeth*, I. vii. 16 ff.)

('High office' is neat with respect to the Prime Minister.)

The most substantial parody after the turn of the century is 'To arm, or not to arm?' (August 1803, 73: 760), another response to fears that Napoleon was going to invade. It does not, however, seem to have made the same impression as 'Buonaparte's Soliloquy at Calais': the novelty of Ford's efforts had obviously worn off and he was on the decline. There were no 'Parodies' in *The Gentleman's Magazine* in 1804 and only a final flourish in December 1805. This last piece, on the death of Nelson at Trafalgar—'Hung be the shrouds with black . . .' (75: 1149)—suggests that technique as well as popularity was failing, for instead of pithily adapting a single well-known speech it is based on *1 Henry VI*, '*1st Act throughout*'. The allusions are consequently too diffuse to be effective. 'Master Shallow' is not heard of again outside his parish in Melton Mowbray.

Testimony to the success of the *Gentleman's Magazine* parodies in their early years is provided by the fact that a number of them were reprinted in the *Scots Magazine* during 1793 and 1794.[12] These include the three anti-radical passages first published in December 1792, which suggests that the political reassurance they offered was appreciated by the gentry even at the confines of the kingdom. A 'Parody on Othello's Account of his Courtship' in the *Anthologia Hibernica* (1793, 1: 152) suggests that they were also well received in Dublin. Then in the early nineteenth century a number of writers made use of the device, the most accomplished pieces being Horace Twiss's version of the Seven Ages—'The Patriot's Progress' from demagogue to Secretary to peerage—and the same author's brief 'Our parodies are ended'.[13]

---

[12] See *Scots Magazine*, 1793, 55: 38, 282; 1794, 56: 97, 337, 774. The short-lived Glasgow periodical the *Culler* (1795) also included a 'Parody on Hamlet's Soliloquy' (p. 144) and 'Parodies of Shakspeare' (p. 208).

[13] Twiss 1814, p. 82. Other early nineteenth-century examples include two parodies by the Shakespeare forger W. H. Ireland in his *Rhapsodies* (1803, pp. 111–12), and one by J. P. Roberdeau in his *Fugitive Verse and Prose* (1804, pp. 75–6). *Covent Garden Journal* of 1810 published 'The Soliloquy of the Moor at Covent Garden' on the OP affair. Parodies of Hamlet's soliloquy continued to multiply: the Hone materials in the British Library also include several further versions of 'To be or not to be', mostly cuttings without date and source. See also Jacobs and Johnson 1976, though their listing is far from complete (Ford's parodies are not mentioned).

Twiss's parodies were published in 1814, but the more interesting development in this decade was the enlisting of Shakespeare in the cause of radicalism. E. P. Thompson has discerned Shakespeare's importance for radical culture: 'The most positive influence upon the sensibility of the Radicals came less from the little theatres than from the Shakespearian revival—not only Hazlitt, but also Wooler, Bamford, Cooper, and a score of self-taught Radical and Chartist journalists were wont to cap their arguments with Shakespearian quotations' (Thompson 1968, p. 809).

In 1818 the radical bookseller Richard Carlile published in the *Independent Whig* an eight-page satire in Shakespearean blank verse, *A Parody of the Tent Scene in Richard the Third*.[14] This attack on Castlereagh's record as Foreign Secretary called him Castlebrag and cast him as Richard, visited by the ghosts of England, Scotland, and Ireland, who claim that he has destroyed the entire United Kingdom. Castlereagh was also the victim of a parody which appeared in the *Black Dwarf* the year after the Peterloo massacre. This time he was cast as another tyrant, Macbeth, soliloquizing as he beheld 'a Vision of the Goddess of Liberty as he rose from his dinner, to proceed to the H——e of C———s, with the new Bills against the remaining liberties of Englishmen':

> Is this the Goddess that I see before me,
> Her back turn'd on herself? soft,—let me stab her.
> I've done it not, and yet I struck with force;
> Art thou not, hateful vision, sensible
> To feeling, as to sight? or art thou but
> Th' effect of indigestion, a false creation
> Proceeding from this overloaded stomach?
> I see thee yet, in form as palpable
> As these six Bills I hold—
> Thou marshals't me the way that I was going;
> And such majority I was to have—
> M[i]ne eyes are made the fools o' th' other senses,
> Or else worth all the rest—I see the[e] still;
> And on thy snow-white garments gouts of blood,
> Which was not so before.—There's no such thing.—
> It is the deeds at Manchester, which inform
> Thus to mine eyes.—Now o'er one half the world,

---

[14] The choice of scene suggests that the author may have known *The Crisis*, No. 6. 'Veritas', who provided Hone with a copy of it, could have been the link: it is noteworthy that the Carlile parody is set 'The Night before Hone's Third Trial'.

Tyranny has sway; now Princes celebrate
Th' Alliance Holy; and starving Radicals,
(Rous'd into action by the sense of right,
And pangs of want) thus with their murd'rous Pikes,
In dread array, tow'rds their foul design
Move like a troup of ghosts. . . .

(*Black Dwarf* 1820, 4: 143)

And so he continues, until he exits 'with a genteel flourish of the body and much self complacency'. By placing the speech between stage directions and by veering from comedy to uncompromising condemnation, from indigestion to Peterloo, the *Black Dwarf* parodist, who signs himself T. H., achieves a much richer, more incisive effect than was ever the case in the *Gentleman's Magazine*. T. H. has a vitality and a comic *élan* that Master Shallow altogether lacks. Such details as the conversion of 'witchcraft celebrates | Pale Hecate's offerings' into 'Princes celebrate | Th' Alliance Holy' show tremendous verve, as the Alliance of European monarchs is rendered *un*holy. The dramatic complexity of Macbeth's character may be lost—we have no sympathy for Castlereagh—but the parody still answers powerfully to its original, matching it metrically and making Castlereagh into something worse than a regicide. Macbeth murders the king; Castlereagh murders the people in the name of the king.

In many respects, this parody is as telling an indictment as Shelley's 'I met Murder on the way— | He had a mask like Castlereagh . . .' (*The Mask of Anarchy: Written on the Occasion of the Massacre at Manchester*, stanza ii). It would also have had more immediate political effect than Shelley's poem: the latter was not published for a long time, whereas the *Black Dwarf* had a wide circulation in radical circles. R. W. Malcolmson says of the early nineteenth century, 'During this period a solid barrier had developed between the culture of gentility and the culture of the people' (Malcolmson 1973, p. 165). This is not so, as far as one aspect of literary culture is concerned: political parodies show that Shakespeare was repossessed both by the gentry and in the radical counter-culture.

The appropriation of Shakespeare in time of war is a tendency that has persisted into our own century. In 1916, a little under two months before the battle of the Somme, every school in England marked 'Shakespeare Day' with the Bible-reading 'Let us now praise famous men', the singing of a Shakespeare song, a discourse on Shakespeare, further songs and selected passages from the plays, and 'God Save the

King'. A beautifully printed sixpenny pamphlet entitled *Shakespeare Tercentenary Observance in the Schools and Other Institutions* had at its centre 'Notes on Shakespeare the Patriot' by Professor Israel Gollancz,[15] who was in no doubt that in *Henry V* 'Shakespeare gives us, in the person of the King, his ideal Patriot-Englishman, and the play rings out to-day as a trumpet-call to all' (Gollancz 1916, p. 15). A similar sentiment lay behind Olivier's great cinematic appropriation of 1944, which was dedicated 'To the Commandos and Airborne Troops of Great Britain' who spearheaded the D-Day landings. Hazlitt, as will be seen, would not have been so sure about this notion of the play as a trumpet-call to patriots.

Shakespeare has been enlisted in lesser wars too. Some lines from *Henry V* were quoted as the caption to *The Peace-Makers* (BMC 4416) of 28 November 1770, a caricature attacking those who did not think it worth going to war over the Falkland Islands. This is a precedent for an extended parody published in *The Economist* of 25 December 1982 under the title *Queen Margaret or Shakespeare Goes to the Falklands*. It carries an explanatory headnote, 'The exclusion of W. Shakespeare from the Task Force press corps has left the nation bereft of its traditional record of heroic British victories. He therefore had to rework his existing material . . .'. The text is composed of two hundred and thirteen extracts from twenty-seven plays, varying in length from single lines to large portions of whole scenes. The history plays provide the most fruitful sources.

Queen Margaret is an interesting combination of traditional appropriations and local detail. Its prophetic prologue by former Prime Minister Edward Heath ends with John of Gaunt's death-bed condemnation of England's decline, a passage frequently invoked in the 1790s, yet it also touches on unemployment in the 1980s by transforming Gonzalo's 'No occupation; all men idle' (*Tempest*, II. i. 155). As in most Shakespearean parodies, the strongest comic effects are achieved by giving new life to specific well-known lines. What better

---

[15] Gollancz was the secretary of the Tercentenary Committee, and the guiding force behind the celebration. By the brilliant stroke of reckoning Shakespeare's birthday according to the old-style calendar (ten days behind the new style), he contrived to make Shakespeare Day coincide with Empire Day. The motivation of the whole business is apparent from a letter that he wrote to *The Times* pub. 23 Dec. 1915: 'It is surely advisable, on the approaching occasion, from many points of view, reverently and in no spirit of festivity, to recall anew, with deeper fervour, the prophetic words of good omen, uttered well-nigh 300 years ago.—"Triumph, my Britain, thou hast one to shew | To whom all scenes in Europe homage owe!" ' (quoting Ben Jonson's commendatory poem on Shakespeare).

exit line for Alexander Haig than 'A plague on both your houses! |
They have made worms' meat of me' (II. ii)? Perhaps the best
example of this effect occurs at the end of the first act:

> GALTIERI [*Produces Exocet*]. Behold I have a weapon
> A better never did itself sustain
> Upon a soldier's thigh.

But there are also some adroit strokes of characterization and plot.
Cecil Parkinson, Chairman of the Conservative Party and sycophantic
admirer of Thatcher, praises his leader through Enobarbus' lines on
Cleopatra in her barge; Thatcher herself is a redoubtable Lady
Macbeth, while Galtieri speaks the language of *Coriolanus*—'Peace is
a very apoplexy, lethargy, mulled, deaf, sleepy, insensible, a getter of
more bastard children than war's a destroyer of men' (I. iv, from
Coriolanus, IV. v. 223). Some identifications are more successful than
others. Lord Carrington's fall from grace is mediated through that of
Wolsey in *Henry VIII* more effectively than through Othello's 'I have
done the state some service'.

Wider dramatic situations also provide material for the parodist.
The scene between Hotspur and his wife (*1 Henry IV*, II. iii) is nicely
inverted to show Denis Thatcher playing the role of Kate, neglected
while a spouse goes to war; the British commanders relive scenes from
the history plays, Admiral Woodward going among his men in
disguise, General Moore converting St Crispian into 'the feast of
Margaret' as he addresses the 'happy few', his 'band of brothers'
consisting of 'assorted paras, marines, journalists' (II. iv). Certain
lines seem uncannily apposite to the Falklands adventure. Nott to
Carrington: 'She'll shake | Your Office about your ears' (I. i);
Parkinson to Thatcher: 'Be it thy course to busy giddy minds | With
foreign quarrels, that action hence borne out | May waste the memory
of the former days?' (I. ii); and, most tellingly, Second Sailor: 'We go
to gain a little patch of ground, | That hath in it no profit but
the name. | To pay five ducats, five, I would not farm it' (II. i). At
a Press briefing during the war, Mrs Thatcher's leaden-voiced
Ministry of Defence spokesman quoted, with unintentional irony,
Hamlet's lines from this scene about finding quarrel in a straw. As
with the Norwegian and the Pole in *Hamlet*, so with the British and
the Argentinian in 1982.

Caricatures and parodies which use Shakespeare as weapons in
their assault on politicians of every hue remain among the most

withering of satirical tools. I use these violent metaphors advisedly, for parody—whether its twists on its originals are crude or sophisticated, verbal, visual, or a combination of the two—is an aggressive art, which answers fire with fire. For all their immediate comic and ironic sharpness, the Shakespearean caricatures and parodies of the later eighteenth and early nineteenth centuries do not answer to what many people value most about Shakespeare. Once set beside the magnanimity and breadth of vision of the plays themselves, they are likely to seem mean and limited. I now wish to turn to a kind of appropriation which, while still speaking to its own time, responds more variously and magnanimously to Shakespeare: the recreative criticism of Hazlitt.

Part II

THE EXAMPLE OF HAZLITT

5

Theatre

ONE of the best-selling Shakespearean editions of the later eighteenth century was that of the plays 'As they are now performed at the Theatres Royal in London', published by John Bell in 1773-4. Fourteen years later, Bell followed up his success by publishing a complete reading text, free from the interference of adapters. But he included among the copperplate embellishments a portrait of Garrick, which, as the contents list explained, 'has no immediate reference to the Work, but may be preserved as the best *acting* Commentator on SHAKSPERE'. There was no question of a complete divorce between acting and reading. Well into the nineteenth century Garrick retained in the popular imagination the special place he had carved for himself as the best commentator on Shakespeare. James Boaden voiced the received opinion in his *Memoirs of Mrs Siddons*: 'If nature wrote through Shakspeare, the poet in his turn spoke best through Garrick' (Boaden 1827, i. 8).

But the early nineteenth century was also marked by important developments in a tradition that questioned whether the stage could do justice to Shakespeare's greatest plays, in particular the so-called four great tragedies and the two 'magical' plays (*A Midsummer Night's Dream* and *The Tempest*), where the imagination was taken to be pre-eminent. Once the imagination is brought to the fore, it is only a short step to the argument that these plays are best served in the imagination of the individual reader. In 1811 Charles Lamb published his essay 'On the Tragedies of Shakspeare, Considered with Reference to their Fitness for Stage Representation'. Though not the unequivocal attack on the stage it is often taken to be,[1] it is the key

---

[1] It is nearly always the first text cited in support of the view that Romanticism was antipathetic to the stage. Park 1982 offers a more measured account than the usual one. Arac 1987 is strong on the difference between Lamb's and Johnson's responses to *Lear* in the theatre, but does not consider the possibility that the two critics shared a scepticism that derived from popular overestimation of Garrick's performance. I think that Lear was very important to both Johnson and Lamb for personal reasons—in

text in this tradition; consideration of it is a necessary preliminary to a discussion of Hazlitt's views on the staging of Shakespeare.

Lamb's apparent scepticism about the stage must be seen in the context of the cult of Garrick. He begins his essay by describing how, when taking a turn in Westminster Abbey, he came across the monument to Garrick which in 1797 had been erected in proximity to that of Shakespeare. It was inscribed with some couplets by one Samuel Jackson Pratt which sought to maintain Garrick's special relationship with the Bard: Shakespeare's forms had lain shrouded in night till 'Immortal Garrick call'd them back to day'. For all eternity, 'SHAKSPEARE and GARRICK like twin stars shall shine, | And earth irradiate with a beam divine'. Lamb calls this a 'farrago of false thoughts and nonsense' (Lamb 1912, i. 113). His essay was originally entitled 'On Garrick, and Acting; and the Plays of Shakespeare, considered with reference . . .'—the initial provocation is the excess of equating Garrick with Shakespeare, not the very principle of staging the plays. Lamb in fact remained a keen theatre-goer throughout his life, and elsewhere he writes warmly of actors and of the necessary complicity between actor and theatre audience in comedy. Here, however, he is so infuriated by the Garrick monument that he responds with a rhetorical excess of his own: 'It may seem a paradox, but I cannot help being of opinion that the plays of Shakspeare are less calculated for performance on a stage, than those of almost any other dramatist whatever' (Lamb 1912, i. 115).

A number of impulses lie behind this paradox. At one level, the essay is an attack on specific conditions in the early nineteenth-century theatre: Lamb is incensed by mangled playhouse texts, especially Tate's version of *King Lear*, by a star system that pays more attention to the actor than the character he personates, by the crudity of delivery that is necessary in a vast building, by cumbersome stage machinery, and by the way the theatre reduces to pantomime such evanescent beings as the witches and Ariel. But, at another level, Lamb is playing with the argument that Shakespeare's major tragedies are *inherently* unperformable: 'the Lear of Shakspeare cannot be acted' (i. 124). This is a paradox because the *Lear* of Shakespeare was written to be acted, and was acted in Shakespeare's own time—though modern theories of revision would now speak of the *Lears* of Shakespeare. On the other hand, from 1681 to 1838, it was

their different ways, each had brushes with madness—and they accordingly disliked the idea that Garrick somehow owned Lear or embodied Lear.

generally agreed that the *Lear* of Shakespeare could not be acted and
that the *Lear* of Tate should be staged instead.[2] In addition, from 1811
to 1820, the *Lear* of Shakespeare could not be acted since the King was
mad. So Lamb's was hardly a lone voice.

Where he was original was in his reasons for believing that *Lear* was
unactable: 'The greatness of Lear is not in corporal dimension, but in
intellectual . . . It is his mind which is laid bare. . . . On the stage we
see nothing but corporal infirmities and weakness, the impotence of
rage; while we read it, we see not Lear, but we are Lear,—we are in
his mind' (ibid.). This is a significant departure because here Lamb
has privatized *King Lear*. Dr Johnson had weighed Tate's *Lear* against
Shakespeare's on the scale of public opinion; he added his own voice
to the 'general suffrage' in favour of Tate (Johnson 1986, p. 240). It
is an affront to society that vice should flourish and virtue perish in a
just cause, so Shakespeare's *Lear* should not be staged. Lamb is not
interested in moral judgements of this sort: for him, *Lear* has more to
do with the mind than with society, so it belongs in the mind. So too
with *Hamlet*: he argues that nine-tenths of the true Hamlet can be
located in the intellect, in 'solitary musings' and 'silent meditations'
(Lamb 1912, i. 116–17), and therefore to embody the character, to
bring it into company and noise, is to make it something other than
what it essentially is—'I am not arguing that Hamlet should not be
acted, but how much Hamlet is made another thing by being acted'
(i. 117). As Lamb puts the general principle, acting offers only 'the
bare imitation of the signs' of the passions, whereas the essence of
Shakespeare's uniqueness resides in 'the motives and grounds of the
passion', 'the internal workings and movements of a great mind'
(i. 113–14). For Lamb, in the theatre a *'symbol of the emotion'* passes
for the emotion itself (i. 119).

The argument has a certain force: just as an allusive caricature
adopts for its own purposes a crude image of a Shakespearean character, so a performance may caricature Shakespeare's psychologically
sophisticated inventions, especially if the conditions of the theatre
allow for little nuance. In his review of G. F. Cooke as Richard III,
Lamb argues that in the imagination Richard is a complex character,
but on stage we see instead of the *'man Richard'* the posturing *'monster*

[2] Kean wanted to restore the original ending in 1820, but met with resistance from
the Drury Lane manager; he did restore it in 1823, but only for 5 performances—its
failure was partly due to the overweight Mrs West's unsuitability in the role of the
dead Cordelia being carried on Kean's arms.

Richard' (Lamb 1912, i. 42)—especially as the version staged was Cibber's. Stage Shakespeare thus panders to the 'popular idea' of the characters and renders them in 'caricature': Lamb used the word when writing to Charles Lloyd on 26 June 1801 of Cooke's perform-ance. If we accept the claim that *Richard III*, *Othello*, and *Macbeth* were the most popular and frequently performed plays in the early nine-teenth century because they were 'the most melodramatic' (Foote 1829, p. 111 n.), we can see Lamb's point; all the more so if we share his presupposition that what is most to be valued in Shakespeare is not melodrama but emotional and intellectual profundity.

What Lamb would call the essential Shakespeare, we would call the Romantic Shakespeare. Nine-tenths of the Romantic Hamlet is solit-ary and meditative, but one could equally well adduce other *Hamlets* that are public and histrionic. Lamb's essay marks a watershed in the history of one particular appropriation of Shakespeare: the tradition which singles out character, which psychologizes and internalizes, which Romanticizes and novelizes. 'On the Tragedies of Shakspeare' was written about forty years after Maurice Morgann's *Essay on the Dramatic Character of Sir John Falstaff* and forty years before Mrs Cowden Clarke's *The Girlhood of Shakespeare's Heroines*, which might be said to mark the sublime germ and the ridiculous fruition of this tradition. It was written four years after *Tales from Shakespear*, in which Lamb and his sister turned the plays into novellas, and three years before Sir Walter Scott embarked on the Waverley Novels, which drew Shakespeare into the mainstream of nineteenth-century British and European fiction.

This novelistic appropriation, which has been very influential, is not without political consequences. Early in his career, Lamb contri-buted to a number of radical newspapers and was accused of Jacobin-ism. But he made the characteristic inward turn of the Romantic. The *Elia* essays which are his most distinctive achievement are supremely private and individualistic, delicate calibrations of personal memory, affection, and loss. They combine consciousness of the self and self-consciousness, confession and irony; they exemplify what has been termed 'The Romantic Ideology'.[3] When Lamb made this turn, he took Shakespeare with him. Crabb Robinson records a conversation of December 1811, when he 'noticed King John and Lewis, as if Shakespeare meant like a Jacobin to shew how base and

---

[3] See McGann 1983*b*; for Elia, see further Bate 1987.

vile kings are'; Lamb, significantly, 'did not remark on this, but said *King John* is one of the plays he likes the least. He praised on the contrary *Richard II'* (Robinson 1938, i. 54). Lamb thus distances himself from the 'Jacobin' Shakespeare, preferring the introspection of Richard II.

The essay 'On the Tragedies of Shakspeare' is not apolitical. Lamb complains that acting 'levels all distinctions' (Lamb 1912, i. 121) in such a way that Mrs Siddons is as much admired in sentimental eighteenth-century dramas as she is in *Macbeth*; readers in the post-revolutionary period would have been likely to recognize that 'levelling' was a politically loaded word (central to the anti-radical movement was the Association for the Preservation of Liberty and Property against Republicans and Levellers, founded by a government officer in 1792). Again, Lamb argues that the truth to nature of Shakespeare's plays is not revealed in the theatre because it is 'so deep that the depth of them lies out of the reach of most of us' (i. 118): this view smacks of the élitism that marks Romantic aesthetics. Coleridge followed the same path as Lamb: in accordance with his political development, his retreat from youthful radicalism into a world of the self, his best Shakespearean criticism is in that most private of forms, the personal marginal annotation.[4] And when he lectured in public it was to a socially élite audience.

Lamb implies that he is troubled by the idea of 'unlettered persons' who do not comprehend *'what an author is'* (i. 114), gaining access to Shakespeare through the theatre. Here there is a private, individualistic notion of 'authorship': Lamb refuses to admit the possibility that much of Shakespeare's power may derive from the fact that he is not in the Romantic sense an 'author' at all. Precisely because his texts are constantly being reinterpreted by actors, adapters, and, in our time, directors, he continues to have a public life. Lamb also complains about the way that a famous speech such as 'To be or not to be' is often 'torn so inhumanly from its living place and principle of continuity in the play' (i. 115). Where the public seemed to have a limitless appetite for the quotation and parody of Hamlet's soliloquy, Lamb, like Coleridge, preferred to see a speech in terms of its organic relationship with the play as a whole. The play is thus read as a hermetic unit, perfect in its inward form—but safely removed from

[4] Hence my near silence about Coleridge: this is a book about *public* appropriations of Shakespeare. Coleridge is only discussed when he and Hazlitt contest Shakespeare's politics in their rival 1818 lectures.

the kind of extrinsic power it may have if selectively applied to contemporary life, as it is by caricaturists and parodists. I would say,
then, that Lamb's reservations about the stage, which Coleridge
shared, are symptomatic of a far-reaching desire to repossess Shakespeare for the self and to remove him from the political appropriators.
Some would praise Coleridge and Lamb for this; others would argue
that the Romantics are themselves engaged in a political appropriation in the name of privacy and individualism.

All this places Hazlitt in a very interesting position, for he both
embraced and assaulted the Romantic ideology: witness, at one
extreme, his *Liber Amoris*, and at the other, his lecture 'On the Living
Poets', with its criticism of the Lake poets' egotism and morbid
sensibility. In certain circumstances he shared Lamb's scepticism
about the capacity of the stage to do justice to Shakespeare. A bad
production made him wonder if Shakespeare should be produced at
all. The attempt to stage the most imaginative, 'Romantic' plays—
The Tempest and *A Midsummer Night's Dream*—led him to write that
'Poetry and the stage do not agree well together' and, like Lamb, to
dismiss performance as 'caricature' (HW v. 274, 234). His review of
Kean's Richard II pursues an argument almost identical to Lamb's.
Richard is read as a meditative, inward-looking character, whereas
the stage offers 'only the *pantomime* part of tragedy': 'all that appeals
to our profounder feelings, to reflection and imagination, to all that
affects us most deeply in our closets, and in fact constitutes the glory
of Shakespear, is little else than an interruption and a drag on the
business of the stage' (HW v. 222). Also like Lamb, he attacked the
theatre and Boydell's Gallery as twin distractions from the essential
Shakespeare: 'Even those daubs of pictures, formerly exhibited under
the title of the Shakespear Gallery, had a less evident tendency to
disturb and distort all the previous notions we had imbibed from
reading Shakespear' (HW v. 234). And, identifying just as strongly
with the Prince of Denmark as Coleridge did, Hazlitt wrote 'We do
not like to see our author's plays acted, and least of all, HAMLET'
(HW iv. 237). Yet in his review of Kean's Hamlet he praised one
particular gesture as 'the finest commentary that was ever made on
Shakespear'.[5] And, with regard to Kean's rendition of the scene in
which Romeo is banished, Hazlitt said, as others had said of Garrick,

---

[5] HW v. 188, with reference to the end of the 'nunnery' scene, where Kean
returned after he had gone 'to the extremity of the stage' and 'from a pang of parting
tenderness' pressed his lips to Ophelia's hand.

that the actor 'treads close indeed upon the genius of his author', and furthermore that 'actors are the best commentators on the poets' (HW iv. 256).

For Hazlitt, this notion of commentary is all-important. He speaks of Kean's 'readings', and sometimes his '*new reading*' (HW v. 188), of certain details. Hazlitt's reviews constitute critical accounts of Kean's readings that are then complemented by his own readings, developed in *Characters of Shakespear's Plays*. Hazlitt often makes a distinction between 'conception' and 'articulation'. Kean's articulations of Shakespeare cannot be improved upon, but his conceptions might be deeper and more varied: 'It is possible to form a higher conception of this character (we do not mean from seeing other actors, but from reading Shakespear) than that given by this very admirable tragedian; but we cannot imagine any character represented with greater distinction and precision, more perfectly *articulated* in every part' (HW v. 181). Hazlitt's reviews of Kean form the core of *A View of the English Stage*, his book of theatre criticism, published in 1818; *A View* should be read beside the better-known *Characters of Shakespear's Plays* of the previous year. The two collections offer, respectively, 'articulations' and 'conceptions' of Shakespeare. Every articulation or conception has the status of commentary; none can be synonymous with the play itself. For Hazlitt, Kean is 'not a literal transcriber of his author's text; he translates his characters with great freedom and ingenuity into a language of his own' (HW v. 190). One might say precisely the same of Hazlitt's own critical practice.

Hazlitt's account of Kean is a model of disinterestedness because he is willing to praise to the sky where he believes that the actor is true to his author—'if Shakespear had written marginal directions to the players . . . he would often have directed them to do what Mr Kean does' (HW v. 202)—but anxious to criticize and correct where he feels that Kean's readings are misreadings or, as in the case of *Lear*, which Kean played when it was restored to the repertory after the king's death in 1820, impoverished readings:

The most that Mr Kean did was to make some single hits here and there; but these did not tell, because they were separated from the main body and movement of the passion. . . . There are pieces of ancient granite that turn the edge of any modern chisel: so perhaps the genius of no living actor can be expected to cope with Lear. Mr Kean chipped off a bit of the character here and there: but he did not pierce the solid substance, nor move the entire mass. (HW xviii. 336, 332–3)

Hazlitt's distinction between true and false, or full and partial, readings of Shakespeare presupposes that there *is* a true reading. In order to reach that truth, he relies on instinct: 'I say what I think: I think what I feel' (HW v. 175). Here he falls into the Romantic trap.

Hazlitt asserted his own independence of mind in response to accusations that he had been put up to 'puff' Kean.[6] It is a fact that Hazlitt's reviews played a major role in precipitating Kean to stardom. Only two other reviewers attended his first performance as Shylock, and their response was lukewarm, whereas for Hazlitt it was an epiphanic event: 'Mr Kean's appearance was the first gleam of genius breaking athwart the gloom of the Stage, and the public have since basked in its ray, in spite of actors, managers, and critics' (HW v. 175). But Hazlitt's motives for praising Kean were wholly principled. He remarks in the preface to *A View* that reactions to Kean tended to be highly partisan; either he could do no wrong or, if one was a supporter of Kemble, he could do no right. Hazlitt, in contrast, attempted to be more judicious. In the end, 'the balance inclines decidedly to the favourable side, though not more I think than his merits exceed his defects' (HW v. 176). The two men barely knew each other but, between them, they revitalized the Shakespearean stage in London.

In what sense was the Hazlitt–Kean version of Shakespeare a product of its age? In the preface to *A View of the English Stage*, Hazlitt staunchly defended the stage as a public arena in which players offered 'the epitome of human life and manners' and 'brief chronicles of the time' (HW v. 173). *A View* is, among other things, an account of the close relationship between the Kean phenomenon and 'the time'—that is to say, the years between the abdication of Napoleon and the Peterloo massacre.

Hazlitt disliked the tendency to interfere with Shakespeare's text

---

6 As Sheridan's *The Critic* reminds us, there was a long tradition of puffing in eighteenth-century theatrical criticism. Hazlitt himself said that Leigh Hunt was the first to introduce a '*pine-apple* flavour' into reviewing, to replace the extremes of puffing and outright condemnation with balanced judgement, 'a pleasant mixture of sharp and sweet' (HW xviii. 381). In this respect, and in the act of dignifying theatrical notices by collecting them into a book, Leigh Hunt is the major influence on Hazlitt's reviewing. There are similarities of substance, too. The image of the lightning-flash, which Hazlitt and then Coleridge applied to Kean, was first used by Hunt with respect to Kemble's limitations: 'I think of Garrick; I think of Mrs Siddons; I think of the lightning which a true actor flashes from *all* corners of his mind and face, and of the thunder that follows such flashes and such only; and it is then that Mr Kemble becomes an actor of very contracted powers indeed' (Hunt 1949, p. 25).

for the sake of contemporary political allusion: reviewing Kemble's *Antony and Cleopatra* in 1813, the year of the first action against the Regent's wife, he complained that 'The piece seems to have been in some measure got up for the occasion, as there are several claptraps in the speeches, which admit of an obvious allusion to passing characters and events, and which were eagerly seized by the audience' (HW v. 190). This is not, however, to deny the pressure of the times, for the contemporary political situation is often alluded to in his reviews. I mentioned in Part I the decisive allusion to habeas corpus with regard to Booth and the managers. A review written late in 1816 sets up a similar parallel: 'We are afraid the junto of Managers of Drury-Lane are not much wiser than the junto of Managers of the affairs of Europe.' And, in the same review, Hazlitt writes with a lightness of touch: 'We see no more reason why Mr Stephen Kemble should play Falstaff, than why Louis XVIII is qualified to fill a throne, because he is fat, and belongs to a particular family' (HW v. 340). The latter phrase alludes to the Kemble family's hegemony in the London theatre.

That hegemony was broken by Kean, and this is one respect in which he was seen as a 'radical' performer. There is a much profounder sense in which Hazlitt's *View of the English Stage* is political than that suggested by the occasional surface allusion. More interesting than the comparisons with *particularities* of contemporary public affairs is the way in which the theatre relates to the *structure* of the early nineteenth-century political debate. The keystone in the structure of *A View* is the dialectical relationship between Kean and Kemble, which is introduced in the second review of Kean's Shylock: 'It is not saying too much of him, though it is saying a great deal, that he has all that Mr Kemble *wants* of perfection' (HW v. 180). The distinction is maintained throughout that part of *A View* which is given over to Kean's Shakespearean roles. As Richard III he has 'a preternatural and terrific grandeur' but is 'deficient in dignity', particularly in the scenes of state business that were Kemble's strength (HW v. 181–2). Kean does not have the royal bearing of Kemble (for one thing he is too short), but he is one of the only two actors in the age—Mrs Siddons is the other—who can convey the Shakespearean preternatural. He is unforgettable in the scene after the murder in *Macbeth*, but cannot catch the 'thoughtful melancholy' of 'My way of life is fallen into the sear', as Kemble could (HW v. 207).

The contest between Kemble and Kean is analogous to that between

Burke and Paine. Although he disagreed completely with the politics of the later Burke, Hazlitt always considered him the greatest prose writer and one of the greatest minds of the age. Part of his admiration derived from a nostalgia for his own youth, the age of Burke. So too with Kemble. For Hazlitt, he embodied the grandeur, dignity, and stability of a past age for ever lost in the turmoil of the early nineteenth century: 'The very tone of Mr Kemble's voice has something retrospective in it—it is an echo of the past' (HW v. 207). The early part of *A View* is given over to the advent of Kean, the spirit of the new age. But, towards the end of the collection, Hazlitt returns to Kemble. His review of Kemble's *King John*, first published on 8 December 1816, begins

We wish we had never seen Mr Kean. He has destroyed the Kemble religion; and it is the religion in which we were brought up. Never again shall we behold Mr Kemble with the same pleasure that we did, nor see Mr Kean with the same pleasure that we have seen Mr Kemble formerly. We used to admire Mr Kemble's figure and manner, and had no idea that there was any want of art or nature. We feel the force of Mr Kean's acting, but then we feel the want of Mr Kemble's person. Thus an old and delightful prejudice is destroyed, and no enthusiasm, no second idolatry comes to take its place. (HW v. 345)

Kemble's force here is like that of Burke; Hazlitt's awakening as a radical precipitated just such a destruction of 'an old and delightful prejudice'. 'No second idolatry' came to take the place of Burke: one senses from the portraits of Paine, Cobbett, and other radicals in *The Spirit of the Age* that Hazlitt did not feel any of them to be a match for Burke.

So it was that a week after reviewing *King John* Hazlitt turned his attention to Kemble's *Coriolanus* and made the claim that anyone who studies the play 'may save himself the trouble of reading Burke's Reflections, or Paine's Rights of Man' (HW v. 347). 'Mr Kemble in the part of Coriolanus was as great as ever' (HW v. 350): Hazlitt's opinion that Kemble was the ideal Coriolanus is closely bound up with his feeling that in the play Shakespeare 'had a leaning to the arbitrary side of the question', and this in turn is closely bound up with his troubled allegiance to Burke. *A View of the English Stage* ends with an elegiac encomium on Kemble, which stresses that Coriolanus was his greatest role (fittingly, it was the one with which he took leave of the stage in June 1817). Kemble's excellence, says Hazlitt, may be summed up in the one word '*intensity*'. The account of his acting style could as well be an account of Burke's prose style, of the technique of his *Reflections on the Revolution in France*: '*intensity*; in the seizing upon some one feeling or idea, in insisting upon it, in never letting it go, and in working it up, with a certain graceful consistency, and conscious grandeur of conception, to a very high degree of pathos or sublimity' (HW v. 379). Conversely, when Hazlitt wrote of Burke's prose style he quoted powerfully from *Coriolanus*:

But Burke's style was forked and playful as the lightning, crested like the serpent. He delivered plain things on a plain ground; but when he rose, there was no end of his flights and circumgyrations—and in this very Letter [i.e. *Letter to a Noble Lord*], 'he, like an eagle in a dove-cot, fluttered *his* Volscians' (the Duke of Bedford and the Earl of Lauderdale) 'in Corioli.' (HW xii. 228)

The Kemble–Coriolanus–Burke association explains why Hazlitt's review of Kean's Coriolanus begins as follows: 'Mr Kean's acting is not of the patrician order; he is one of the people, and what might be termed a *radical* performer. . . . That is, he cannot play Coriolanus so well as he plays some other characters, or as we have seen it played often'—played often by Kemble, that is (HW xviii. 290). In what sense is Kean a '*radical*' performer, save in the obvious one that he came from and moved in lower social circles than Kemble did? It is not that Hazlitt saw him as a Tom Paine of the stage, but that the language used to describe his acting made him into the theatrical equivalent of certain key figures in the radical pantheon. Hazlitt and others thought of Kean as an *electrical* performer. Sir George Beaumont found 'a fire in his acting that was electric'; Hazlitt persistently applied to his performances such phrases as 'electrical effect', 'bursts', 'energy', 'electrical shocks'.[7] The metaphor would have had a freshness in 1814, so soon after Franklin's and Priestley's experiments with electricity, that it lacks now. The association with Franklin and Priestley, one synonymous with the American Revolution and the other victim of the anti-radical 'Church and King' backlash in 1791, would also have had a sharp political edge. To be electrical was to be radical. Even Jean-Paul Marat had written a treatise on electricity. I suspect that other terms which Hazlitt applied to Kean would also have had an edge that they now lack: 'enthusiastic' and 'enthusiasm' (HW v. 181, 185, and elsewhere) were epithets frequently used

[7] Beaumont, recorded in Farington 1978–84, xiii. 4518, 20 May 1814; HW v. 188, xviii. 332, v. 203, v. 223.

in attacks on radicals, partly because of the association between Jacobinism and dissenting circles; 'animation' (HW v. 179, 182, and elsewhere) carried a set of associations with Mesmerism, which was thought of as a suspiciously French, even Jacobinical phenomenon. Words like 'boldness', 'power', and 'violent' speak for themselves. One begins to see that there was more than one respect in which Kean *revolutionized* the London stage, and to understand why his Iago led Hazlitt to the conclusion that the character was 'a true prototype of modern Jacobinism' (HW v. 212).

Hazlitt's conception of the spirit of the age was not merely political. His image of Kean as a pure emanation of that spirit also had an aesthetic motivation. In his first review of Kean's Richard, Hazlitt argued that 'to be perfect' the performance 'should have a little more solidity, depth, sustained, and impassioned feeling, with somewhat less brilliancy, with fewer glancing lights, pointed transitions, and pantomimic evolutions' (HW v. 181). Hazlitt returned to Drury Lane just under a week later to review Kean's second performance of the role. He still felt that it was not sufficiently *sustained*, but instead of repeating the images of sudden evolutions and glancing lights which prefigure Coleridge's famous remark that watching Kean act was like reading Shakespeare by flashes of lightning, he introduced a comparison with the visual arts that he had used in his review of Kean's debut as Shylock: 'a succession of striking pictures' (HW v. 179, 184). The review ends, 'He bids fair to supply us with the best Shakespear Gallery we have had!' (HW v. 184). Like the Shakespeare Gallery paintings, Kean's performances alight on individual moments of excitement at the expense of a unified vision of the whole play. For Hazlitt, this is a basic characteristic and a major deficiency of the age's approach to Shakespeare.

That Kean's technique was characterized by extremes was a major problem as well as a source of the actor's power and fascination. He would plummet from a shout to a whisper, use inarticulate sounds and exaggerated facial expressions, and vary his pace, rushing carelessly through passages he thought unimportant so that he could force the audience's attention on certain crucial moments. It was these rapid transitions that Coleridge had in mind when he said 'His rapid descents from the hyper-tragic to the infra-colloquial, though sometimes productive of great effect, are often unreasonable. To see him act, is like reading Shakspeare by flashes of lightning' (*Table Talk*, 27 April 1823). The emphasis on key moments was partly a practical consideration. It would have been impossible to sustain throughout a performance the energy and passion which Kean wished to infuse into his tragic heroes; it was a shrewd decision to stress certain hyperdramatic effects, for that would have been the best way to catch the attention of audiences who, owing to conditions in the theatres, would have found it difficult to concentrate throughout. The problem, however, was that 'hits' would be emphasized out of all proportion, with scenes punctuated by applause; the continuity of the play would thus be lost. This is what lies behind Coleridge's criticism: the structure, the organic unity of Shakespeare's plays, so central to his and Schlegel's readings, was destroyed by the Kean method.

J. W. Donohue (1970, pp. 184–6) has argued persuasively that a major factor contributing to the failure of the Romantic drama was the way that the work of the major poets tended towards the fragmentary; plays need to be sustained and organized, they cannot follow the model of the lyric which crystallizes and magnifies a specific memory or perception, investing a single moment with cosmic proportions. For Hazlitt, Kean was in this respect typical of the spirit of the age (or, as we would now say, a typical 'Romantic'): he is unable to *sustain* his moments of penetrating truth to Shakespeare. His performances may be likened to *The Excursion*, a combination of dull stretches and wonderfully heightened passages, Wordsworthian moments of vision. There are many equivalents in the poetry of the age for both Kean's dazzling moments and Kemble's brooding introspection. Neither Kean nor Kemble, however, quite mastered the creation who seemed to embody Romanticism, Hamlet. Kean electrified when jumping into Ophelia's grave, crying 'This is I, Hamlet the Dane!', while Kemble cut the right dark figure standing apart from everyone else in the opening court scene and during the play within the play. But neither of them seemed wholly adequate in soliloquy: the Romantic Hamlet existed only in the mind.

Hazlitt's ideal performance would have been achieved through some combination of Kean's energy and Kemble's intensity. Mrs Siddons's last years were a disappointment; Hazlitt felt that it was a mistake for her to return to the stage in 1816, three years after her first retirement (HW v. 312–14). But, until she became too old and slowed down her delivery excessively, she came closest to achieving this union. In addition, she combined compelling stage presence, psychological insights, and sensitivity to Shakespeare's language. Among actresses she was unrivalled. Garrick's Mrs Pritchard now seemed stiff and formal in comparison, and among the younger generation there was no obvious successor. For a time Hazlitt hoped that Eliza O'Neill might become a second Siddons. His review of her Juliet begins 'We occasionally see something on the stage that reminds us a little of Shakespear', implying that she has a little of Siddons's capacity to do justice to Shakespearean tragedy in the theatre. But Hazlitt then makes it clear that she falls short of the Siddons ideal: 'Miss O'Neill's Juliet, if it does not correspond exactly with our idea of the character, does not degrade it. We never saw Garrick; and Mrs Siddons was the only person who ever embodied our idea of high tragedy' (HW v. 198). Hazlitt constantly asks whether individual performances match up to his 'idea' of character or tragedy, ideas that will eventually be written down in *Characters of Shakespear's Plays*. Mrs Siddons alone *embodies* these on stage; Hazlitt's praise of O'Neill is that she is in the Siddons tradition: 'We have, we believe, been betrayed into this digression, because Miss O'Neill, more than any late actress, reminded us in certain passages, and in a faint degree, of Mrs Siddons' (HW v. 199). But O'Neill never fulfilled her promise, and by 1820 she had married and left the stage. 'A husband, like death, cancels all other claims', remarks Hazlitt in his essay on her retirement (HW xviii. 281).

It is striking that Hazlitt responds to O'Neill and even to Siddons entirely in emotional terms. It is their rendering of *passion* that interests him. There is no sense in which their characteristics can be translated into political terms, as those of Kean and Kemble can. For Hazlitt, the high point of Mrs Siddons's repertoire was that most intimate moment, Lady Macbeth's sleep-walking, where the character is revealed as vulnerable woman rather than scheming politician. To put this another way, it is a mark of the spirit of the age that women, even when they appear on the public stage, are confined to the private sphere. If it is granted, as I think it must be, that Siddons was the most admired Shakespearean performer of the age, then this has important consequences. Even so politically conscious a critic as Hazlitt ends up saying that only the apolitical Mrs Siddons embodies his idea of high tragedy. Given that Shakespeare's high tragedies had by this time come to be regarded as his greatest achievement, it follows that the age's strongest embodiment of Shakespeare was an apolitical one. For the nineteenth century, it was very convenient to forget about the politicized Shakespeare and to claim instead that the true Shakespeare was the passionate but private version embodied by

Siddons. Hazlitt viewed her as somehow above temporality—'as if a being of a superior order had dropped from another sphere to awe the world with the majesty of her appearance'—and as 'the idol of the people', capable of hushing 'the tumultuous shouts of the pit in breathless expectation' (HW v. 312). Hazlitt is usually suspicious of those who are in the business of quelling the masses. Not so in the case of the great actress: when he sees her as a Queen in the theatre, the metaphor has none of the sceptical overtones that there are in his references to her brother's aristocratic bearing.

Kean's startling success was confined to the period of radical ferment, 1814 to 1819. Thereafter, William Charles Macready became an increasingly dominant figure in the London theatre. Although his acting style owed something to the example of Kean, he was really the successor to Kemble—actor, producer, restorer of texts (he it was who finally produced an authentic *Lear*, complete with Fool, in 1838), manager of first Covent Garden and then Drury Lane. Kean is conspicuous by his absence from Tennyson's sonnet of 1851 on Macready's retirement:

> Farewell, Macready, since this night we part,
>   Go, take thine honours home; rank with the best,
>   Garrick and statelier Kemble, and the rest
> Who made a nation purer through their art.

The purification of the nation through art is an image that applies even more fittingly to Mrs Siddons. She was a very successful Volumnia: in such a role she could embody a conception of duty to the nation, and thus defuse and tame the potentially radical Shakespeare. Through Siddons's Volumnia, *Coriolanus* could be made into a play less about patricians and plebeians than about family values and a form of matriarchy that is in fact profoundly patriarchal. In short, it could be made conformable to the age of Queen Victoria.

6

Criticism

HAZLITT matters as a Shakespearean critic not only because of his responsiveness to the theatre and his role in the promotion of Kean. *A View of the English Stage* has claims to be the finest volume of theatre criticism in the language, but as literary criticism *Characters of Shakespear's Plays* is more significant. It needs to be reread in detail because it is usually regarded as 'the culmination of the eighteenth-century emphasis on character in Shakespeare',[1] whereas it was in fact a new kind of critical book in which Hazlitt invented, which is to say discovered, a number of readings which are still important to us today. He was the first to write sympathetically of Shylock and unsympathetically of Henry V, the first to read *The Tempest* in terms of imperialism. He was the first to elevate *Lear* to the position it still retains in many people's minds as the supreme Shakespearean drama. He advanced one of the most convincing readings of the character of Iago, and was one of the first to see the problematic nature of the Duke and Isabella in *Measure for Measure*, and the strengths of less well-known plays like *Cymbeline* and *Timon of Athens*. He wrote not only of particular characters but of how similarities and antitheses between characters are a formative structural principle in the plays. And in his essays on *Coriolanus* he confronted more directly than anyone else in the age the deeply troubling relationship between artistic and political power.

The one-volume critical introduction to Shakespeare which surveys the full range of the plays has become a genre in itself. Such studies continue to proliferate—three of them were published within the space of a few months early in 1986.[2] *Characters of Shakespear's Plays* was the book that initiated the genre. Although the Shakespeare industry developed in the eighteenth century, no one published an introductory critical survey for the general reader. From their titles, Charles Gildon's *Remarks on the Plays of Shakespear* (1710) and John Upton's

---

[1] R. A. Foakes, in his introduction to Coleridge 1987, p. liii.
[2] Eagleton 1986; Edwards 1986; Greer 1986.

Critical Observations on Shakespeare (1746) might appear to be surveys of this kind, but Gildon did not progress beyond plot summaries, occasional remarks on sources, and the quotation of select 'beauties', while Upton, like so many men of the eighteenth century, was concerned with textual matters.[3]

As the art of the novel and the science of psychology developed in the last quarter of the century, so did 'character' criticism. But such studies as William Richardson's *Philosophical Analysis and Illustration of some of Shakespeare's Remarkable Characters* (1774) and Thomas Whately's *Remarks on some of the Characters of Shakespeare* (1785) focused on a small number of plays; the finest work of this sort offered an exhaustive analysis of a single character—Maurice Morgann's *Essay on the Dramatic Character of Sir John Falstaff* (1777). There were also books which aimed to justify Shakespeare's achievement from the point of view of art or ethics: a representative artistic defence was Mrs Elizabeth Montagu's 1769 riposte to the French neo-classical denigration of the plays, *An Essay on the Writings and Genius of Shakespear*, an ethical one Mrs Elizabeth Griffith's 1775 *The Morality of Shakespeare's Drama Illustrated*, which adduced a code of behaviour from select quotations. But writers like Mrs Montagu again restricted themselves to a small number of plays; only *Henry IV*, *Macbeth*, and *Julius Caesar* receive detailed treatment in her *Essay*. Other books belonged to scholarship rather than interpretative criticism—thus, for example, the study of Shakespeare's sources had its origin in Charlotte Lennox's *Shakespear Illustrated: or, The Novels and Histories, on which the Plays of Shakespear are Founded, Collected and Translated from the Original Authors. With Critical Remarks* (3 vols., 1753–4) and Richard Farmer's *An Essay on the Learning of Shakespeare* (1767).

This is not to say that evaluative literary criticism and close reading of Shakespeare's poetry are not to be found in the eighteenth century. Far from it. But most criticism of this sort was carried out in the periodical literature, in editions of the plays, or in the course of more general critical works. The latter would sometimes be focused on a form, a tradition going back to Thomas Rymer's 1692 *Short View of Tragedy* and including, for example, William Guthrie's *Essay upon English Tragedy* of 1747. Other general works were more theoretical in

---

[3] Gildon's *Remarks* were published as a supplementary volume to the first edited text of the plays, that of Nicholas Rowe (1709). Sherbo 1986 provides a good introduction to that quintessentially eighteenth-century activity, the elucidation of minutiae in Shakespeare's text.

their emphasis, in the manner of Lord Kames's three-volume *Elements of Criticism*, first published in 1762. Neither sort of study could serve as a popular introduction to Shakespeare. Equally, to put together a one-volume introduction to Shakespeare from the writings of the greatest eighteenth-century critic, Dr Johnson, the modern editor has to yoke together the preface, general observations on each play, and selected notes from the 1765 edition, together with extracts from periodical essays. The only separate critical book on Shakespeare which Johnson published in its own right was again focused on a single play, the *Miscellaneous Observations on the Tragedy of Macbeth* (1745), a slim volume much concerned with textual matters.

The first work which bears some resemblance to our idea of a critical introduction came from Germany: A. W. von Schlegel touched on all the plays in his *Lectures on Dramatic Art and Literature*, first delivered in Vienna in 1808, published soon after,[4] and translated into English in 1815. Two great unwritten books also belong to this period: Ludwig Tieck, Schlegel's collaborator on the definitive German translation of the plays, planned a wide-ranging *Buch über Shakespeare*, and Coleridge intended to work up his lectures, marginalia, and notebook jottings into a book—it is typical of his failure to complete his projects that his letters reveal him planning this work as early as 1804 and still speaking in 1820 of how he will shortly publish his 'Characteristics of Shakespear's Dramatic Works, with a Critical Review of each Play'.[5] But by then Hazlitt had beaten him to it: Coleridge's projected title is suspiciously close to *Characters of Shakespear's Plays*.

The history that I have been unfolding is covered in part by Hazlitt in the preface to his book. Those who wish to maintain a sharp distinction between 'Augustan' and 'Romantic' readings of Shakespeare would do well to note that Hazlitt's preface begins with a quotation from Pope's preface to his 1725 edition of the plays, a classic elevation of Shakespeare to the status of 'nature': 'he is not so much an imitator, as an instrument of nature'. Pope is fulsome in his praise of Shakespeare's characters; Hazlitt writes that the object of his book is to illustrate Pope's generalizing remarks 'in a more particular manner by a reference to each play'. He mentions the limitations in scope of Richardson's and Whately's work (Whately is mistakenly called

[4] In 1809, then revised in 1811.
[5] To Beaumont, 1 Feb. 1804; to Allsop, 30 Mar. 1820: Coleridge 1956–71 ii. 1054, v. 25.

24. John Nixon, The Ireland family manufacturing Shakespearean relics (1796)

The MAGICAL INSTALLATION or MACBETH Invested.

Bute installed. K.G. 22 Sept. 1762.   Bute.

Deluded by Lust, Religion and Pride
Macbeth even and Damn'd on def'd;
As Shakespear had told us the fatal disaster,
The Thane was a rite who murderd his Master,
And tho' with false Trs he his could moan,
Yet he seizd on his & mount his throne!
Beware ye MonArchs of rites ware!
Remember poor Dun, and only curst Snare,
For ah w Glory such M aspire,
Unfounded Ambition blows up the;
With smling & cringing & soft Adulation,
They pamper up Princes sure Ruination;
And oft a good like a Victim has bled,
That his might devolve a proud Re;

1762

25. Anonymous broadside, The Earl of Bute as Macbeth (1762)

26. William Dent, Fox & Co. as Falstaff & Co. (1786)

27. James Gillray, Fox & Co. as Falstaff & Co. (1788)

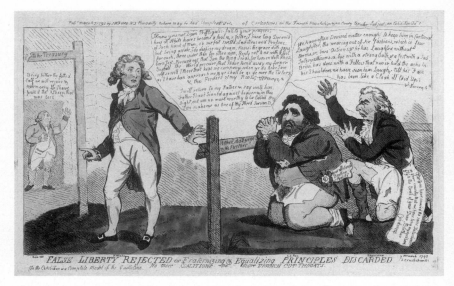

28. Isaac Cruikshank, The Prince of Wales rejects Falstaff-Fox and Bardolph-Sheridan (1793)

29. Anonymous caricature of the Prince of Wales rejecting his erstwhile followers (1811)

Mason), then acknowledges Schlegel—'The only work which seemed to supersede the necessity of an attempt like the present was Schlegel's very admirable Lectures on the Drama, which give by far the best account of the plays of Shakespear that has hitherto appeared' (HW iv. 171).

It is a mark of Hazlitt's respect for the German critic that he gives over much of his preface to a transcription of Schlegel's general account of Shakespeare. His only reservations concern a certain characteristically German 'mysticism' in the style, 'not very attract-ive to the English reader', and the lack of specific examples, made inevitable by the wide range of the lectures. As Wordsworth does in his 1815 'Essay, Supplementary to the Preface', Hazlitt expresses indignation over the fact that it has taken a German to do justice to Shakespeare: 'We will at the same time confess, that some little jealousy of the character of the national understanding was not without its share in producing the following undertaking, for "we were piqued" that it should be reserved for a foreign critic to give "reasons for the faith which we English have in Shakespear"' (HW iv. 172). But the political motives here are different from those of Wordsworth. Where the latter was merely saying what a true-born Englishman—or, in Wordsworth's case, a reborn Englishman—could be expected to say in the year of Waterloo, Hazlitt, knowing that the radical's loyalty to his country will always be called into question, was reassuring his readers with a nationalistic-sounding statement of his own credentials in order to pre-empt the accusation that the liberal rereadings of the plays in the body of *Characters* were unpatriotic.

Hazlitt had already expressed his admiration for Schlegel's Shake-spearean criticism in a long review for the *Edinburgh* of the English translation of the lectures. Henry Crabb Robinson thought that there was a symbiosis between the two critics: 'Hazlitt's review of Schlegel's lectures on the drama is a capital article, and Hazlitt's own share of the excellent matter is by no means small. He has entered into the sense of the author and evinces a kindred spirit' (Robinson 1938, i. 182). Hazlitt later claimed that he had 'done something (more than any one except Schlegel) to vindicate' Shakespeare from 'the stigma of French criticism' (HW xii. 122), and Schlegel returned the compli-ment, speaking to Tom Moore 'of Hazlitt, who, he said, *l'avoit dépassé* in his critical opinions, and was an ultra-Shakspearian'.[6] Although

---

[6] *Diary*, May 1821, in Moore 1853–6, iii. 235.

there are some direct debts,[7] Schlegel's influence on *Characters* is general rather than specific, turning on a shared admiration for Shakespeare's formal artistry rather than a series of particular insights.

'We have the rather availed ourselves of this testimony of a foreign critic in behalf of Shakespear, because our own countryman, Dr Johnson, has not been so favourable to him' (HW iv. 174). The latter part of the preface to *Characters* is given over to an attack on Dr Johnson as a Shakespearean critic. 'Let those who have a prejudice against Johnson read Boswell's Life of him: as those whom he has prejudiced against Shakespear should read his Irene', writes Hazlitt, turning against Johnson a sentence that is superbly Johnsonian in its *gravitas* and its balance. A critic brings his own predispositions to the text that he is reading: Hazlitt felt that Johnson 'found the general species or *didactic* form in Shakespear's characters, which was all he sought or cared for; he did not find the individual traits, or the *dramatic* distinctions which Shakespear has engrafted on this general nature, because he felt no interest in them' (HW iv. 176). For Hazlitt, there is a fundamental unlikeness of mind and style which separates Johnson from Shakespeare. 'To weigh his excellences and defects in equal scales', as Johnson does in the 1765 Preface, is, for Hazlitt, a very un-Shakespearean activity. Hazlitt does Johnson an injustice when he claims that 'All his ideas were cast in a given mould, in a set form: they were made out by rule and system, by climax, inference, and antithesis', but he is right to assert that Shakespeare's way of thinking was 'the reverse' of this (HW iv. 175). The greatness of Johnson's Shakespearean criticism derives from an awareness of Shakespeare's resistance to system. Johnson is at his most interesting when he is under stress, as when he is struggling with the painfulness of the end of *Lear* and *Othello*. He is a great antithetic critic, where Hazlitt is a great sympathetic one.

Hazlitt's case against Johnson is perhaps stronger on the question of style. There is something constricting, something that does not answer to Shakespearean fluidity, about the Johnsonian period. This is especially the case in Johnson's brief summary judgements, for example that on *Cymbeline*:

This play has many just sentiments, some natural dialogues, and some pleasing scenes, but they are obtained at the expence of much incongruity.

---

[7] Listed, though exaggerated, in Schnöckelborg 1931. See also Sauer 1981, pp. 100–9.

To remark the folly of the fiction, the absurdity of the conduct, the confusion of the names and manners of different times, and the impossibility of the events in any system of life, were to waste criticism upon unresisting imbecillity, upon faults too evident for detection, and too gross for aggravation. (Johnson 1986, p. 307)

Johnson's style seems to make a balancing act inevitable—one knows that after the three epithets of praise there will be a 'but'. Again, when Johnson seeks to justify Shakespeare's mixed form, the fact that his plays are 'not in the rigorous and critical sense either tragedies or comedies, but compositions of a distinct kind; exhibiting the real state of sublunary nature, which partakes of good and evil, joy and sorrow, mingled with endless variety of proportion and innumerable modes of combination', he does so by saying that in the world as it is 'at the same time, the reveller is hasting to his wine, and the mourner burying his friend' (Johnson 1986, p. 14). Peter Conrad sees the limitation when he remarks that in Johnson's image the reveller and the mourner do not 'as they always do in Shakespeare, meet: Johnson's syntax preserves a segregation'.[8] It is this tendency which Hazlitt has in mind when he writes, 'Another circumstance which led to Dr Johnson's indiscriminate praise or censure of Shakespear, is the very structure of his style. . . . He no sooner acknowledges the merits of his author in one line than the periodical revolution of his style carries the weight of his opinion completely over to the side of objection, thus keeping up a perpetual alternation of perfections and absurdities' (HW iv. 177). What Johnson says of Shakespeare may be applied to Johnson on Shakespeare: 'What he does best, he soon ceases to do. He no sooner begins to move than he counteracts himself; and terror and pity, as they are rising in the mind, are checked and blasted by sudden frigidity' (Johnson's preface, quoted, HW iv. 178). Hazlitt's Shakespearean criticism, on the other hand, though it sometimes misfires, always has a Shakespearean vitality.

Generally speaking, Hazlitt discusses the tragedies before, and in more detail than, the histories and comedies. But, as if to challenge Johnson, he begins his book with a surprise: a chapter on *Cymbeline* (HW iv. 179–86). Johnson's view of *Cymbeline* was an orthodox one,

---

[8] Conrad 1985, p. 179, in the course of a chaotic but stimulating chapter on 'Shakespeare's After-Life', which is helpful on Shakespeare's incorporation into the novel, first in Fielding and Sterne, then in Dickens and eventually Virginia Woolf—the novelization of Shakespeare is a subject for a book in itself (in Hazlitt's period, Scott would be the key figure, *Measure for Measure* and *The Heart of Midlothian* key texts).

shared by most eighteenth-century commentators,[9] but Hazlitt regards the play as 'one of the most delightful . . . a favourite with us'. This opening achieves a number of things. By giving prominence to a previously little-known play, Hazlitt forces his reader to think afresh about the canon of Shakespeare, to go beyond the dozen or so universally acknowledged favourites. By praising *Cymbeline*, he vigorously detaches himself from eighteenth-century orthodoxy and aligns himself with Schlegel, who had overturned that orthodoxy by describing the play as 'one of Shakspeare's most wonderful compositions' (Schlegel 1846, p. 397). And, by speaking of a personal favourite, he announces that his book will record what he feels about Shakespeare as much as what he thinks about him and more than what he knows about him—that he is writing a work of creative criticism, not one of historical scholarship, an account of Shakespeare's present significance, not his past meaning.

Hazlitt understood the structure of *Cymbeline*. He called it a 'dramatic romance', and perceived that it works on a 'principle of perspective'. It is a play that contains many journeys, and watching or reading it is 'like going on a journey'. For all the variety of incident on the way, the end is always in sight: 'Though the events are scattered over such an extent of surface, and relate to such a variety of characters, yet the links which bind the different interests of the story are never entirely broken. The most straggling and seemingly casual incidents are contrived in such a manner as to lead at last to the complete developement of the catastrophe' (HW iv. 179). Johnson was of the opinion that Shakespeare was inattentive to the winding-up of his plots; Hazlitt follows Schlegel in arguing that the contrary is true.

This attention to structure is typical of *Characters of Shakespear's Plays*. Towards the end of the opening essay, Hazlitt articulates a central principle: 'as it happens in most of the author's works, there is not only the utmost keeping in each separate character; but in the

---

[9] Eighteenth-century orthodoxy does not mean universal eighteenth-century opinion: consensus in eighteenth-century Shakespearean criticism is easy to find, unanimity almost impossible. The experience of reading *Cymbeline* criticism from the period is altogether characteristic: just as one comes to think that every critic will join the chorus of voices (e.g. Charles Gildon, Charlotte Lennox, William Hawkins) condemning the play's 'irregularity', one discovers a little-known critic in an obscure periodical stoutly defending it (John Potter in *The Theatrical Review; or, New Companion to the Play-House* 1771–2, repr. in Vickers 1974–81, v. 432–3). But this is not to deny the originality of the early nineteenth-century critics: Potter praises *Cymbeline* in spite of its plot, Schlegel and Hazlitt because of it.

casting of the different parts, and their relation to one another, there is an affinity and harmony, like that we may observe in the gradations of colour in a picture' (HW iv. 183). It is a misunderstanding of Hazlitt to say that he was a character critic in the tradition that runs from Morgann to Bradley and which was exploded by L. C. Knights in 'How Many Children Had Lady Macbeth?'. As the simile of the gradations of colour in a picture reminds us, Hazlitt was an art critic before he was a literary critic, and what he learnt as an art critic was to look at a painting whole, to see it as a unified structure. An art critic does not take the human figures out of a painting, nor does Hazlitt take the characters out of a Shakespearean play. He writes about Shakespeare's characters because they constitute the heart of the play, but he writes about them in relation to each other because it is from their relationships that the play derives its wholeness.[10] When Hazlitt puts his principle into practice, he is doing something new and strong in Shakespearean criticism. Certainly, none of his predecessors had written like this of *Cymbeline*[11] (notice the recurrence of the pictorial metaphor):

The striking and powerful contrasts in which Shakespear abounds could not escape observation; but the use he makes of the principle of analogy to reconcile the greatest diversities of character and to maintain a continuity of feeling throughout, has not been sufficiently attended to. In CYMBELINE, for instance, the principal interest arises out of the unalterable fidelity of Imogen to her husband under the most trying circumstances. Now the other parts of the picture are filled up with subordinate examples of the same feeling, variously modified by different situations, and applied to the purposes of virtue or vice. The plot is aided by the amorous importunities of Cloten, by the persevering determination of Iachimo to conceal the defeat of his project by a daring imposture: the faithful attachment of Pisanio to his mistress is an affecting accompaniment to the whole; the obstinate adherence to his purpose in Bellarius, who keeps the fate of the young princes so long a secret in resentment for the ungrateful return to his former services, the incorrigible wickedness of the Queen, and even the blind uxorious confidence of Cymbeline, are all so many lines of the same story, tending to the same point. (HW iv. 183-4)

[10] Wells 1982 argues that 'characters' refers to the overall character of each play as well as the dramatis personae; for Hazlitt's interest in the 'design' of Shakespearean tragedy, see also Kinnaird 1978, pp. 175-95. Other strong examples of his handling of structure include accounts of the intimate relationship between Ariel and Caliban, and of the interplay between the Lear plot and the Gloucester plot.

[11] Schlegel praises the *dénouement* and the 'blend[ing] together into one harmonious whole the social manners of the newest times with olden heroic deeds', but he foregrounds Imogen in such a way as to diminish the other characters (Schlegel 1846, pp. 397-9).

Here we have something very different from the appropriation of Shakespeare into contemporary life or the reconstitution of his plays according to the tenets of later aesthetic theory (a fate to which *Cymbeline* was peculiarly susceptible—it was rewritten by Thomas D'Urfey in about 1673, Charles Marsh in 1755, William Hawkins in 1759, David Garrick in 1761, Henry Brooke in 1778, and Ambrose Eccles in 1793). Hazlitt is not so much appropriating *Cymbeline* as allowing it to appropriate him; he submits himself to the play, thinks with it, and thus inhabits its structure. Intuition is perhaps the key to the critical disposition of this essay: a delicate *feeling with* the play replaces the robust, obtruding purposefulness of active appropriation. The 'continuity of feeling' which Hazlitt finds *within* the play is maintained *between* the reader and the play. A good reader reads as Shakespeare writes—the 'principle of analogy' is not impressed upon the surface, but evolves below the level of consciousness. Hazlitt is putting into practice Schlegel's theory of organic form:

The effect of this coincidence is rather felt than observed; and as the impression exists unconsciously in the mind of the reader, so it probably arose in the same manner in the mind of the author, not from design, but from the force of natural association, a particular train of thought suggesting different inflections of the same predominant feeling, melting into, and strengthening one another, like chords in music. (HW iv. 184)

Hazlitt was not only an art critic but also a philosopher before he was a literary critic, and here he has clearly learnt from the theory of association which was so widespread in eighteenth-century British philosophy. More significantly, the process by which he is entering into the mind of his author is a living example of that other philosophic principle, sympathy, which is the ultimate grounding of his politics and aesthetics.

As should be expected of one who responded with gusto to landscape and landscape painting, Hazlitt also wrote suggestively of place in Shakespeare. In a few sentences, he sketched out a reading of *Cymbeline*'s pastoral which prefigures one of the most widely favoured twentieth-century approaches to the play. He contrasts the 'romantic scenes' in which Belarius, Guiderius, and Arviragus appear with 'the intrigues and artificial refinements of the court from which they are banished'. But he recognizes that theirs is no soft pastoral: 'They follow the business of huntsmen, not of shepherds; and this is in keeping with the spirit of adventure and uncertainty in the rest of the story' (HW iv. 184). Hazlitt sees that the mountain scenes in *Cymbeline* and the forest of Arden in *As You Like It* are the two supreme examples in Shakespeare of a realized pastoral world (we learn less of the geography of Bohemia, which is a more symbolic country, as Hazlitt perceived when he compared Perdita and Florizel's courtship in the sheep-shearing scene to 'the return of spring', HW iv. 326). But the richness of Hazlitt's criticism lies in the capacity to distinguish between as well to compare Wales and Arden: 'the gallant sportsmen in CYMBELINE have to encounter the abrupt declivities of hill and valley: Touchstone and Audrey jog along a level path' (HW iv. 185). *Cymbeline* is a vertical play, *As You Like It* a horizontal one.

Most readers have remembered Hazlitt's *Cymbeline* essay for the least original part of it: the praise of Imogen (with whom male critics have always tended to fall in love). As a result, Hazlitt's attempt to lay out a case for the whole of the play has had little influence. In claiming that *Lear* was the greatest of all Shakespeare's plays, Hazlitt was going with the tide, and his opinion rapidly gained, and has long retained, wide acquiescence; in making claims for *Cymbeline* as a unified work of art, rather than merely a show-case for the charms of Imogen, he was out on his own. As will be seen, Hazlitt anticipated the twentieth century in his admiration of *Measure for Measure*; in the case of *Cymbeline*, however, our century has not done the play justice—perhaps in this instance Hazlitt is anticipating eyes not yet created and tongues to be.

As Hazlitt's *Cymbeline* is built on 'the principle of analogy', so his *Macbeth* 'is done upon a stronger and more systematic principle of contrast than any other of Shakespear's plays' (HW iv. 191). The account of Macbeth in this second essay in *Characters* consists mainly of a contrast with Richard III that is very much in the manner of Whately's 1785 *Remarks on Some of the Characters of Shakespeare* and Kemble's reply of the following year, *Macbeth Reconsidered*. What is original about Hazlitt's analysis is, again, his sense of the structure of the play, and in particular the relationship between scenic contrast and verbal equivocation:

It moves upon the verge of an abyss, and is a constant struggle between life and death. The action is desperate and the reaction is dreadful. It is a huddling together of fierce extremes, a war of opposite natures which of them shall destroy the other. There is nothing but what has a violent end or violent beginnings. The lights and shades are laid on with a determinate hand; the transitions from triumph to despair, from the height of terror to the repose of death, are sudden and startling; every passion brings in its fellow-contrary, and the thoughts pitch and jostle against each other as in the dark. The whole play is an unruly chaos of strange and forbidding things, where the ground rocks under our feet. Shakespear's genius here took its full swing, and trod upon the farthest bounds of nature and passion. This circumstance will account for the abruptness and violent antitheses of the style, the throes and labours which run through the expression, and from defects will turn them into beauties. 'So fair and foul a day I have not seen,' etc. 'Such welcome and unwelcome news together.' 'Men's lives are like the flowers in their caps, dying or ere they sicken.' 'Look like the innocent flower, but be the serpent under it.' The scene before the castle-gate follows the appearance of the Witches on the heath, and is followed by a midnight murder. (HW iv. 191)

Not only does Hazlitt have a wonderful sense of the tactile, the astonishingly physical, quality of the play's imagery—it is apropos of *Macbeth* that he says that Shakespeare's plays 'have the force of things upon the mind' (HW iv. 186)—but his own language seems to take on the energy of his subject. Like Schlegel and Coleridge, he emphasizes the rapidity of *Macbeth*, and that rapidity seems to be enacted in his own verbal constructions: 'driven along', 'reels', 'staggers', 'throw', 'baffling', 'entangling', 'blindly rushing forward', and 'recoiling' occur in swift succession (HW iv. 187). As he does when he allows Shakespearean quotations to speak through him, Hazlitt gives himself up to and re-expresses the language of the text.

Emphasis falls on powerful dramatic moments as well as particular verbs and verbal constructions. Hazlitt says that he cannot speak of Lady Macbeth without speaking of Mrs Siddons, and in alighting on certain moments, such as Lady Macbeth's letting slip 'Thou'rt mad to say it' on hearing of Duncan's impending arrival, he is clearly influenced by his experience in the theatre. He is able to see what a superb moment this is because he has seen Mrs Siddons many times, and is aware that she had thought hard about how as an actress she could animate the line. Mrs Jameson, Hazlitt's successor as both Shakespearean critic and admirer of Siddons, has an interesting note on another short line that is profound in its simplicity:

In her impersonation of the part of Lady Macbeth, Mrs Siddons adopted successively three different intonations in giving the words *we fail*. At first, a quick, contemptuous interrogation—'*we fail?*' Afterwards, with the note of admiration—*we fail!* and an accent of indignant astonishment, laying the principal emphasis on the word *we*—*we* fail! Lastly, she fixed on what I am convinced is the true reading—we fail. With the simple period, modulating her voice to a deep, low, resolute tone, which settled the issue at once—as though she had said, 'if we fail, why then we fail, and all is over'.[12]

There is a force in Mrs Jameson's conviction that the third reading is the most powerful, but it is questionable to call it the 'true' one, for the dramatic richness of the moment lies precisely in the multiplicity of possible renderings of the two words. The emotion—the 'reality'— of the line is created by the performer as much as it is by the author, and no two performances will be the same.

Mrs Jameson is an important figure in that, whilst a modern woman would disapprove of some of her views on the 'Characteristics of Women', she was the first critic to treat Shakespeare's female characters with the kind of seriousness which had been accorded to his male ones (the treatment of women is about the one respect in which Hazlitt is not exemplary to an emancipated consciousness). She called her book on Shakespeare's heroines *Characteristics of Women, Moral, Poetical, and Historical*, and made it clear in the introduction that she was thinking about Shakespeare in the context of the nineteenth-century woman's question:

It appears to me that the condition of women in society, as at present constituted, is false in itself, and injurious to them,—that the education of women, as at present conducted, is founded on mistaken principles, and tends to increase fearfully the sum of misery and error in both sexes; but I do not choose presumptuously to fling these opinions in the face of the world, in the form of essays on morality, and treatises on education. I have rather chosen to illustrate certain positions by example, and leave my readers to deduce the moral themselves, and draw their own inferences. (Jameson 1832, vol. i, p. viii)

Jameson also recognizes the role of appropriation in Shakespearean criticism: 'We hear Shakspeare's men and women discussed, praised and dispraised, liked, disliked, as real human beings; and in forming our opinions of them, we are influenced by our own characters, habits of thought, prejudices, feelings, impulses' (Jameson 1832, vol. i, p. xx). The climax of her book is an impassioned defence of Lady Macbeth, but perhaps her most 'modern' analysis is that of the relationship between Beatrice and Benedick: 'It is observable, that the power is throughout on her side, and the sympathy and interest on his: which, by reversing the usual order of things, seems to excite

---

[12] This note is from the 2nd (1833) edn. of Jameson's *Characteristics of Women* (originally 1832), 'corrected and enlarged' (repr. 1904, p. 321).

us *against the grain*, if I may use such an expression' (Jameson 1832, i. 66).

As Hazlitt does, Jameson measures her reading of Lady Macbeth against Mrs Siddons's performance. The sheer memorability of Siddons's Lady Macbeth is again and again remarked upon in the period. Hazlitt says that to have seen it 'was an event in every one's life, not to be forgotten' and we should take him at his word. Even in years as eventful as those between the fall of the Bastille and the battle of Waterloo, the memory of an evening in the theatre watching a great actress could permanently mark a man or woman's life. Ruskin's father, writing in 1853, was typical: 'Mrs Siddons Lady Macbeth and Keans Othello dwell in my memory for ever' (quoted, Hilton 1985, p. 23). It is also important to recognize that there are many kinds of performance which a public may value, may want to retain in the consciousness as cherished experiences—I am thinking for example of sporting performances, and in particular of Hazlitt's admiration for the art of John Cavanagh, the fives player. It is wholly characteristic of Hazlitt's catholicity and vitality that his magnificent encomium on Cavanagh belongs to 1819, the year in which he collected his *Political Essays* and wrote his *Letter to Gifford*. One should, however, note that in 'The Indian Jugglers', the finest essay ever written on the physical dexterity of the sportsman, Hazlitt concludes that performance is ultimately inferior to composition because 'No act terminating in itself constitutes greatness' (HW viii. 85). Shakespeare's continuing productivity elevates him above the individual performer whose productions cannot be preserved for posterity (the advent of film and sound-recording may alter this argument). Hazlitt's admiration for Siddons is such that she is the exception which proves this rule: 'I must make an exception for Mrs Siddons, or else give up my definition of greatness for her sake' ('The Indian Jugglers', HW viii. 85). The theatre can be the life-blood of a culture; to have seen Mrs Siddons might, for a moment, have been enough to make life seem worth the living.

Though Hazlitt admired Siddons above all other actors, he also had far-reaching respect for the art of acting in general. He especially valued actors because he believed that they embody the principle of sympathy: 'The height of their ambition is to be *beside themselves*' (HW iv. 153). Hazlitt hoped that he would be remembered above all for the 'metaphysical discovery' (HW ix. 51) he made early in life and articulated in his early philosophical work, *An Essay on the Prin-*

ciples of Human Action. The argument of the *Essay*, namely that the
human mind is naturally disinterested—not self-interested, as
Hobbes had argued—and that it has the capacity for sympathy, or
what we would now call empathy, is the key to Hazlitt's aesthetics
and politics. He took sympathy to be the basis of all moral action;
the act of imagination is fundamentally sympathetic because it is a
reaching out from present self-interest to identification with others
and with one's own future. Imagination leads to understanding and
fellow-suffering; art is essentially moral and liberal because it takes
the observer beyond himself. The co-existence of understanding,
which necessitates distance, and fellow-feeling or identification makes
drama, tragedy especially, the highest form of art. In the theatre one
suffers with the tragic protagonist but also remains detached from the
fictions played out on stage. In his essay on *Othello*, Hazlitt rewrites
Aristotle's poetic of tragedy in terms of the sympathetic imagination:

It has been said that tragedy purifies the affections by terror and pity. That is,
it substitutes imaginary sympathy for mere selfishness. It gives us a high and
permanent interest, beyond ourselves, in humanity as such. . . . It makes
man a partaker with his kind. It subdues and softens the stubbornness of his
will. It teaches him that there are and have been others like himself, by
showing him as in a glass what they have felt, thought, and done. It opens the
chambers of the human heart. . . . It is the refiner of the species; a discipline
of humanity. (HW iv. 200)

Shakespearean tragedy becomes for him the supreme artistic achievement, for nowhere is the sympathetic imagination better exemplified.
'The capacious soul of Shakspeare had an intuitive and mighty
sympathy with whatever could enter into the heart of man in all
possible circumstances' (HW xix. 83): sympathy is embodied in the
practice of the dramatist, the response of the audience in the theatre,
and the good actor's identification of himself with his role. Hazlitt
would have found confirmation for this notion of tragedy as the most
sympathetic genre in his reading of Schlegel's *Lectures*: 'When we
take a warm interest in the persons of a tragedy, we cease to think of
ourselves' (Schlegel 1846, p. 68). It was because he did not 'consider
comedy as exactly an affair of the heart or the imagination' (HW vi.
38)—as wholly sympathetic, that is—that Hazlitt gave less emphasis
to Shakespeare's achievement in comedy. The treatment of some of
the comedies, towards the end of *Characters*, is disappointingly per-
functory.

The comedy about which he wrote most effectively was *Measure for Measure*. His reading of this play owes its strength to the principle of sympathy. Hazlitt argued that 'fellow-feeling' provides a morality that is lacking if the play is viewed in terms of conventional codes of behaviour:

> Shakespear was in one sense the least moral of all writers; for morality (commonly so called) is made up of antipathies; and his talent consisted in sympathy with human nature, in all its shapes, degrees, depressions, and elevations. The object of the pedantic moralist is to find out the bad in everything; his was to shew that 'there is some soul of goodness in things evil.' . . . In one sense, Shakespear was no moralist at all: in another, he was the greatest of all moralists. . . . He shewed the greatest knowledge of humanity with the greatest fellow-feeling for it. (HW iv. 346–7)

As originally written for a theatre review published in the *Examiner* of 11 February 1816, this passage included an additional sentence aimed at contemporary moralism: 'We would recommend it to the Society for the Suppression of Vice to read Shakespear' (HW v. 283). There is a similar passage in Hazlitt's lecture on Shakespeare and Ben Jonson in his series *On the English Comic Writers*: 'I have more sympathy with one of Shakespeare's pick-purses, Gadshill or Peto, than I can possibly have with any member of the Society for the Suppression of Vice, and would by no means assist to deliver the one into the hands of the other' (HW vi. 33). Those of a conservative disposition did not approve of such allusions to the contemporary scene—a letter to the editor of *The Times* (12 November 1818, p. 3) attacked Hazlitt for introducing politics into this lecture. As will be seen in the case of William Gifford's attack on Hazlitt's reading of *Coriolanus*, ethics and politics were inextricable in matters such as this.

The principle of sympathy furnished Hazlitt with a new reading of *Measure for Measure*. He did not condemn Lucio, Pompey, and Froth as previous critics, even Schlegel, had done. In an especially brilliant stroke, he saw that Barnardine is a central figure because 'he is a fine antithesis to the morality and the hypocrisy of the other characters in the play'. Barnardine is, Hazlitt suggests, Caliban transposed to a Viennese prison: the play is thus turned upside down and seen from the point of view of a subversive underdog whom the 'legitimate' characters in the play—and the 'legitimate' critics—attempt, not wholly successfully, to suppress. Hazlitt also questioned the strict moral code of Isabella, saying that he was not 'greatly enamoured' of her 'rigid chastity'.[13] And he offered a brief but decisive account of the Duke: 'he is more absorbed in his own plots and gravity than anxious for the welfare of the state; more tenacious of his own character than attentive to the feelings and apprehensions of others' (HW iv. 346).

In a single page Hazlitt has drawn the outlines of a 'modern' reading of *Measure for Measure*. Viewed in terms of traditional morality, it is an extremely troubling reading. Mrs Jameson saw it as an instance of 'that strange perversion of sentiment and want of taste which sometimes mingle with [Hazlitt's] piercing and powerful intellect' (Jameson 1832, i. 57). From the very start of his essay Hazlitt turns the comfortable reading of the play upside down: the 'original sin in the nature of the subject' is not sex, as a 'pedantic moralist' would have it, but 'want of passion' (HW iv. 345). Where Coleridge was deeply offended and pained by *Measure for Measure* (Coleridge 1960, i. 102), Hazlitt refashioned and liberated the play. It was a bold act, which predictably provoked the wrath of the critical establishment: in his review of *Characters*, William Gifford quoted the definition of Shakespearean morality from this essay and remarked that 'Mr Hazlitt's notions of *natural morality* may be gathered from' his refusal to condemn the play's bawds and pimps (Gifford 1818, p. 463). In his reply to Gifford, Hazlitt argued that anyone who shows human sympathy may be seen as a radical: 'Jacobin sentiments sprout from the commonest sympathy, and are even unavoidable in a government critic, when the common claims of humanity touch his pity or his self-love' (HW ix. 24 n.). It was as much the implied politics of Hazlitt's principle of sympathy as any overt political statement that led the *British Critic* reviewer to fulminate that *Characters* was 'stuffed with dull common place, Jacobin declamation. . . . tirades of democratic trash' (*British Critic* 1818, 9: 15–22).

It is characteristic of the political polarization of the period that a journal such as the *British Critic* should damn democracy as Jacobinism and treat Hazlitt as a dangerous revolutionary. Since terms like 'Jacobin' and 'radical' were never used disinterestedly in the period, there are problems in employing them in a relatively dispassionate analysis. Anybody who criticized the government or said anything in

[13] There is a hint of a similar critique in Dr Johnson's 'In Isabella's declamation there is something harsh, and something forced and far-fetched' (Johnson 1986, p. 84). But characteristically Johnson swiftly suppresses this disturbing thought.

favour of the French Revolution would in certain quarters be branded a 'Jacobin', but this is not to say that someone like Hazlitt looked back uncritically on the Terror. There were many shades of 'radical' opinion, as may be seen from Cruikshank's *Coriolanus Addressing the Plebeians*, where, as the eye moves from left to right, the plebeians become more and more respectable. The Leigh Hunt circle might better be called 'liberal' than 'radical'. Hazlitt, however, not only contributed to Hunt's *Liberal* and *Examiner*, but also co-founded the *Yellow Dwarf*, the title of which expresses affinity with T. J. Wooler's far more radical *Black Dwarf*. I have called Hazlitt a 'radical' critic, since it seems to me that 'liberal' is now too tame a term—one thinks of modern Liberalism or of Matthew Arnold's liberal humanism—for the author of, say, the *Yellow Dwarf* essay 'What is the People?'

The epithet 'Jacobin' was used by Hazlitt himself in one of his reviews of Kean's performances as Iago. The chapter on *Othello* in *Characters* was worked up from these reviews, but with some interesting revisions. Surprisingly, Hazlitt suppressed a paragraph that was in line with his reading of morality in *Measure for Measure*. He writes astutely about how Iago 'turns the character of poor Desdemona, as it were, inside out' by suggesting to Othello that there is something unnatural about her not marrying a man 'Of her own clime, complexion, and degree' (HW iv. 208). But, in the review of Kean, he then turns the play inside out: 'For our own part, we are a little of Iago's council in this matter.' Hazlitt grants Desdemona 'infinite credit for purity and delicacy of sentiment', but suggests that 'purity and grossness sometimes "nearly are allied, | And thin partitions do their bounds divide" ', since 'moral character' is 'so uncertain and undefinable a thing' (HW v. 217). This is, I think, the first time a critic has begun to question Desdemona; in Johnson, Coleridge, and Schlegel, she is artless and angelic in purity. Hazlitt is not taking the side of Iago, but he is recognizing that Desdemona is neither artless nor an angel but a woman endowed with a sexuality which contributes to her own destruction. He does not gloss over, as other critics tended to, the sexually 'liberal' language that she uses in dialogue with both Iago and Emilia. Why Hazlitt omitted this passage from *Characters* in 1817 and restored it when the review of Kean was reprinted in *A View* in 1818, I do not know. Perhaps he wondered about the decorum of including even so brief a critique of Desdemona when elsewhere in *Characters* Shakespeare's heroines are read as wholly innocent beings who become themselves by loving their husbands. But, in the light of his remarks about *Measure for Measure*, the idea of the close relation-ship between 'purity' and what pedantic moralists call 'grossness' does make sense.

One thing that we can be sure about is that it was Kean's acting that led Hazlitt to think hard about Iago. Acting is the key here, for Hazlitt—in another ground-breaking analysis—reads Iago as an actor, and thus breaks with the tradition of criticism that took him to be 'motiveless':

Some persons, more nice than wise, have thought this whole character *unnatural*, because his villainy is *without a sufficient motive*. Shakespear, who was as good a philosopher as he was a poet, thought otherwise. He knew that the love of power, which is another name for the love of mischief, is natural to man. . . . Iago in fact belongs to a class of character, common to Shakespear and at the same time peculiar to him; whose heads are as acute and active as their hearts are hard and callous. . . . He is quite or as nearly as indifferent to his own fate as to that of others; he runs all risks for a trifling and doubtful advantage; and is himself the dupe and victim of his ruling passion—an insatiable craving after action of the most difficult and dangerous kind. 'Our ancient' is a philosopher, who fancies that a lie that kills has more point in it than an alliteration or an antithesis; who thinks a fatal experiment on the peace of a family a better thing than watching the palpitations in the heart of a flea in a microscope . . . He is an amateur of tragedy in real life; and instead of employing his invention on .imaginary characters, or long-forgotten incidents, he takes the bolder and more desperate course of getting up his plot at home, casts the principal parts among his nearest friends and connections, and rehearses it in downright earnest, with steady nerves and unabated resolution. (HW iv. 206–7)

This is an utterly new interpretation: the forensic Iago, the self-consciously theatrical Iago, the Iago who is more interested in the process than the outcome of his schemes, the ultimately self-destructive Iago, one might almost say the existential Iago. It is Iago the 'practical joker' of W. H. Auden's essay. But it is also an Iago of Hazlitt's own age: 'the love of power' as synonymous with 'the love of mischief' was something Hazlitt was writing about in his political essays at this time. The characterization of Iago is developed from that first published in a review of Kean in the *Examiner* of 24 July 1814. There, Hazlitt's example of the love of power which Iago embodies is Jacobinism. What Hazlitt has in mind is the 'distrust', 'hatred', and 'anxious and corroding thoughts' (HW v. 212) which marked the extreme Jacobinism of the Terror. That power corrupts is a lesson which must be learnt by the predominantly pro-radical readership of the *Examiner* as well as by the forces actually in power. When Hazlitt reprinted the analysis in *Characters* in 1817 at a time when the *ancien régime* was reasserting itself, he removed the reference to Jacobinism, and the attack on the mischief of the powerful was implicitly turned against the 'Legitimate' rulers at home and in Europe.

When reading *Characters* it is important to remember that it was written in the winter of 1816–17 and published during the year of the suspension of habeas corpus, the Seditious Meetings Bill, and the execution in Derby of Jeremiah Brandreth and the other leaders of the Pentrich rising. It could not have been disinterested to speak at such a time of how Shakespeare 'has entered at once into the manners of the common people, and the jealousies and heart-burnings of the different factions', of how he has shown 'penetration into political character and the springs of public events' (HW iv. 195, 198). These quotations are from the essay on *Julius Caesar*, in which Hazlitt describes how Brutus embodies the perennial dilemma of those who wish to overcome autocracy without themselves resorting to autocratic violence:

That humanity and honesty which dispose men to resist injustice and tyranny render them unfit to cope with the cunning and power of those who are opposed to them. The friends of liberty trust to the professions of others, because they are themselves sincere, and endeavour to reconcile the public good with the least possible hurt to its enemies, who have no regard to any thing but their own unprincipled ends, and stick at nothing to accomplish them. (HW iv. 198)

To a politically conscious reader in 1817, that phrase 'The friends of liberty' could only mean one thing, for it was a tag which revolutionary sympathizers such as Thelwall and the London Corresponding Society had made their own in the 1790s. Because of the way that Shakespearean criticism developed in the later nineteenth century, it is all too easy for us to overlook such phrases and to read *Characters of Shakespear's Plays* in the context of A. C. Bradley's *Shakespearean Tragedy*. It would be truer to Hazlitt to read it in the context of other publications of the same year, such as Shelley's pamphlets *A Proposal for Putting Reform to the Vote* and *'We Pity the Plumage, but Forget the Dying Bird': An Address to the People on the Death of Princess Charlotte*.

If we are to set *Characters* in the context of another book on Shakespeare, we could not do better than consider one which also belongs to 1817. Nathan Drake's *Shakspeare and his Times* appeared just over six months after *Characters*. It was aimed at the kind of well-to-do reader who in the eighteenth century would have subscribed to new editions of the complete works, and perhaps dabbled in amateur textual criticism in the pages of the gentlemen's monthlies. Indeed, Drake was welcomed by those monthlies: 'The publication of this work will form an epoch in the Shakespearean History of this Country', proclaimed the *Gentleman's Magazine* (1818, 88: 334); 'a literary treasure, for the benefit of future ages,—to which many an unborn admirer of Shakespeare will resort with feelings of gratitude to the founder', prophesied the *Monthly Magazine* (1817, 44: 540–1). The latter review was written from the traditionalist critical mentality that took the purpose of reading Shakespeare to be the experience of 'mental delight' and the gathering of 'moral instruction'. Drake's book was ignored by the serious literary quarterlies, such as Jeffrey's *Edinburgh Review*, just as Hazlitt's was ignored by most of the gentlemen's monthlies and execrated by those that did not ignore it, such as the *New Monthly*. *Shakspeare and his Times* was published in two handsome quarto volumes, one of over seven hundred pages and the other of over six hundred, at a cost of five guineas, or seven guineas for a large paper edition. *Characters of Shakespear's Plays* was published in octavo at 10*s*. 6*d*. Drake wrote from a genteel provincial background—he was a Suffolk physician—for a traditional provincial readership. Hazlitt wrote from a dissenting urban background for a new London readership which was well represented by the men and women who, excluded by their nonconformity from a traditional education, would attend lectures at the Surrey Institution. Drake speculated for his gentle readers on such subjects as Elizabethan belief in fairies and the identity of the fair youth in the sonnets. He tried to bring alive the Elizabethan world—and to keep Shakespeare there. The contemporary world only intruded with regard to *Coriolanus*, a 'very peculiar' play which 'affords a picture of what may be termed a Roman electioneering mob', attacks 'popular anarchy', and lauds the hero's 'undisguised contempt of all that is vulgar, pusillanimous, and base' (Drake 1817, ii. 493–4). For Drake, Shylock is a 'Satanic character' and Isabella 'a lovely example of female excellence' (1817, ii. 389, 454). Henry V is 'the darling offspring of his bard', 'a noble and chivalrous hero', 'endowed with every regal virtue', 'magnanimous, eloquent, pious, and sincere' (1817, ii. 426). Set *Characters* beside these orthodoxies and it becomes something new, contemporary and dangerous.

In the essay on *Julius Caesar* Hazlitt has little difficulty in addressing the problem of the relationship between violence and 'the friends of liberty'. There is a problem, but there is no question as to where he stands on the issue. Hazlitt does not have to force his reading in order to argue that Brutus is on the side of liberty and the play sympathizes with Brutus' dilemma. *Coriolanus* is a different matter. The chapter on this play, developed from an *Examiner* review of Kemble's Covent Garden production of December 1816, begins in laconic, almost bantering fashion, but as the opening paragraph unfolds over several pages it becomes more and more problematic:

SHAKESPEAR has in this play shewn himself well versed in history and state-affairs. CORIOLANUS is a store-house of political common-places. Any one who studies it may save himself the trouble of reading Burke's Reflections, or Paine's Rights of Man, or the Debates in both Houses of Parliament since the French Revolution or our own. The arguments for and against aristocracy or democracy, on the privileges of the few and the claims of the many, on liberty and slavery, power and the abuse of it, peace and war, are here very ably handled, with the spirit of a poet and the acuteness of a philosopher. (HW iv. 214)

So far, so good: Shakespeare is shown to put both sides of the question; his capacious sympathy enables him to enter into the minds of both Coriolanus and the people. Initially, then, this reading falls in with Hazlitt's cardinal principle that Shakespeare himself is disinterested, that, as the following essay, on *Troilus and Cressida*, puts it, 'Shakespear never committed himself to his characters. . . . He saw both sides of a question, the different views taken of it according to the different interests of the parties concerned, and he was at once an actor and spectator in the scene' (HW iv. 225).

But suddenly Hazlitt makes a turn that subverts this principle: 'Shakespear himself seems to have had a leaning to the arbitrary side of the question, perhaps from some feeling of contempt for his own origin; and to have spared no occasion of baiting the rabble. What he says of them is very true: what he says of their betters is also very true, though he dwells less upon it' (HW iv. 214). From this conclusion arises a general principle which seems to undermine the whole project of Hazlitt's writing by calling into question the belief that art is 'a discipline of humanity', that 'the spirit of poetry' is 'favourable to liberty and humanity' (HW ix. 50): 'The cause of the people is indeed but little calculated as a subject for poetry . . . The language of poetry naturally falls in with the language of power' (HW iv. 214). Perhaps with half of an eye on the political apostasy of Wordsworth, Coleridge, and Southey (there is a telling quotation from Wordsworth's 'Ode: 1815'), Hazlitt then sets up a dichotomy between the imagination and the understanding: 'The one is a monopolising faculty, which seeks the greatest quantity of present excitement by inequality and disproportion; the other is a distributive faculty, which seeks the greatest quantity of ultimate good, by justice and proportion. The one is an aristocratical, the other a republican faculty' (ibid.). 'The principle of poetry is a very anti-levelling principle', he continues, introducing a series of images that unequivocally place poetry on the side of arbitrary monarchical power:

It rises above the ordinary standard of sufferings and crimes. It presents a dazzling appearance. It shows its head turretted, crowned, and crested. Its front is gilt and blood-stained. Before it 'it carries noise, and behind it leaves tears.' It has its altars and its victims, sacrifices, human sacrifices. Kings, priests, nobles, are its train-bearers, tyrants and slaves its executioners.— 'Carnage is its daughter.' [Wordsworth]—Poetry is right-royal. It puts the individual for the species, the one above the infinite many, might before right. A lion hunting a flock of sheep or a herd of wild asses is a more poetical object than they; and we even take part with the lordly beast, because our vanity or some other feeling makes us disposed to place ourselves in the situation of the strongest party. (HW iv. 214–15)

This last image is referred back to Coriolanus and the citizens. Hazlitt then undertakes a crisp analysis of the play which leads him to the conclusion that

The whole dramatic moral of CORIOLANUS is that those who have little shall have less, and that those who have much shall take away all that others have left. The people are poor; therefore they ought to be starved. They are slaves; therefore they ought to be beaten. They work hard; therefore they ought to be treated like beasts of burden. They are ignorant; therefore they ought not to be allowed to feel that they want food, or clothing, or rest, that they are enslaved, oppressed, and miserable. This is the logic of the imagination and the passions; which seek to aggrandize what excites admiration and to heap contempt on misery, to raise power into tyranny, and to make tyranny absolute; to thrust down that which is low still lower, and to make wretches desperate: to exalt magistrates into kings, kings into gods; to degrade subjects to the rank of slaves, and slaves to the condition of brutes. (HW iv. 216)

The analysis then ends with a comparison between poetry and history which makes it quite clear that Hazlitt is thinking as much about the condition of the people in England in 1816 and 1817 as he is about the interpretation of *Coriolanus*. It is essential to keep in mind the conjunction between the dispute about the availability of grain in the first scene of *Coriolanus* and the principal cause of popular discontent in the years immediately after the Napoleonic wars: the 1815 Corn Law.

Where it is customary to appropriate Shakespeare's plays in such a way that they support one's own positions, here Hazlitt has interpreted *Coriolanus* in such a way that it explains a condition that he deplores. Indeed, when he writes 'We may depend upon it that what men delight to read in books, they will put in practice in reality' (ibid.), he appears to be suggesting that poetry is responsible for repression. Hazlitt seems to be one step away from becoming a kind of radicalized Plato arguing that poetry should be banned because it is harmful to the ideal republic.

Lionel Trilling, one of our century's strongest liberal critics, saw that Hazlitt has here raised some very difficult problems for 'the liberal imagination'. He writes, apropos of Henry James:

Hazlitt said that 'the language of poetry naturally falls in with the language of power,' and goes on to develop an elaborate comparison between the processes of the imagination and the processes of autocratic rule. He is not merely indulging in a flight of fancy or a fashion of speaking; no stancher radical democrat ever lived than Hazlitt and no greater lover of imaginative literature, yet he believed that poetry has an affinity with political power in its autocratic and aristocratic form and that it is not a friend of the democratic virtues. We are likely not to want to agree with Hazlitt; we prefer to speak of art as if it lived in a white bungalow with a garden, had a wife and two children, and were harmless and quiet and co-operative. But James is of Hazlitt's opinion; his first great revelation of art came as an analogy with the triumphs of the world; art spoke to him of the imperious will, with the music of an army with banners. Perhaps it is to the point that James's final act of imagination, as he lay dying, was to call his secretary and give her as his last dictation what purported to be an autobiographical memoir by Napoleon Bonaparte. (Trilling 1950, pp. 81–2)

Had he had a secretary, Hazlitt would probably have done the same on his death-bed.

How, then, can poetry—can Shakespeare—be repossessed for the cause of liberty? First, I think it must be accepted that Hazlitt has shown that if we are to have poetry in our ideal republic, then we cannot have 'levelling' in every respect. He is surely right to argue that it is in the nature of art to sympathize with the lion more than the flock of sheep or herd of wild asses. James Barry saw which of George Stubbs's paintings exercised the strongest hold on the imagination: 'His "Lion Killing a Horse"; a "Tiger Lying in his Den", as large as life, appearing, as it were, disturbed and listening, which were in the last year's exhibition, are pictures that must rouse and agitate the most inattentive; he is now painting a lion, panting and out of breath, lying with his paws over a stag he has run down: it is inimitable' (Redgrave 1981, p. 136). The pull of power, in life as well as art, cannot be gainsaid. Hazlitt's own admiration for Napoleon, manifested in his biographical labours, is symptomatic. But does it necessarily follow from this that the principle of power, the aristocratic principle, must operate in the body politic so as to maintain enslavement, oppression, and misery?

Hazlitt addressed the problem of the aristocratic principle in a number of ways. He made it clear that, when it came to value-judgement in art, there was no connection between the social and the literary élite. In his essay 'On the Aristocracy of Letters' he attacked the idea, all too prevalent at the time, that a man deserved the name of a poet simply because he visited at Holland House. Hazlitt speaks here of 'the commonwealth of letters', and argues that 'There can be no true superiority but what arises out of the presupposed ground of equality' (HW viii. 208). But to say that a 'powerful' or 'superior' writer need not come from a position of power and superiority in society is not to question the pre-eminence of the principle of power. To get at that, one needs to return to Hazlitt's own central philosophical principle, his denial of the Hobbesian and Mandevillean notion that human action—and hence human society—is built on the self-interested exercising of power. For Hazlitt, man has the potential to be a Leviathan, but he also has the potential to be sympathetic, the power to negate his own power. The *Round Table* essay 'On Classical Education' argues that those who make up 'the commonwealth of letters' have a *benevolent* power because they induce sympathy: 'By conversing with the *mighty dead* . . . we become strongly attached to those who can no longer either hurt or serve us . . . We feel the presence of that power which gives immortality to human thoughts and actions, and catch the flame of enthusiasm from all nations and ages' (HW iv. 5). 'The flame of enthusiasm' has strong radical overtones. 'That power which gives immortality to human thoughts and actions' is the greatest power of all; it more than compensates for poetry's tendency to fall in with self-interested political power in the way that the essay on *Coriolanus* suggests. Coriolanus himself shows little interest in anyone other than those who can hurt or serve him (his mother's power lies in her capacity to hurt him), but in reading the play *we* are given 'liberal views' as our minds are enabled 'to take an interest in things foreign to' themselves (these terms of reference are also from 'On Classical Education'). One is thus brought back to a traditional humanism which argues that the study of literature affords a kind of salvation. Clearly Hazlitt did believe this at times, and would have liked to believe it all the time, but in 1816 and 1817 he could not consistently believe it—not least because Southey and Coleridge had destroyed much of his faith in contemporary poetry.

A similar argument might be played out in slightly different terms: the language of poetry may fall in with the language of power, but poetry, and still more drama, also has the capacity to anatomize power. By educating us in the ways of power, it may liberate us, since, as Hazlitt wrote in another essay, 'Knowledge is power' (HW xii. 296–7).[14] It is possible, then, that the essay on *Coriolanus* is not so pessimistic after all. The imagination may identify with Coriolanus, but Shakespeare also addresses the understanding in such a way that the play is no mere glorification of its hero but a lesson in the workings of power and the disastrous consequences of political polarization. As the essay on *Macbeth* is written in the precipitate style of that play, so the account of *Coriolanus* is written in the brusque, polarized style of this one. Hazlitt's version of *Coriolanus* as a battle between Burke and Paine is crude, and deliberately so. It is a performance designed to raise the political stakes in the discussion of Shakespeare at a time of high political tension.

Hazlitt achieved precisely what he set out to do: provoke the Establishment. William Gifford, the most powerful Tory editor of the day, rose to the bait and assaulted *Characters* in the *Quarterly Review*. Hazlitt replied, pressing home his argument, in his *Letter to William Gifford, Esq.*, one of the great neglected texts of the early nineteenth century.

---

[14] This Baconian phrase was also one of the slogans of the young Coleridge's *Prospectus* to his radical journal the *Watchman* and, later, of the German Social Democratic movement in which Eduard Fuchs participated (see Benjamin 1979, p. 356).

Gifford argues in his review that 'In his remarks upon Coriolanus, which contain the concentrated venom of his malignity [Hazlitt] has libelled our great poet as a friend of arbitrary power, in order that he may introduce an invective against human nature' (Gifford 1818, p. 464). It is to Gifford's credit that he sees how central the *Coriolanus* essay is to the book. He also sees the contemporary overtones: 'It is true [Shakespeare] was not actuated by an envious hatred of greatness; he was not at all likely, had he lived in our time, to be an orator in Spa-fields, or the editor of a seditious Sunday newspaper.' Gifford takes the opportunity to make Shakespeare into a writer of whom the government would approve: 'he knew what discord would follow if degree were taken away; and therefore, with the wise and good of every age, he pointed out the injuries that must arise to society from a turbulent rabble instigated to mischief by men not much more enlightened, and infinitely more worthless than themselves' (Gifford 1818, p. 465). He then turns to Hazlitt's generalization about poetry and power, suggesting that it offers a 'new theory of the "pleasures of the imagination" ' which would make us sympathize with 'the cruelties of Domitian or Nero' or the 'still blacker' 'crimes of revolutionary France' (pp. 465–6). He concludes by saying that he would not have condescended to notice Hazlitt's 'senseless and wicked sophistry' but that 'it might not be unprofitable to show how very small a portion of talent and literature was necessary for carrying on the trade of sedition' (p. 466).

Hazlitt hit back at the claim that *Characters* was a seditious book, not least because he felt that Gifford's review had destroyed his work's public reputation, just as the *Quarterly* and *Blackwood's* destroyed Keats: 'Taylor and Hessey [the publishers] told me that they had sold nearly two editions . . . in about three months, but that after the Quarterly Review of [it] came out, they never sold another copy' (HW viii. 99). A *Plain Speaker* essay makes the point in explicitly political terms:

I had endeavoured to guide the taste of the English people to the best of the old English writers; but I had said that English kings did not reign by right divine . . . I had done something (more than any one except Schlegel) to vindicate [Shakespeare] from the stigma of French criticism: but our Anti-Jacobin and Anti-Gallican writers soon found out that I had said and written that Frenchmen, Englishmen, men were not slaves by birth-right. This was enough to *damn* the work. (HW xii. 122)

So it was that in 1819 he published his reply to Gifford, which opens with a devastating account of the impulses behind the latter's criticism:

You are the *Government Critic*, a character nicely differing from that of a government spy—the invisible link, that connects literature with the police. It is your business to keep a strict eye over all writers who differ in opinion with his Majesty's Ministers, and to measure their talents and attainments by the standard of their servility and meanness. . . . The distinction between truth and falsehood you make no account of: you mind only the distinction between Whig and Tory. (HW ix. 13)

Hazlitt excoriates the 'mob of well-dressed readers' of the *Quarterly*, as well as its editor: 'They come to you for a scale not of literary talent but of political subserviency. . . . When you say that an author cannot write common sense or English, you mean that he does not believe in the doctrine of *divine right*. Of course, the clergy and gentry will not read such an author' (HW ix. 14). Having exposed the political nature of the *Quarterly*'s criticism and branded Gifford as a literary police officer, Hazlitt then turns to the specifics of the attack on his own works.

If *Characters of Shakespear's Plays* contains as 'small a portion of talent and literature' as Gifford claims it does, why does he bother to assault it so vigorously? Hazlitt answers this question by suggesting that Gifford's motivation was fear that a radical reading of Shakespeare was gaining ground:

The greater the shock given to the complacency of servility and corruption, by an opinion getting abroad that there was any knowledge of Shakespear or the English language except on the minister's side of the question, would it not be the more absolutely incumbent on you as the head of the literary police, to arrest such an opinion in the outset, to crush it before it gathered strength, and to produce the article in question as your warrant? (HW ix. 33)

As Gifford did, Hazlitt sees that the question of *Coriolanus* is central; he needs to tread carefully, since this is the play in which he has said that Shakespeare perhaps *was* 'on the minister's side of the question'. In order to attack Hazlitt, Gifford had been forced into the (for him) awkward position of arguing that Shakespeare was *not* on the side of arbitrary power. Hazlitt cites Gifford's argument, lacing it with triumphant interjections in square brackets, thus creating a dialogic effect:

'Who has painted with more cordial feelings the tranquil innocence of humble life?' [True.] 'Who has furnished more instructive lessons to the great upon "the insolence of office"—"the oppressor's wrong"—or the abuses of brief authority'—[which you would hallow through all time]—'or who has more severely stigmatised those "who crook the pregnant hinges of the knee where thrift may follow fawning?"' [Granted, none better.] 'It is true he was not actuated by an envious hatred of greatness'—[so that to stigmatise servility and corruption does not always proceed from envy and a love of mischief]— 'he was not at all likely, had he lived in our time, to be an orator in Spa-fields or the editor of a seditious Sunday newspaper'—[to have delivered Mr Coleridge's *Conciones ad Populum*, or to have written Mr Southey's Wat Tyler]— 'he knew what discord would follow if degree were taken away'—[As it did in France from the taking away the degree between the tyrant and the slave, and those little convenient steps and props of it, the Bastile, Lettres de Cachet, and Louis XV's *Palais aux cerfs*]—'And *therefore*, with the wise and good of every age, he pointed out the injuries that must arise to society from a turbulent rabble instigated to mischief by men not much more enlightened, and infinitely more worthless than themselves.' (HW ix. 36)

By breaking down the argument sentence by sentence, Hazlitt has shown how Gifford has started out to show that Shakespeare does *not* have a leaning to the arbitrary side of the question, so that he can prove Hazlitt wrong, and ended up by arguing that Shakespeare *does* have a leaning to the arbitrary side, so that he can be seen to be on the right side in the present discontents. Hazlitt has produced an extraordinary composite text, consisting of quotation from Gifford, quotation within quotation from Shakespeare, parenthetic comment, and contemporary allusion. The politics of Shakespeare are contested and updated before the eyes of the reader.

Hazlitt then restates his own position, that Shakespeare has described *both* sides but seems to have given the arbitrary side 'more quarter than it deserved' (ibid.). Further illumination of his general principle is provided: 'the imagination, generally speaking, delights in power, in strong excitement, as well as in truth, in good, in right, whereas pure reason and the moral sense approve only of the true and good' (HW ix. 37). Hazlitt reiterates a very painful truth. Just how painful it is may be suggested by a modern instance: is it not the case that, in both his own time and ours, Adolf Hitler has fascinated the imagination? In Hazlitt's words, 'Is it a paradox of my making, that "one murder makes a villain, millions a hero!" Or is it not true that here, as in other cases, the enormity of the evil overpowers and makes a convert of the imagination by its very magnitude?' (HW ix. 37–8). Hazlitt can do nothing to change this, but he can fulfil a service to humanity by drawing attention to it. He can be an anatomist of power and that is why the literary police are troubled by him:

My offence against purity in the passage alluded to, 'which contains the concentrated venom of my malignity,' is, that I have admitted that there are tyrants and slaves abroad in the world; and you would hush the matter up, and pretend that there is no such thing, in order that there may be nothing else. Farther, I have explained the cause, the subtle sophistry of the human mind, that tolerates and pampers the evil, in order to guard against its approaches; you would conceal the cause in order to prevent the cure. (HW ix. 38)

Hazlitt's role as an anatomist—a critic—is decisive in that it enables him to warn against both actual tyranny and the dangerous tendency of the human mind to submit to all kinds of manifestation of power. He argues that the reason he has not changed his principles, as Coleridge and Southey have, is that he is a metaphysician, not a poet, 'and I suspect that the conviction of an abstract principle is alone a match for the prejudices of absolute power'—'The love of truth is the best foundation for the love of liberty' (HW ix. 50). Hazlitt's abstract principle is that of sympathy, which he had first articulated in his early essay on *Human Action*; he ends the *Letter to Gifford* by summarizing the argument of that essay and thus introducing a note of hope.

I am not the first to quote the *Letter to Gifford* at length: on 12 and 13 March 1819, John Keats copied pages and pages of it into his journal-letter to his brother and sister-in-law. He was particularly impressed by the opening account of Gifford as the invisible link that connects literature with the police, and the defence of the reading of *Coriolanus*: 'The manner in which this is managed: the force and innate power with which it yeasts and works itself up—the feeling for the costume of society; is in a style of genius—He hath a demon as he himself says of Lord Byron' (Keats 1958, ii. 76). It makes us think afresh about Keats to see him in spring 1819 reading Hazlitt, thinking about 'the costume of society', and being led by Hazlitt's argument to question his own vocation, to propose that poetry 'is not so fine a thing as philosophy—For the same reason that an eagle is not so fine a thing as a truth' (ibid., ii. 81). This is another of those occasions—a slightly unexpected one—in which Keats's instincts seem to me to be absolutely right: he has proved upon his pulses that in the *Letter to Gifford*, and especially that part of it which grapples with

Coriolanus and power, Hazlitt has produced one of the crucial texts of the age.

Gifford said that 'the mention of a king or a court always throws [Hazlitt] into a fit of raving' (Gifford 1818, p. 464). He had in mind the end of the essay in *Characters* on *Henry VIII*, in which it is argued that kings in the abstract 'are very disagreeable characters' and that it is only their 'power', their 'splendour', which 'dazzles the imagination and suspends the judgment' of those who are exposed to them. Shakespeare's eye, however, penetrates 'the pomp of circumstance and the veil of opinion' (HW iv. 305). Hazlitt thus argues that, on the one hand to represent kings on stage is to mythologize monarchy by dazzling the imagination of the audience with its power and splendour, but that on the other hand Shakespeare's plays expose the corruption and absurdity of kings. Reason would dictate that Henry VIII, as portrayed by Shakespeare, should be condemned, but in the theatre the audience is enthralled by him. This sense of a double response is especially apparent in the essay on *Henry V*, in which, far from 'raving', Hazlitt engages in a temperate and deft critique of the king.

Hazlitt acknowledges that Henry V is 'a very favourite monarch with the English nation' and that 'We like him in the play' where he is 'a very amiable monster, a very splendid pageant' (HW iv. 286–7). But the moment one begins to think of him in life instead of in art, it is a different matter:

> we take a very romantic, heroic, patriotic, and poetical delight in the boasts and feats of our younger Harry, as they appear on the stage and are confined to lines of ten syllables; where no blood follows the stroke that wounds our ears, where no harvest bends beneath horses' hoofs, no city flames, no little child is butchered, no dead men's bodies are found piled on heaps and festering the next morning—in the orchestra! (HW iv. 286)

This is stirring but hardly eye-opening—it is self-evident that war on the stage or on Olivier's screen in *Henry V* may be romantic, heroic, and patriotic whereas in a real war crops are trampled, children are killed, and bodies fester. Where Hazlitt is original is in his account of Henry V's *realpolitik*.[15] The king is 'fond of war and low company', 'careless, dissolute, and ambitious'; he rules not by a sense of right but by 'brute force, glossed over with a little religious hypocrisy and

---

[15] As on a number of occasions, his reading draws in one or two particulars on hints in Schlegel.

archiepiscopal advice'; the rejection of Falstaff hangs over the play ('The truth is, that we never could forgive the Prince's treatment of Falstaff'); Agincourt is but Gadshill writ large; because he does not know how to govern his own kingdom, Henry makes war upon another; because his claim to the English throne is doubtful, he makes an even more doubtful claim to the French one; 'Because he did not know how to exercise the enormous power, which had just dropped into his hands, to any one good purpose, he immediately undertook (a cheap and obvious resource of sovereignty) to do all the mischief he could' (HW iv. 285).

The analogy with contemporary Europe is made explicit: 'Such is the history of kingly power, from the beginning to the end of the world;—with this difference, that the object of war formerly, when the people adhered to their allegiance, was to depose kings; the object latterly, since the people swerved from their allegiance, has been to restore kings and to make common cause against mankind' (HW iv. 286). Neither the contemporary application nor Hazlitt's rapid shifts between the historical and the dramatic Henry detract from the reading of the play: there *is* a critique of the king built into *Henry V*, and twentieth-century criticism has come increasingly to value it. *Henry V* is a play that is now admired by many for its two faces, its simultaneous glorification and condemnation of the code of war or, as Burke would have said, of 'chivalry'.[16] Hazlitt was the first to draw one of those faces, the first to activate a certain potential latent in the play, and for this we should be grateful whatever we think of his politics.

It was Hazlitt's willingness to allow his own politics and his own age to shape his reading that enabled him to throw new light on the play. One of the main reasons for modern scepticism about the behaviour of the king is the business of killing the French prisoners. Dr Johnson's sharp eye saw the problem here: 'Unhappily the King gives one reason for his order to kill the prisoners, and Gower another. . . . The King is in a very bloody disposition. He has already cut the throats of his prisoners, and threatens now to cut them again' (Johnson 1986, p. 203). But, with a characteristic, and perhaps politically evasive, manœuvre, Johnson concluded that the problem lay in the text and not the king: 'No haste of composition could produce such negligence; neither was this play, which is the second

---

[16] I have in mind the reading of *Henry V*, and Shakespearean drama generally, as a Wittgensteinian 'duck-rabbit' put forward by Rabkin 1981.

draught of the same design, written in haste. There must be some dislocation of the scenes' (ibid.). Thanks to the tradition, initiated by Hazlitt, of questioning the king's motives, Gary Taylor can show that there is strong dramatic justification for what Johnson took to be dislocations (see Taylor 1982, pp. 32–3). Criticism at its best is the activation of latent potential, and this instance suggests that such activation is dependent on a paradox: precisely because Hazlitt's criticism is responsive to the form and pressure of his own time, it is revelatory in its opening up of a text from another time.

Hazlitt's scepticism about Shakespeare's kings is also bound up with his anger at Coleridge's conversion to the cause of legitimacy. 'Do you then really admire those plague spots of history, and scourges of human nature, Richard II, Richard III, King John, and Henry VIII?', he asks Gifford, 'Do you with Mr Coleridge, in his late Lectures, contend that not to fall down in prostration of soul before the abstract majesty of kings as it is seen in the diminished perspective of centuries, argues an inherent littleness of mind?' (HW ix. 35). Coleridge's 1818 and 1819 lectures are only imperfectly preserved, so we do not know to precisely what Hazlitt refers— perhaps a passage in the lecture of 31 December 1818 on *Richard II*, in which Coleridge seems to have argued that 'patriotic reminiscence' was the 'all-permeating Spirit' of the play and that it would 'fall dead on the hearts of Jacobinized Englishmen' (Coleridge 1987, ii. 283). Hazlitt's jibe at Coleridge's politics must, however, be seen in the broader context of the London lecturing scene at this time.

Hazlitt probably only attended one of Coleridge's lectures. He was ill during the 1808 course, but either went to or was told about the lecture of 16 December 1811, when Coleridge singled out the word 'crying' in Prospero's account of his flight from Milan with Miranda; in his lecture 'On Shakspeare and Milton', Hazlitt acknowledged that an earlier critic had 'ingeniously remarked' on this (HW v. 48). Where Coleridge is unquestionably a finer critic than Hazlitt is in his attention to the texture of Shakespeare's poetic language. That is why he is the father of twentieth-century apolitical 'practical criticism'. But Hazlitt was by no means immune to verbal finesse or insensitive to the movement of verse: he writes excellently of, for example, the relationship between style and psychology in Leontes: 'the crabbed and tortuous style of the speeches of Leontes, reasoning on his own jealousy, beset with doubts and fears, and entangled more and more in the thorny labyrinth, bears every mark of Shakespear's peculiar manner of conveying the painful struggle of different thoughts and feelings, labouring for utterance, and almost strangled in the birth' (HW iv. 324). There are many good things of this sort in *Characters*, but they do not constitute the peculiar distinction of Hazlitt's criticism.

Early in 1818 Coleridge and Hazlitt were lecturing simultaneously, acting as rival authorities. On 27 January Crabb Robinson heard Hazlitt's lecture 'On Shakspeare and Milton' at the Surrey Institution, then rushed off to attend the opening lecture of Coleridge's series at the London Philosophical Society on Shakespeare and other poets; he also attended both lectures on 17 and 24 February (Robinson 1938, i. 218–19). John Thelwall's remark about Coleridge's *Hamlet* lecture a year later at once obscures and reveals the true state of affairs: 'In many particulars Mr C. at least accords with, if he has not availed himself of the opinions of Hazlitt, and of another Lecturer, whose disquisitions on the character of *Hamlet*, during the last season, excited very popular attention' (*The Champion*, 10 January 1819, p. 29). Coleridge and Hazlitt are broadly in accord over the character of Hamlet, but this is one occasion where plagiarism on Coleridge's part is most unlikely, for he had lectured on *Hamlet* several times before Hazlitt did so. Thelwall's accusation is a device designed to draw attention to, and reflect credit upon, 'another Lecturer': himself (his Shakespearean lectures are, alas, now lost). There was, then, an extraordinary amount of Shakespearean activity in London in the turbulent final years of the Regency: *Characters* was published in 1817, Gifford's attack in 1818, and Hazlitt's defence in 1819; and in early 1818 Thelwall, Coleridge, and Hazlitt were all lecturing on the plays. The presence of Thelwall, 'Citizen John' of the heady 1790s when Coleridge had been 'Citizen Samuel', must have been an acute embarrassment to the Coleridge who was now bowing down before 'the abstract majesty of kings'. Taken together, Thelwall and Hazlitt must have constituted powerful testimony to the 'opinion getting abroad' that there could be 'knowledge of Shakespear' which was most certainly *not* 'on the minister's side of the question'.

The fragmentary state of Coleridge's lectures and the total loss of Thelwall's mean that we cannot reconstruct what must have been a fascinating and urgent contestation for political possession of Shakespeare. One thing we do know about Thelwall is that he was convinced of the political significance of the theatre. In 1795 he had delivered a pair of lectures 'On the POLITICAL PROSTITUTION of our PUBLIC THEATRES'. The subject, he claims, is a political one 'for it is connected, in a considerable degree with the morals, manners and interests of society . . . Indeed, if we consider seriously any subject whatever, though it may seem to the superficial observer as far removed from politics as the equator from the poles, we shall find, if it is a subject that has any meaning or connection whatever with any principle of common sense or morality, that it is in reality a question of politics' (Thelwall 1795-6, iii. 279-80). Thelwall's analysis bears out a number of important points: that the structure of the theatre in the period was 'intimately connected with the political system' (he attacks the 'system of monopoly' in the London theatre), that the show of parliamentary democracy is but a kind of theatre (an inferior kind, at that—'As for theatrical exhibitions in themselves, I venerate them more than all the mock realities, or real mockeries, of St Stephen's Chapel'), and that the theatre could be used as an instrument of State control (in Shakespeare's time, 'public exhibitions were made use of as vehicles of fulsome adulation to tyranny and oppression' so that the theatres were 'powerful vehicles for the suppression of every generous principle of liberty'). Most interestingly, Thelwall argues that it was because they were 'friends of liberty' that the puritans disliked the theatre; Shakespeare, on the other hand, embodied the servility of the theatre in that he 'too often wielded the pen of political prostitution' (Thelwall 1795-6, iii. 280-2, 301-2).

This view of Shakespeare's politics is based primarily on *Coriolanus*. Thelwall, who called his journal the *Tribune*, could not abide Shakespeare's portrayal of the representatives of the people: 'Who can behold without indignation the contemptible light in which he has exhibited those virtuous tribunes to whom Rome owed so large a portion of her liberty?' Thelwall nevertheless believed that the drama could be an instrument of popular liberation: Ben Jonson, it is claimed, 'felt the principles of liberty' and showed in his plays 'frequent flashes of political truth' (iii. 302-3). It is possible that in his lost lectures of 1817-18, under the influence of Hazlitt's radical reappraisal of the plays in *Characters*, Thelwall revised his own notions of Shakespeare's 'political prostitution'. We know that one of his lectures was on *King Lear*,[17] and we know the kind of passage he liked to quote from that play: 'Take physic Pomp—Expose thyself to feel what wretches feel' (epigraph to lecture 'On the proper means of arresting National Calamities', *Tribune*, No. 1, 14 March 1795). But,

---

[17] See the *Champion*, No. 268, 22 Feb. 1818, p. 115.

whatever new conclusions Thelwall came to about the nature of Shakespeare's politics, his very presence in London as a lecturer constituted a politicization of the plays, a placing of them in the public sphere. It is telling that in one of his reports on Coleridge's Shakespearean lectures, Thelwall *begins* with Coleridge's political apostasy and only subsequently gives an account of his poetic and dramatic readings (*The Champion*, 21 December 1818).

The *Champion* was a radical journal edited by Thelwall himself. The politicization of Shakespearean criticism at this time is also demonstrable from newspaper reporting. An excellent example is provided by Hazlitt's response to Coleridge's reading of Caliban.[18] The *Courier* was among the most vigorously pro-Establishment papers. On 9 February 1818 it included the following detail in its account of Coleridge's lecture of the previous Friday evening: 'The character of Caliban, as an original and caricature of Jacobinism, so fully illustrated at Paris during the French Revolution, he described in a vigorous and lively manner, exciting repeated bursts of applause' (Coleridge 1987, ii. 124). Clearly, there was a patriotic audience: Coleridge addressed his lectures to the 'higher and middle classes of English society' and prided himself on the 'respectability' of those who attended (Coleridge 1987, ii. 39, 45), whereas Hazlitt's audience at the Surrey Institution included many Nonconformists who shared his anti-Castlereagh and anti-slavery views (see Talfourd 1848, ii. 174). The Jacobin Caliban sits uneasily beside a note in another report of the 6 February lecture to the effect that Coleridge credited Shakespeare with having 'no sectarian character of Politician or religion' despite writing 'in an age of political and religious heat' (Coleridge 1987, ii. 120). Coleridge contrives to render Shakespeare both apolitical and anti-Jacobin.

Hazlitt read the *Courier* report and published a reply on 14 February in the pro-radical journal he had helped to found, the *Yellow Dwarf*. As so often, he chid Coleridge with his own former Jacobinism, reminding him of the anti-government lectures he had published in 1795 under the title *Conciones ad Populum*. But he also produced a counter-reading of *The Tempest*. This takes the form of an ironic amplification of Coleridge's comparison with modern France. Hazlitt reads Caliban as the 'legitimate' ruler of the isle, who has been usurped by Prospero; Prospero is therefore the Jacobin, or the Bona-

---

[18] Ably discussed, though not set in the broader context of Shakespearean politics, by Bromwich 1983, pp. 270–4.

30. Anonymous caricature reading the trial of Queen Caroline through *Hamlet* (1820)

31. William Dent, A revolutionary brew from *Macbeth* (1791)

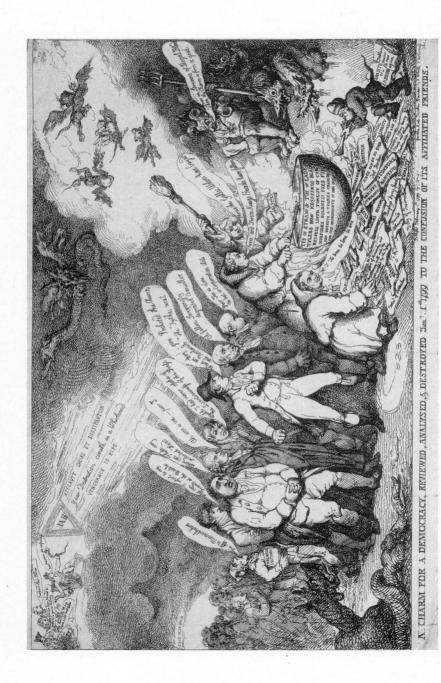

32. Thomas Rowlandson, Another revolutionary brew from *Macbeth* (1799)

Pub.d Jan.y 5.th 1803, by J. Gillray. 27. St. James's Street.

A PHANTASMAGORIA:—Scene—Conjuring up an Armed-Skeleton.

33. James Gillray, A political phantasmagoria from *Macbeth* (1803)

34. James Gillray, Ministerial *Wierd-Sisters*—Dundas, Pitt, Thurlow (1791)

35. Henry Fuseli, *The Three Witches* (1783)

parte, and Caliban the Bourbon, 'the Louis XVIII of the enchanted island in *The Tempest*' (HW xix. 207). The initial purpose of this is to debunk Coleridge's 'caricature', but parts of Hazlitt's self-consciously provocative reading have an irrefutable force:

Caliban is so far from being a prototype of modern Jacobinism, that he is strictly the legitimate sovereign of the isle, and Prospero and the rest are usurpers, who have ousted him from his hereditary jurisdiction by superiority of talent and knowledge. 'This island's mine, by Sycorax my mother;' and he complains bitterly of the artifices used by his new friends to cajole him out of it. (ibid.)

If we are to speak of usurpation, does it not come from the court rather than the native, from not Caliban but Prospero's brother and 'those finished Court-practitioners, Sebastian and Antonio, who wanted to murder the sleeping King'? 'Were they Jacobins like Caliban, or legitimate personages, like Mr Coleridge? Did they belong to the new school or the old? That is the question; but it is a question which our lay-preacher will take care not to answer' (HW xix. 208). A partisan critic will always take care not to ask certain questions which might upset his appropriation of a Shakespearean text for his own cause. It is to Hazlitt's credit that he recognizes that *The Tempest* can only be appropriated for his cause by being read against the grain, just as it is to his credit that he recognizes that *Coriolanus* will not fall in with his own cause. But a reading *against the grain*, that provocative phrase of Mrs Jameson's, is not a misreading. The analysis of *The Tempest* in *Characters* points to the fact that Prospero is 'arbitrary, tetchy, and impatient of opposition' (HW iv. 242); if this insight is put beside the counter-reading of Caliban in the *Yellow Dwarf*, with its reference to his 'natural sovereignty' over the isle, one is then furnished with an account of *The Tempest* as an affair of imperialism and power politics, not a rarefied Romantic effusion of pure imagination.

Hazlitt was far ahead of his time here: in our post-imperial age it has become fashionable to read *The Tempest* in terms of colonialism, but in an (albeit limited) inspection of early nineteenth-century pamphlets and speeches regarding slavery, I have not found pro- and anti-abolitionists contesting the character of Caliban. Thomas Clarkson devoted chapter 3 of his *History of the Rise, Progress, and Accomplishment of the Abolition of the African Slave-Trade by the British Parliament* (1808) to anti-slavery sentiments in classic English authors, such as

Milton, Thomson, and Cowper—but here Shakespeare is conspicuous by his absence. It was much later in the century that Ruskin read Caliban as the type of slavery and Sycorax as the mother of it; and this was an unsympathetic reading, since Ruskin saw slavery not as a political institution but as the '*inherent, natural, and eternal inheritance* of a large portion of the human race' (Ruskin 1872, ch. 5, sec. 134).

A modern liberal-minded approach to Caliban inevitably raises the issue of race. Hazlitt saw that in *Othello* Shakespeare inverted the traditional association of external blackness with internal evil, an association used uncritically in *Titus Andronicus*, by giving a black heart to a man with a white skin and vice versa. Edward Young's play *The Revenge* is, he argues, 'an obvious transposition of Othello: the two principal characters are the same; only their colours are reversed'; this is an alteration that is 'in conformity to our prejudices' (HW v. 227). Hazlitt thus implies that Shakespeare's play does *not* conform to our prejudices, a position he also adopted in his essay on *The Merchant of Venice*.

In 1741 Charles Macklin had humanized Shylock, converted him from a pantomime villain to an impassioned and dignified, though still malevolent, creature. In 1814 Edmund Kean had played him with a fierceness and single-mindedness. Many reviewers and theatre-goers testified to the energy of Kean's Shylock and the way in which he played the character as 'a man brooding over one idea, that of its wrongs, and bent on one unalterable purpose, revenge' (HW v. 179).[19] This quotation is from Hazlitt's review of Kean's debut on 26 January 1814. When Hazlitt reviewed the performance again in April 1816 he introduced a new perspective that is absent from other commentators on Kean. He criticized his own earlier review on the grounds that he had 'formed an overstrained idea of the gloomy character of Shylock, probably more from seeing other players perform it than from the text of Shakespear'; he continued to the effect that Kean was 'nearer the mark' of the true Shakespearean Shylock:

Shakespear could not easily divest his characters of their entire humanity: his Jew is more than half a Christian. Certainly, our sympathies are much oftener with him than with his enemies. He is honest in his vices; they are hypocrites in their virtues. In all his arguments and replies he has the advantage over them, by taking them on their own ground. (HW v. 296)

---

[19] Accounts of Macklin's and Kean's performances are helpfully discussed by Brown 1961.

It is this defence of Shylock which Hazlitt reiterates in *Characters*. Here, he writes of the Jew's 'strong, quick, and deep sense of justice', and of his mistreatment at the hands of the Christians; here, decisively, he quotes the great speech, 'Hath not a Jew eyes . . .' (HW iv. 320-1).

David Bromwich argues that 'Between Kean's performance and Hazlitt's description, an evil character whose humanity had at last been shown, was transformed into one whose wrongs outweigh his faults, the most nearly heroic character in a play without a hero' (Bromwich 1983, p. 403). Hazlitt the critic has built upon the work of Kean the actor and developed a new reading of the part. Something similar had happened when Charles Lamb extrapolated from the performance of Robert Bensley a reading of Malvolio as a tragic character.[20] I share Bromwich's sense that Hazlitt is the first to read Shylock with unequivocal sympathy, though I would want to note Richard Hole's 'Apology for the Character and Conduct of Shylock', published in Exeter in 1796. One cannot take Hole entirely seriously— he also set out to apologize for the character and conduct of Iago—but his *jeu d'esprit* does draw attention to the double standards of the Christians in the play, and to the injuries and public insults heaped upon Shylock by Antonio and others. Hole produces a thought-provoking plot summary of an imagined rewritten Jewish version of the play with Shylock as hero, but in the end his essay is written in a spirit more of ingenuity than of passion. Writing for 'a Society of Gentlemen at Exeter', Hole was a marginal figure; it was Hazlitt who reconstituted Shylock and brought into the public sphere a new reading of the play, one which for obvious reasons has been very important to the twentieth century.[21]

Hazlitt's essay on *The Merchant of Venice* is in the broad sense, as those on *Coriolanus* and *Henry V* are in the narrow sense, political. I believe that this is the strand of Hazlitt's criticism which we should value most, and which should make us think most, today. It is a disappointment to return to the essay on *Hamlet*, a piece which tells us more about Hazlitt than Shakespeare. This is what we now think of as characteristic 'Romantic' criticism: a rhapsody on how Hamlet has entered our consciousness, how we seem to know all his thoughts 'as

[20] See Lamb's essay 'On Some of the Old Actors', repr. in *Elia*; Barnet 1954 shows that others did not respond to Bensley's Malvolio as tragic, and that the reading is more an 'invention' (I prefer 'extrapolation') of Lamb's.

[21] Bromwich (1983, pp. 406-7) goes on to relate Hazlitt's sympathetic reading of Shylock to his late essay on 'Emancipation of the Jews'.

well as we do our own'. His words are merely 'the idle coinage of the poet's brain', yet 'They are as real as our own thoughts. Their reality is in the reader's mind. It is *we* who are Hamlet. The play has a prophetic truth, which is above that of history' (HW iv. 232). Here *Hamlet* is 'prophetic' not of contemporary public affairs but of the Romantic artist's own troubled personal life. After touching on the process of sympathy ('the distresses of Hamlet are transferred, by the turn of his mind, to the general account of humanity'), on Shakespeare's 'magnanimity', and on the sensitive pacing of the play, Hazlitt undertakes a reading of the character of Hamlet which falls in with the Goethe–Coleridge axis: Hamlet is 'incapable of deliberate action', he is 'the prince of philosophical speculators', his refusal to kill Claudius while he is praying is 'only an excuse for his own want of resolution' (HW iv. 233–4). Hamlet is above all a creature of the mind, who transfers uneasily to the stage; 'Mr Kean's Hamlet is as much too splenetic and rash as Mr Kemble's is too deliberate and formal' (HW iv. 237). Hazlitt here shares Lamb's sense of the insufficiency of the stage to hold those characters such as Hamlet with whom the writer feels that he himself has a peculiar affinity. Thus the essay in *Characters* begins 'This is that Hamlet the Dane, whom we read of in our youth, and whom we may be said almost to remember in our after-years' (HW iv. 232), while in his review of Kean's performance Hazlitt distinguishes between the actor's Hamlet and the 'very' Hamlet: 'Mr Kean's representation of the character had the most brilliant success. It did not indeed come home to our feelings, as Hamlet (that very Hamlet whom we read of in our youth, and seem almost to remember in our after-years), but it was a most striking and animated rehearsal of the part' (HW v. 187). That last figure suggests that in the theatre Hazlitt found only 'rehearsals', in both senses of the word, of Hamlet. The finished performance took place in his own mind and life: Hazlitt's account of 'the true Hamlet'—a man who has 'known "the pangs of despised love" ', whose 'powers of action have been eaten up by thought' (HW iv. 232)—is also an account of the emotional life of Hazlitt.

The pull of Hamlet was such that when Hazlitt wrote of him he could not escape precisely the morbid egotism for which he so frequently castigated the poets of his own age. *Lear* offers something of an antidote, for what it teaches Hazlitt above all else is the need for sympathy, for a going-out from the self. Hazlitt is modest in his claims for what he can say about the play, immodest in his claims for the play. That is to say, he begins his essay by saying that *Lear* baffles criticism, that 'all that we can say must fall far short of the subject', and then he asserts that it is 'the best of all Shakespear's plays' (HW iv. 257). He is the first to say unequivocally in print that *Lear* is Shakespear's greatest play. *Characters* thus paves the way for Shelley's claim that *Lear* is 'the most perfect specimen of the dramatic art existing in the world' ('A Defence of Poetry'—Shelley 1909, p. 134). But somehow Hazlitt is inadequate to the task of showing *why* it is the best of Shakespeare's plays. He finds himself leaning heavily on Lamb,[22] and ending with a rather attenuated list of 'four things [that] have struck us in reading LEAR' (HW iv. 271–2). The first of these attempts to remove poetry from the aristocratic cause and restore it to all humanity ('Whoever therefore has a contempt for poetry, has a contempt for himself and humanity'), and the last to restate the principle of sympathy ('our sympathy with actual suffering is lost in the strong impulse given to our natural affections, and carried away with the swelling tide of passion, that gushes from and relieves the heart'). It is symptomatic of this essay's insufficiency that Hazlitt here falls back on vaguely rhapsodic language. The play has eluded his grasp. Obviously there is a sense in which to read or see *King Lear* makes us human—Keats had something of the sort in mind when, after reading and annotating Hazlitt's essay, he reread the play and transcribed his sonnet on it into his facsimile Shakespeare First Folio. But nowhere in his treatment of *Lear* does Hazlitt get to grips with the problem of power. His feelings seem to have got the better of his understanding.

Yet maybe this failure was another success, for it suggests a source of the play's greatness: its intractability. Hazlitt found himself appropriating *Coriolanus* for the wrong side; he cannot appropriate *King Lear* at all. As he said of Kean's performance, he only chips off a bit of the play here and there; he does not 'pierce the solid substance, nor move the entire mass'. *Lear* is a piece of ancient granite

---

[22] He quotes the passage 'The LEAR of Shakespear cannot be acted. . . . while we read it, we see not Lear, but we are Lear;—we are in his mind . . .' from Lamb's essay on the tragedies. *Characters* is dedicated to Lamb, in acknowledgement of Hazlitt's more general debt. Coleridge said that he preferred Lamb's 'exquisite criticisms on Shakspeare' to 'Hazlitt's round and round imitations of them' (*Table Talk*, 6 Aug. 1832). I think that Lamb made a major contribution to Romantic Shakespearean criticism but that he did so principally in conversation: the esteem in which his contemporaries held him far outstrips that warranted by his published essays. Elsewhere, I have argued this case, and tried to catch something of the flavour of Lamb's criticism (Bate 1985).

that turns the edge even of Hazlitt's modern chisel. Despite the fact that during the years of the king's madness it had a peculiar contemporary force, the unaccommodated play, 'the thing itself', defied appropriation.

7

Quotation

KARL KRAUS, apophthegmatic satirist, stood in the same relationship to early twentieth-century Austrian culture as William Hazlitt
did to early nineteenth-century English culture: he embodied the
spirit of the age at its most creative, while he castigated the forces
which destroyed that spirit and precipitated the age into tyranny and
philistinism. Of Kraus, Brecht is reported as saying 'When the age
died by its own hand, he was that hand' (Benjamin 1979, p. 271).
David Bromwich has applied these words to Hazlitt; I wish to pursue
the comparison further by drawing together two strands of Walter
Benjamin's great essay on Kraus.

'Shakespeare had foreknowledge of everything'—yes. But above all of Kraus.
. . . A fool, a Caliban, a Timon—no more thoughtful, no more dignified or
better—but, nevertheless, his own Shakespeare. All the figures thronging
about him should be seen as originating in Shakespeare. Always he is the
model, whether Kraus speaks with Weininger about man or with Altenberg
about woman, with Wedekind about the stage or with Loos about food, with
Else Lasker-Schüler about the Jews or with Theodor Haecker about the
Christians. (Benjamin 1979, pp. 280-1)

'Shakespeare had foreknowledge of everything': the notion that one
may find oneself in a character such as Caliban or Timon would have
been understood by Hazlitt. And Hazlitt shared both the catholicity
of Kraus's interests and the capacity to bring Shakespeare to bear on
every subject—'Always he is the model.'

Benjamin, who thought that the ideal book would have consisted
entirely of quotations, saw quotation as Kraus's essential polemical
procedure. 'Kraus's achievement exhausts itself at the highest level
by making even the newspaper quotable': Kraus punishes the journ-
alism of his contemporaries for its linguistic poverty by 'swoop[ing]
on the wings of the word to drag it from its darkness' (Benjamin
1979, p. 285). But his art of quotation saves as well as punishes,

as it does on the Shakespearean wings of the lines in which, before Arras,
someone sends word home of how in the early morning, on the last blasted

tree before the fortifications, a lark began to sing. A single line, and not even one of his, is enough to enable Kraus to descend, as saviour, into this inferno, a single italicization: 'It was a nightingale and not a lark which sat there on the pomegrana[d]e tree and sang.' (Benjamin 1979, pp. 285–6)

The pun does not quite work in English: in German, *Granat* means 'pomegranate' and *Granate* means 'grenade' or 'shell'. Kraus's wit transforms a moment of pathos and destruction in the Great War into a monument of linguistic creation and plenitude. Furthermore, the evocation of the *aubade* in *Romeo and Juliet* forces the reader to think of love in the context of violence and destruction, a juxtaposition that can only damage the political and military Establishment which has a vested interest in war. Benjamin continues:

In the quotation that both saves and chastises, language proves the matrix of justice. It summons the word by its name, wrenches it destructively from its context, but precisely thereby calls it back to its origin. It appears, now with rhyme and reason, congruously in the structure of a new text. As rhyme it gathers the similar into its aura; as name it sounds alone and expressionless. In quotation the two realms—of origin and destruction—justify themselves before language. And conversely, only where they interpenetrate—in quotation—is language consummated. (p. 286)

Benjamin's high claims for the art of quotation provide strong justification for the extensive quotations from Hazlitt in this book: by wrenching passages creatively from their context, it is possible both to call back the origin of certain Shakespearean readings in Hazlitt and to enable his voice to be heard in a contemporary critical context.

Hazlitt shares with Kraus not only a way of using Shakespeare to illuminate the modern world, but also the art of quotation. When the painter William Bewick described him as 'the Shakespeare prose writer of our glorious country', he meant that Hazlitt outdid all others in 'truth, style, and originality' (Landseer 1871, i. 42). But there is a more specific sense in which he is a 'Shakespeare prose writer', for the language of the plays works like yeast in Hazlitt's prose. Shakespearean quotations bring to consummation Hazlitt's own language, which is always aphoristic like a quotation and imagistic like Shakespearean verse. And through quotation Hazlitt both saves and chastises his own age.

Good quoters are made not born. It is instructive to trace Hazlitt's 'First Acquaintance' with Shakespeare. His sister, Margaret, testifies to the family's fondness during William's early years for Shakespeare, Sterne, and print-shops, such as that of John Boydell at the Shakespeare Gallery (M. Hazlitt 1967, p. 101; W. C. Hazlitt 1897, i. 65–6). The two latter interests serve to remind us that, although Hazlitt referred to Shakespeare far more frequently than to any other writer, his inveterate use of quotation and literary allusion was not restricted to one author, and that he moved easily between literature and graphic art (and, indeed, that Boydell's Gallery was a focal point for London literary life in the 1790s). Shakespeare did not, however, figure especially prominently in Hazlitt's early life and work. Looking back on his youth, Hazlitt concluded that two factors combined to give him a voice of his own: learning to paint and meeting Coleridge (HW xvii. 312). Among his early paintings, now lost, was a 'King Lear—head and shoulders, small size', described by his grandson as follows: 'It is a sketch of the head and shoulders of the old mad king, with his white hair waving in the wind, very characteristic and Shakespearian' (W. C. Hazlitt 1867, vol. i, pp. xvi, 109). But there are few other indications of an early interest in Shakespeare; surprisingly, he plays little part in 'My First Acquaintance with Poets'—indeed, Hazlitt does not question Coleridge's remark that, compared with Milton, Shakespeare appears to be 'a mere stripling in the art' (HW xvii. 120–1; also HW xx. 216).

The turning-point came in Paris in 1802. Hazlitt had gone to the Louvre to study the old masters, but as an Englishman in the land of Voltaire he inevitably found himself embattled on the literary front. Twenty years later, he remembered reading Shakespeare in Paris when he remarked in one of his *Sketches of the Principal Picture-Galleries in England* for the *London Magazine* that 'books, pictures, and the face of nature' were the only three enduring pleasures in life: 'And there that fine passage stands in Antony and Cleopatra as we read it long ago with exulting eyes in Paris, after puzzling over a tragedy of Racine's, and cried aloud: "Our Shakspeare was also a poet!" These feelings are dear to us at the time; and they come back unimpaired, heightened, mellowed, whenever we choose to go back to them' (HW x. 27). Here, the recollection of Shakespeare takes on the status of a Wordsworthian 'spot of time'. Whether spoken at the time or only in retrospect, that possessive 'our', reminiscent of the great seventeenth-century apologists for Shakespeare, suggests that from this point on Hazlitt's commitment to the English Bard will be both deeply personal and fiercely evangelical.

The reading of *Antony and Cleopatra* first surfaced in a footnote to

An Essay on the Principles of Human Action, Hazlitt's early philosophical inquiry, published in 1805. The note criticizes the French for their generalizing tendency, their inability to combine 'a great variety of complicated actions to correspond with the distinct characters and complex forms of things'; French poetry, argues Hazlitt, therefore wants 'imagination', that associative faculty through which our feelings are 'modified by the objects exciting them' (HW i. 24 n.–25 n.). There is consequently nothing in French drama that belongs 'to the same class' as Antony's lines comparing himself to shifting clouds (*Antony and Cleopatra*, IV. xiv. 1–13). Quotation is rare in the *Essay*, so the reference stands out; it is especially telling in this context because, in imagining that the clouds resemble a variety of animals and objects, Antony himself is exemplifying the associative power of the imagination. This single invocation of Shakespeare in the essay where Hazlitt first develops his theory of the sympathetic imagination gives a hint of the central position the plays would occupy in his later deliberations on this all-important subject.

It should surprise no one that Hazlitt quotes from Shakespeare—which eighteenth- or nineteenth-century English prose writer does not?—but the frequency with which he does so throughout his original writing subsequent to the *Essay on the Principles of Human Action* is quite exceptional. Some bare statistics will reveal the extent of the phenomenon. Setting aside references where Hazlitt is discussing some specific point in Shakespeare, there are about two and a half thousand quotations from the plays in Howe's edition of the *Complete Works*. Hazlitt quotes from a wide range of authors; the second highest frequency belongs to Milton, but the total number of Miltonic phrases is outweighed by those, over five hundred, from *Hamlet* alone. Every play is used, with the exception of *1 Henry VI*; apart from confirming the old saying that *Hamlet* is full of quotations, their relative frequency reveals almost as great an obsession with *Macbeth*, cited over three hundred times, and the popularity of *Othello* (especially resonant for the Hazlitt who wrote *Liber Amoris*), *As You Like It*, and *Henry V*, each of which is invoked on more than a hundred occasions.

Hazlitt does not quote Shakespeare in *every* piece he writes: a two-part review of George Ensor's *On the State of Europe*, published in the *Examiner* on 29 September and 13 October 1816, is packed with suggestive political quotations from the plays, but the article of the week in between, 'A Modern Tory Delineated', does not contain a single one (HW xix. 161–76). Nevertheless, nearly every book, every collection of essays, no matter how far removed its subject is from Shakespeare, yields up scores of quotations. The only exceptions are the works in which Hazlitt is more editor than author, such as *A New and Improved Grammar*, the *Life of Holcroft*, which was in part a reproduction of Holcroft's diary, and the three-volume *Life of Napoleon*, much of which consists of translations or paraphrases of French histories.

A specific example will put the figures in perspective. In 1819 Hazlitt published his *Political Essays*, mainly reprinted from contributions to the *Morning Chronicle* and the *Examiner*. Ostensibly they have little to do with poetry or drama, but this does not prevent Hazlitt from weaving into his prose quotations from Wordsworth, Spenser, and many eighteenth-century poets, as well as the more obvious authorities, Burke and the Bible. The two deities of English poetry are quoted more frequently than anybody else, Milton nearly forty times, Shakespeare over two hundred, thirty-two of his plays being represented.[1]

The quotations in *Political Essays* are qualitatively as well as quantitatively telling. A strong instance of how they are deployed is provided by the essay 'What is the People?'—the title perhaps glances at *Coriolanus*, 'What is the city, but the people?' (III. i. 198)—which was first published in the *Yellow Dwarf* of 7 March 1818. It is one of Hazlitt's scathing attacks on 'Legitimacy', the concept that summed up for him the Europe-wide reaction of the post-Napoleonic years—the Bourbon restoration, the alliance of crowned heads, repression at home. The essay begins with an address to those who espouse the cause of Legitimacy:

. . . you would tear out this mighty heart of a nation, and lay it bare and bleeding at the foot of despotism: you would slay the mind of a country to fill up the dreary aching void with the old, obscene, drivelling prejudices of superstition and tyranny: you would tread out the eye of Liberty (the light of nations) like 'a vile jelly,' that mankind may be led about darkling to its endless drudgery. (HW vii. 259)

---

[1] These figures include one or two phrases which are not strictly quotations, such as 'like Timon . . .' and a name for Castlereagh that is familiar to us from the *Craftsman*: 'My Lord Shallow' (HW vii. 129, 98). The 5 plays not represented are *The Comedy of Errors*, *1 Henry VI*, *3 Henry VI*, *Pericles*, and *Richard III*; the first 4 of these are, with *Two Gentlemen*, *2 Henry VI*, and *Titus Andronicus*, the 7 plays quoted from less than 10 times in HW—they were also out of favour in the early nineteenth-century theatre. *Richard III* is a freak result, for overall I make it the 16th most frequently cited play.

The allusion to *Lear* incisively associates the supporters of Legitimacy with Cornwall and Regan. Liberty is stamped out, like Gloucester's eyes. Characteristically, a direct quotation leads to an embedded allusion, 'vile jelly' to the Fool's image of dispossession, 'we were left darkling' (I. iv. 217). Often, once a play enters a particular passage it remains there. At the beginning of his second paragraph, Hazlitt writes that Legitimacy is nothing other than 'the old doctrine of Divine Right, new vamped-up'. He then pauses to relish the word: ' "Fine word, Legitimate!" We wonder where our English politicians picked it up. Is it an echo from the tomb of the martyred monarch, Charles the First?' (HW vii. 260). The reader is invited to consider from where the echo is in fact picked up. It is from Edmund's first soliloquy in *King Lear*. Like so many strong Shakespearean quotations, it may be read in two ways. At one level, it makes 'English politicians' into Edmunds, thus reiterating the association with the destroyers of Gloucester. But Hazlitt read Edmund as a more sympathetic character than Regan and Goneril, for he does not have their hypocrisy: 'Their deliberate hypocrisy adds the last finishing to the odiousness of their characters. It is the absence of this detestable quality that is the only relief in the character of Edmund the Bastard, and that at times reconciles us to him. . . . His religious honesty in this respect is admirable. One speech of his is worth a million' (HW iv. 258–9; 'he is not a hypocrite to himself', Hazlitt adds in the *Letter to Gifford*, HW ix. 40). Edmund's opening speech, with its vigorous debunking of the hypocrisies implicit in his being excluded from inheritance because of 'illegitimacy', is just what Hazlitt has in mind. In saying 'Fine word, Legitimate!' he is adopting the role of the Edmund who anatomizes the *ancien régime*.

There are two further powerful Shakespearean quotations in 'What is the People?' Hazlitt argues that the tendency to absolutism is built into the system of monarchy: 'A King cannot attain absolute power, while the people remain perfectly free; yet what King would not attain absolute power? While any trace of liberty is left among a people, ambitious Princes will never be easy, never at peace, never of sound mind' (HW vii. 264). One does not have to go far to find a model for the ambitious ruler not resting until he has absolute power:

Till all distinctions of right and wrong, liberty and slavery, happiness and misery, are looked upon as matters of indifference, or as saucy, insolent pretensions,—are sunk and merged in their idle caprice and pampered self-will, they will still feel themselves 'cribbed, confined, and cabin'd in': but if they can once more set up the doctrine of Legitimacy, 'the right divine of Kings to govern wrong,' and set mankind at defiance with impunity, they will then be 'broad and casing as the general air, whole as the rock.' (ibid.)

Macbeth's restlessness on discovering that Fleance has escaped is invoked in order to imply that all kings are usurpers and tyrants in quest of absolute power, and that they will not be content until they have achieved this—even at the expense of killing a child, or of snuffing out all liberty.[2]

The other allusion relates interestingly to the reading of *The Tempest* which Hazlitt was contesting with Coleridge around the time he wrote 'What is the People?' (his contribution to the debate, we recall, was published, also in the *Yellow Dwarf*, in February 1818). He says that on waking from the dream of Legitimacy, 'you may say with Caliban, "Why, what a fool was I to take this drunken monster for a God!"' (HW vii. 263). Legitimacy is thus again seen as a form of usurpation, in that it is associated with Stephano. Hazlitt compounds his effect by removing 'monster' from Caliban and adding it to 'drunkard', the original epithet for Stephano. Once Caliban, who here stands for the people, has been freed from his slavery to Legitimacy, he may take possession of the isle that is rightly his.

The centrality of quotation to Hazlitt's dazzling style is demonstrable from the fact that quotation was used as a tool to attack him. The *Monthly Review* (1820, 93: 250–8) assaulted his *Political Essays* by means of a review that parodied their style, turning Shakespeare's language against Hazlitt. On a more personal note, when Leigh Hunt fell out with Hazlitt over the *Table Talk* essay 'On Paradox and Common-place', which attacked Shelley for harming the cause of reform through his fanaticism, he hit back with a Shakespearean allusion: 'There are more things in heaven and earth than are dreamt of even in your philosophy' (quoted, Howe 1949, p. 319). There could be no more telling stroke than the accusation that Hazlitt was *not being Hamlet*.

Both Thomas De Quincey and Thomas Noon Talfourd dwelt on the matter of quotation in their assessments of Hazlitt.[3] Their respective

---

[2] The other quotation in the passage—'the right divine of Kings to govern wrong'—is a tag from *The Dunciad* (iv. 188), much used in political polemic at this time.

[3] Modern Hazlitt scholars divide equally on the merits of his quotations. Wardle 1971 proffers only half a sentence on the subject; Albrecht 1965 merely states 'The

arguments deserve to be quoted at length. 'In general', writes Talfourd,

the force of his expostulation, or his reasoning, was diverted (unconsciously to himself) by figures and phantasies, by fine and quaint allusions, by quotations from his favourite authors, introduced with singular felicity, as respects the direct line of association, but tending, by their very beauty, to unnerve the mind of the reader, and substitute the sense of luxury for clear conviction, or noble anger. In some of his essays, where the reasoning is most cogent, every other sentence contains some exquisite passage from Shakspeare, or Fletcher, or Wordsworth, trailing after it a line of golden associations . . . till, in the recurring shock of pleasurable surprise, the main argument is forgotten.[4]

As an example, he takes Hazlitt's allusion—Talfourd uses the word— to a moment in *Clarissa* when the heroine is about to be ravished, arguing that it makes us think of the novel, not of the political waverers who are being compared to Clarissa. There is for Talfourd a pleasure in the recognition of a fine quotation and a further pleasure in being reminded of one's own favourite texts; certain quotations and allusions recover a full context, 'a line of golden associations'. It is argued that Hazlitt knows Shakespearean and other texts so well that he may allude to them 'unconsciously'.

Talfourd's criticism of the device is a subtle one. He does not argue that Hazlitt's quotations are inapposite, though occasionally they are; far from it, 'the *direct* line of association' is singularly felicitous. Talfourd's concern is rather that the 'shock of pleasurable surprise'[5] and the attractions of the earlier text back to which we are transported distract us from the argument in hand. But for Hazlitt all arguments, even political ones that are not directly literary, benefit from being brought into relation with the writings of the mighty dead who remain the ultimate authority for his beliefs. Hazlitt ascribes 'author-

integrity of Hazlitt's essays, it must be admitted, is sometimes marred by his use of quotations' (p. 168); McFarland 1987 is dismissive. Conversely, Bromwich 1983 is astute on the politics of the many quotations from Burke, and Kinnaird 1978 argues cogently that for Hazlitt quotation is bound up with emotional, even bodily, possession of works of genius; he quotes (p. 292) an extremely relevant sentence from *The Plain Speaker*: 'The excellence that we feel, we participate in as if it were our own—it becomes ours by transfusion of mind—it is instilled into our hearts—it mingles with our blood' (HW xii. 101).

[4] Talfourd 1848, ii. 161; repr., with minor alterations, from Talfourd 1836.

[5] An interestingly self-performative phrase that summons up the golden associations of Wordsworth's 'a gentle shock of mild surprize' ('There was a Boy').

ity' to the geniuses of the past, Shakespeare foremost among them, instead of to reason, external nature, government, the Church, or whatever—poets are the *acknowledged* legislators of his world. Talfourd believed that the constant play of earlier texts within the texture of Hazlitt's prose exposed a want of unifying, organizing imagination. He took this to be Hazlitt's principal weakness. Hazlitt, I think, would have replied that quotation constituted an act of sympathy with the immortals in the 'commonwealth of letters' which in his ideal republic would replace the aristocracy of rank.

De Quincey stated his opinion in a review of Talfourd. He had always been sceptical about the use of direct quotations; they 'express a mind not fully possessed by its subject', he had said when discussing the allusion to *Hamlet* in Wordsworth's 'Immortality Ode' (De Quincey 1889–90, v. 100–1). In his article on Talfourd's *Final Memorials of Charles Lamb* in the *North British Review* of November 1848, he assented to the remarks about the fractured, discontinuous nature of Hazlitt's mind, but intensified the criticism of his quotations, arguing that it was by no means a 'felicitous' fault.

For De Quincey, 'the habit of trite quotation' is a common vice; it would not be worth noticing but that Talfourd seems to 'countenance that paralytic "mouth-diarrhoea" (to borrow a phrase of Coleridge's) . . . which places the reader at the mercy of a man's tritest remembrances from his most school-boy reading'.[6] This criticism on the grounds of vulgarity is incidental; De Quincey's claim that in 1848 the habit of quotation 'has taken refuge among the most imbecile of authors' does not have any bearing on the sophisticated use of the habit by Hazlitt in his prime. But it leads into more general reflections. De Quincey contends that 'to express one's own thoughts by another man's words' is 'at war with sincerity, the foundation of all good writing'; further,

to throw one's own thoughts, matter and form, through alien organs so absolutely as to make another man one's interpreter for evil and good, is either to confess a singular laxity of thinking that can so flexibly adapt itself to any casual form of words, or else to confess that sort of carelessness about the expression which draws its real origins from a sense of indifference about the thing to be expressed. Utterly at war this distressing practice is with all simplicity and earnestness of writing . . .

[6] This, and subsequent quotations from the review, are from De Quincey 1889–90, v. 236–8. 'Mouth-diarrhoea' is rich, coming from Coleridge.

If De Quincey's long sentence is 'simplicity', one might legitimately crave the 'complexity' of Hazlitt's quotations, which so often help the reader to place an argument.

But is 'sincerity' necessarily 'the foundation of all good writing'? Does it not smack of being bound within the self, of that 'egotism' which Hazlitt saw as the dangerous limitation of Wordsworth and his followers? (De Quincey shared none of Hazlitt's reservations about the Lake poets; that is why the two critics are mighty opposites among English Romantic prose writers.) Hazlitt stressed again and again that throwing 'one's own thoughts, matter and form, through alien organs', the 'ventriloquism' that marked the truly sympathetic imagination, bespoke neither 'laxity' nor 'indifference' but that disinterestedness most to be desired in poet and critic alike. For Hazlitt, quotation is strong identification.

De Quincey's crowning criticism can therefore be turned into praise. Quotation is a form of stealing; those 'golden associations' make the reader think he is reading a fine book when in fact the author is taking credit for his forebears' eloquence. 'Meantime,' De Quincey concludes, 'the whole is a series of mosaics, a tessellation made up from borrowed fragments; and, first when the reader's attention is expressly directed upon the fact, he becomes aware that the nominal author has contributed nothing more to the book than a few passages of transition or brief clauses of connexion.' If, however, one takes the foundation of good writing to be not sincerity and individuality but responsiveness to the geniuses of the past, then quotation is not stealing from earlier writers but acknowledging their superior eloquence. What better activity for the critic than making 'connexions' between different works of genius, and between the mighty dead and the contemporary world?

De Quincey's phrase 'a tessellation made up from borrowed fragments' raises the issue of 'intertextuality'. For a post-structuralist like Roland Barthes all texts consist of quotations without quotation marks. But Hazlitt's texts are formed in part of quotations within quotation marks. They are not anonymous and untraceable; they name Hazlitt's admired forefathers. If self-sufficiency is impossible, fragmentariness inevitable, then at least the use of quotation enables readers to complete the text by connecting it with a beloved earlier text. I use words like 'admired' and 'beloved' because it seems to me that so open a form of 'intertextuality' as quotation implies willing and purposeful, not troubled or parasitic, dependence—dependence, furthermore, which affords release from the literary and political self-interest that mark the spirit of the later age.

Hazlitt was aware of criticism of his quotations, mentioning it in his replies to assaults on him by right-wing journalists. In the *Letter to Gifford*, for example, he writes 'There is one objection however which you make to me which is singular enough: viz. that I quote Shakespear. I can only answer, that "I would not change that vice for your best virtue" ' (HW ix. 43). Hazlitt stands by his practice, damning both Gifford and another of his assailants, *Blackwood's Magazine*'s 'Z', through wonderful quotations—Keats spoke of their 'feu de joie'—from *Lear*: 'I cry you mercy then: I took you for the Editor of the Quarterly Review!', ' "thou whoreson Z., thou unnecessary letter" ' (HW ix. 34, 3). He points out that Gifford, who is fond of quoting Greek, is hardly qualified to condemn him for quoting Shakespeare. That it is seen as a 'singular' objection suggests that Hazlitt felt it was perfectly natural and unexceptionable to use Shakespeare's words. It was common during this period to quote from Shakespeare in conversation and informal writings, such as letters; in 'On Familiar Style', Hazlitt argues that the proper style for the familiar essay is the conversational idiom: Shakespearean quotation is therefore wholly appropriate in his essays and reviews.[7] As always when Hazlitt crosses swords with Gifford, there is a political twist to the argument: to write in a high style and to quote Greek was to mark oneself off as a member of the cultural aristocracy, whereas to write in a 'familiar' style and to quote Shakespeare was to address the people.

De Quincey's argument assumes that Hazlitt's quotations are 'casual', that 'it argues a state of indolent ease inconsistent with the pressure and coercion of strong fermenting thoughts before we can be at leisure for idle or chance quotations'. But in the *Table Talk* essay 'On Familiar Style' Hazlitt himself rejects 'loose, unconnected, *slipshod* allusions' (HW viii. 242). Very few of his quotations are 'idle

---

[7] Curiously, Hazlitt's own surviving letters are less packed with Shakespearean quotations than Keats's or Byron's. They are, however, generally more concerned with business matters than the discussion of critical principles or methods of writing; Hazlitt's thinking in these areas was done in *conversation*. Significantly, Shakespearean quotation is more frequent in the letters to Patmore about Sarah Walker, which form the basis of *Liber Amoris*, as if Hazlitt is trying to mediate painful experience through the plays. The doomed romance is frequently referred to *Othello*, telling use is made of Lear's 'That way madness lies', and part one of *Liber Amoris* itself ends with 'A Proposal of Love' in the language of Troilus.

or chance'; their effectiveness often lies in the carefulness with which
they are chosen, in—to borrow from Benjamin on Kraus—the way
that they appear 'congruously in the structure of a new text'. What
could be more apposite in a discussion of how short-lived the fame of
the Shakespeare Gallery painters has been than passages on transience and death from *Macbeth* and *Romeo*?[8]

Hazlitt's most revealing comment on the desirability, the necessity
even, of quoting Shakespeare occurs in his tenth conversation with
Northcote. The remark is put into Northcote's mouth, but Hazlitt is
sympathetic to it; it may even be his own idea, given to Northcote in
retrospect to instil it with extra authority. Hazlitt mentions that 'a
translation of a French work' had very effectively 'applied to those
who adhered to Buonaparte in his misfortunes' Enobarbus's lines on
retaining allegiance to his 'fallen lord' Antony (HW xi. 247). It can
hardly be coincidental that in his *Life of Napoleon*, itself largely translated from various French works, he quotes the line from *Antony and
Cleopatra* in exactly this context (HW xv. 209). Northcote replies that,
being Shakespeare's lines, they are sure to come in 'finely':

What a power there always is in any *bit* brought in from him or Milton among
other things! How it shines like a jewel! I think Milton reads best in this way;
he is too fine for a continuance. Don't you think Shakspeare and the writers
of that day had a prodigious advantage in using phrases and combinations of
style, which could not be admitted now that the language is reduced to a more
precise and uniform standard, but which yet have a peculiar force and felicity
when they can be justified by the privilege of age? (HW xi. 247)

The idea that Milton 'reads best' when appropriated phrase by
phrase into contemporary works does a lot to quell the criticism that
the process somehow performs a disservice to the earlier author. To
pick up the metaphor, his light is so bright that continuous exposure
to it is damaging; Northcote prefers the single piercing image shining
from an alien context.

But it is the second idea that is pure Hazlitt. Shakespeare's
'phrases and combinations of style' are an ideal, but they cannot be
'admitted' in original writing now that the language is fixed. Quotation offers a solution to this problem because Shakespearean phrases
are 'privileged'—they retain their power despite being archaic. Thus,
Hazlitt attacks Coleridge's play *Remorse* for its neo-Shakespearean
blank verse, but in reviewing *The Statesman's Manual* protests that

[8] See HW iv. 149–50.

Coleridge need not apologize for quoting Shakespeare (HW xviii. 465; xvi. 108). Hazlitt would distinguish between strong quotation and weak imitation; quotation is necessary because it legitimizes a relationship with the language of an earlier, superior age, and enables the repossession of Shakespeare for one's own self and society. This form of 'privilege' and 'legitimacy', being open to all who can read, may serve to undo the privilege and legitimacy of arbitrary power.

Nowhere does Hazlitt undertake this repossession more fully than in *The Spirit of the Age*, published early in 1825 as an anonymous octavo volume with the epigraph 'To know another well were to know one's self' (HW xi. 2). Hazlitt, the former painter, subtitles his collection 'Contemporary Portraits': he draws his age by means of pen-portraits. One of the most telling brush-strokes is the Shakespearean parallel. By making contemporary figures into Shakespearean characters, producing verbal caricatures as incisive as, though far more generous than, Gillray's visual ones, Hazlitt fulfils his own role as Hamlet. 'To know a man well, were to know himself': the quotation, now corrected, is attributed to Hamlet (V. ii. 139) on the title-page of the second edition, published some months later, as if Hazlitt wishes to force home the point.

The first portrait is of Jeremy Bentham. Hazlitt concludes that Bentham, with his reduction of everything to Utility, is too parochial, too narrow; he 'has not "looked enough abroad into universality"' (HW xi. 16). The quotation is from Bacon—Shakespeare is never the exclusive point of reference—but for Hazlitt Shakespeare and universality were almost interchangeable terms, and so it is that one of the factors leading to this conclusion is that Bentham 'has no great fondness for poetry, and can hardly extract a moral out of Shakespeare' (ibid.). 'Extract a moral' is a sharp thrust indeed: even compilers of 'Select Beauties' like William Dodd and Mrs Elizabeth Griffith had been able to *extract* morals out of Shakespeare back in the mid-eighteenth century. A contrast to Bentham is provided by the parliamentary reformer Sir Francis Burdett, who is portrayed later in the collection: he is praised as one of the best speakers in the House because he quotes Shakespeare 'often' and 'with extreme aptness and felicity' (HW xi. 140).

While the characterization of Bentham depends partly on the subject's overt relationship with Shakespeare, that of Godwin employs a subtler method. Hazlitt makes a case for Godwin as a thinker and writer who has undergone typically harsh treatment at the hands of the fickle spirit of an age which had him blazing in the height of reputation one moment, forgotten the next: 'His bark, after being tossed in the revolutionary tempest, now raised to heaven by all the fury of popular breath, now almost dashed in pieces, and buried in the quicksands of ignorance' (HW xi. 16). Quotation is woven into the texture of this passage, but if it is recalled that the *Macbeth* witches' 'tempest-toss'd' is a presence behind Coleridge's 'Ancient Mariner' (see Bate 1986, pp. 59–61), it is possible to unravel the allusion: Godwin is both the Mariner and the Master of the *Tiger*, who is himself identified with Macbeth. He is the man of destiny who will be cast up and then dashed down by the conditions of the age. The 'tempest' also brings Prospero into play. Thus, in the following paragraph a quotation from Pope proves insufficient, a reference to *The Tempest* thoroughly resounding: 'Was it for this, that Mr Godwin himself sat with arms folded, and, "like Cato, gave his little senate laws?" Or rather, like another Prospero, uttered syllables that with their enchanted breath were to change the world, and might almost stop the stars in their courses?' (HW xi. 18). Here, Godwin is a magician conjuring up the spirit of *Political Justice* which is then in the era of reaction buried deeper than did ever plummet sound.

From Godwin Hazlitt proceeds to Coleridge. The essay opens, 'The present is an age of talkers, and not of doers': the subtext of this must read something like 'the present is an age of Hamlets, Coleridge foremost among them'. A network of associations is quickly established. 'Mr Coleridge has "a mind reflecting ages past"; his voice is like the echo of the congregated roar of the "dark rearward and abyss" of thought' (HW xi. 29). The first quotation is from the poem on Shakespeare, prefixed to the Second Folio, that Coleridge admired and, according to Collier, attributed to Milton; the second is adapted from *The Tempest* (I. ii. 50), carrying with it the implication that Coleridge's voice is an echo of Prospero's.

There are a dozen Shakespearean quotations in the essay on Coleridge, most frequently from *Hamlet* and *The Tempest*; half of them are juxtaposed with Miltonic ones. The appropriations of Hamlet and Prospero, the juxtaposition of the twin presiders over the English poetic pantheon: Hazlitt has caught some essentials of Coleridge. The most wonderful passage in the portrait is a single sentence which lasts for two pages describing, and in so doing enacting, the way in which Coleridge's mind darts from subject to subject. At last we run out of breath, the sentence ends, and of Coleridge Hazlitt can only say,

adapting Hamlet, 'Alas! "Frailty, thy name is *Genius!*" ' (HW xi. 34).
Hazlitt does not damn Coleridge with faint praise. Instead, through
evoking Hamlet's chastisement of Gertrude, but with 'woman'
changed to 'Genius', he redeems him with strong criticism. It is a
superb example of quotation's capacity to 'both save and chastise'.

After this *tour de force* one would expect the following essay, on the
Revd Mr Irving, to be an anticlimax. But it is not, for, as Hazlitt
remarks elsewhere, Irving is a Kean among clerics, a man who has
scoured the works of Shakespeare for quotations he can appropriate
(HW xx. 114). So it is that he can 'spout Shakspeare (and that not in
a sneaking under-tone, but at the top of his voice, and with the full
breadth of his chest) from a Calvinistic pulpit' (HW xi. 38–9). He is
brought alive as another latter-day Coriolanus: 'It was rare sport to
see him, "like an eagle in a dovecote, flutter the Volscians in Corioli" '
(HW xi. 41). Then he is compared to a rival preacher, Dr Chalmers.
But the latter proves a worthy match:

'By his so potent art,' the art of laying down problematical premises, and
drawing from them still more doubtful, but not impossible, conclusions, 'he
could bedim the noonday sun, betwixt the green sea and the azure vault set
roaring war,' and almost compel the stars in their courses to testify to his
opinions. (HW xi. 46)

The age was large enough for Coriolanus and Prospero to stall
together in the pulpit.

These are merely a handful of the most striking effects of characterization through quotation in the first few essays of *The Spirit of the Age*.
Every person portrayed in the collection has his relationship with
Shakespeare. Often there is merely a passing identification: Byron is
Prince Hal, a 'chartered libertine'; Crabbe, like Falstaff, turns
'diseases to commodities', and stands in relation to the poetry of the
age as Audrey does to the pastoral of *As You Like It* (HW xi. 76,
164–5). But sometimes there is an extended comparison, as between
Scott and Shakespeare. This becomes a version of the celebrated
distinction between imagination and fancy, Scott being credited with
the latter but not with Shakespeare's imagination, a quality defined
through quotation of Theseus' 'the poet's eye' (HW xi. 60); elsewhere, however, Hazlitt makes Scott into a man of full imagination
by calling him 'the Scottish Prospero, old Sir Walter' (HW xix. 85).

The only figure for whom Hazlitt feels utter scorn is his old enemy
William Gifford, reactionary editor of the *Quarterly*. His portrait is

stripped of all Shakespearean lustre save a curse from *Lear*, a comparison with Stephano, that dog of *The Tempest*, and a quotation from *Romeo and Juliet* that makes him into 'an envious worm' biting the sweet bud of Keats's poetry. Where most of the Shakespearean quotations in *The Spirit of the Age* give a sense of the flawed greatness of the contemporary figure portrayed, these wholly diminish Gifford. The damnation of Gifford by means of Shakespearean quotation is a device that Hazlitt had already used extensively in the 1819 *Letter*. There, he had been determined to show that Gifford was not in tune with Shakespeare: 'You, Sir, have no sympathy in common with Hamlet; nothing to make him ever "present to your mind's eye" ' (HW ix. 42). Hazlitt has everything that Gifford has not: 'sympathy' in its full philosophical sense, and sympathy with Hamlet in particular. As the quotation suggests, Shakespeare is a ghost of old Hamlet, a fatherly presence in Hazlitt's imagination. And Hazlitt, as the epigraph to *The Spirit of the Age* proclaims and the analysis in *Characters of Shakespear's Plays* reveals, identifies himself with Hamlet above all others.

That act of identification is a going-out from the self which is to be desired both morally and politically—as has been seen, sympathy is the basis not only of Hazlitt's philosophical principles but also of his radical politics—but the fact that it is an identification with the aristocratic mind of Hamlet, so supreme in thought and feeling yet so ineffectual in action and government, suggests that in the end Hazlitt failed to overcome the spirit of the age which he so ably analysed. That spirit has become known as Romanticism and is associated with the retreat from public life, the movement inward, and the privileging of the individual consciousness. Hazlitt devotes much space in his *Political Essays* to the apostasy of Southey and Coleridge. He never became apostate himself, and yet his Hamlet-mind came to outweigh his concern for the body politic. His actual political influence proved minimal. *A View of the English Stage* raised the possibility of politicizing the theatre, *Characters of Shakespear's Plays* of politicizing literary criticism, but neither the theatre nor criticism developed along radical lines. *Characters* was probably the most widely read book on Shakespeare for the rest of the nineteenth century, but it was usually depoliticized.

There are some notable exceptions: I take the book's political aspect to be a formative influence on the analysis of *Coriolanus* in Charlotte Brontë's *Shirley*: ' "you must not be proud to your work-people; you must not neglect chances of soothing them, and you must not be of an inflexible nature, uttering a request as austerely as if it were a command." "That is the moral you tack to the play." ' (*Shirley*, 1849, ch. 6). Generally, however, Victorian readers made Hazlitt into a character critic, whereas in his own time he was acknowledged as a political critic. He is now thought of in relation to the psychological criticism of Shakespearean character initiated by Richardson and Morgann, consummated by Bradley, and reconstituted by contemporary Freudian readings. But, in 1817, he was thought of as a Jacobinical critic rather than a psychological one.

Hazlitt was caught between *Coriolanus* and the Goethe–Coleridge version of Hamlet. It was Hamlet who won: sensitivity to feeling, the anguish of self-consciousness, and the isolation of soliloquy became dominant values among nineteenth-century intellectuals. Freud would have been the first to admit that the Romantic Hamlet helped him to invent psychoanalysis: 'Freud is a kind of codifier or abstractor of William Shakespeare. . . . it is Shakespeare who gives us the map of the mind. It is Shakespeare who invents Freudian psychology. Freud finds ways of translating it into a supposedly analytic vocabulary.'[9] But if Freud was one of the nineteenth century's obsessive readers and quoters of Shakespeare, Marx was another. According to his daughter Eleanor, Shakespeare 'was the Bible of our house, seldom out of our hands or mouths. By the time I was six I knew scene upon scene of Shakespeare by heart.' Marx did not, however, seem to have been especially interested in *Coriolanus*— the two Shakespearean characters about whom he wrote most extensively were, as might be expected of the author of *Capital*, Shylock and Timon.[10] If Marx had grappled with Hazlitt's essay on *Coriolanus*, the course of Shakespearean appropriation might have been very different.

[9] Harold Bloom, in Salusinszky 1987, p. 55. Where Bloom says 'William Shakespeare', I would say 'Romantic Shakespeare'.

[10] See Prawer 1976, p. 386 for the Eleanor Marx quotation, ch. 3. for Karl Marx on Shylock and Timon.

Epilogue

GERMAINE GREER is optimistic about England: 'As long as Shakespeare remains central to English cultural life, it will retain the values which make it unique in the world, namely tolerance, pluralism, the talent for viable compromise, and a profound commitment to that most wasteful form of social organization, democracy' (Greer 1986, p. 125). Shakespeare would perhaps be surprised to know that he stood for such values. One could just as well argue that his plays— *Coriolanus*, for instance—stand for another set of values, namely intolerance, singularity, refusal to compromise, and a profound contempt for democracy. Hazlitt's insight that *Coriolanus* contains within itself the politics of both Burke and Paine is fundamental. That a work of art may simultaneously appear to endorse conflicting value-schemes is a strong indicator of its own value. This provides as good an answer as any to the hoary old problem of the grounds for value-judgement in art: faced with the question 'Why is a Shakespeare play more valuable than a Mills and Boon novel?', as good an answer as any is that a Mills and Boon novel is not likely to contain within itself the politics of both Burke and Paine.

Shakespeare's plays have a profound commitment to and a profound contempt for both democracy and autocracy. Accordingly, the one term in the quotation from Greer which has an irresistible force is 'pluralism'. Shakespeare is plural because his plays have a pervasive political doubleness: Gillray turned him against both Pitt and Fox; the tragedies were accommodated on stage by both the patrician Kemble and the radical Kean; *Characters of Shakespear's Plays* and Drake's *Shakspeare and his Times* were published in the same year; the next year, Thomas Bowdler published the ten volumes of his complete *Family Shakespeare*, that ultimate moral, and hence political, policing of Shakespeare's text; but, the year after that, the *Black Dwarf* parodist enlisted *Macbeth* in the fight against Castlereagh's post-Peterloo gagging acts.

This plurality springs from that capaciousness which Hazlitt called 'sympathy'. Hazlitt shared both the eighteenth-century belief that all

criticism is ethical and the modern belief that all criticism is political;
his 'sympathy' is a philosophical and moral theory that furnishes him
with both a literary critical method and a political standpoint. One of
the paradoxes of literary history is that in its own time Hazlitt's
notion of Shakespearean sympathy was perceived as radical and even
seditious, whereas in the present critical climate it is perceived as
complacent and outmoded to admire the plays for their multiplicity of
viewpoints and their sensitivity towards every human dilemma. This
furnishes another instance of Shakespearean doubleness: yesterday's
radical interpretation is today's conservative one.

Perhaps where today's rearguard of liberal humanist critics have
become vulnerable is in giving the impression that Shakespeare can
somehow transcend the particularities of the historical moment—the
moment both of production and of interpretation. Hazlitt would not
have acknowledged the possibility of such a transcendence; his criticism is always charged with the energies of his own contentious age.
He would have understood the thesis of this book, namely that if
'political' is understood in its broad sense—as referring to relations
within the body politic, not merely to party politics—then the valuation and appropriation of Shakespeare is always political. The
Romantic 'privatization' of Shakespeare, the valuation of *Hamlet*
above *Coriolanus*: these are political manœuvres. *King John* was central
to the canon of Shakespeare's plays between 1791 and 1820: one
recalls Jane Austen wishing to see it instead of *Hamlet*. Why is it no
longer thought of as a central play? Presumably because it does not
have the richness of language and characterization that we now take
to be the central Shakespearean qualities. But it is political to value
these things more than, say, the anatomy of kingship that is offered
by *King John*.[1]

There will always be those who resist the view that Shakespeare's
texts are constituted by a series of historical moments, by their own
afterlife of performance and interpretation. Shakespeare's texts, it
will be argued, belong to Shakespeare and mean what he intended
them to mean, and by an effort of historical scholarship we may

---

[1] I would say that the turning-point in the fortunes of *King John* came with J. R.
Planché's Covent Garden production of 1823-4, which was marked by extreme
antiquarianism. According to the playbill, 'The whole of the Dresses and Decorations
[were] executed from indisputable Authorities, such as Monumental Effigies, Seals,
Illuminated MSS., etc.'. This seems to be an attempt to put Shakespeare safely back
in the past (cf. Nathan Drake's book), thus effectively depoliticizing him. Antiquarianism became the hallmark of subsequent productions of *King John*.

recover that meaning and we will then have the 'truth' of the matter. When Nigel Lawson, as Mrs Thatcher's Chancellor of the Exchequer, put on record his opinion that Shakespeare was a Conservative, he was probably remembering a piece of historical scholarship of this sort which was influential in his youth, E. M. W. Tillyard's *The Elizabethan World-Picture*.[2] Contemporary scholars of a left-wing persuasion reply that Tillyard's book reveals more about the need to assert an 'ordered' world-picture in the early 1940s than it does about the state of the world (one gets the impression that for Tillyard England was the world) in the late sixteenth century. The 'new historicism' currently fashionable argues that the construction of a hierarchical world-picture during the Elizabethan age was authority's way of underwriting its own power, but that any such act of inscription contains within itself the seeds of its own subversion—for Stephen Greenblatt, the image of authority in the Renaissance 'involves as its positive condition the constant production of its own radical subversion and the powerful containment of that subversion' (Dollimore and Sinfield 1985, p. 30). This position may reveal more about the need for contemporary academics to assert a 'subversive' world-picture in the age of Reagan and Thatcher than it does about England, Europe and the New World (the perspective is wider than Tillyard's) in the Renaissance. As historiography since Collingwood has told us, historical scholarship can never be disinterested: 'the historian himself, together with the here-and-now which forms the total body of evidence available to him, is a part of the process he is studying, has his own place in that process, and can see it only from the point of view which at this present moment he occupies within it'; 'We may say, then, that in history—as in the human sciences in general—every representation of the past has specifiable ideological implications' (Collingwood 1946, p. 248; White 1978, p. 69).

The fact that the past can only be recovered in the light of the present is not the sole problem facing anyone who wishes to discover the 'truth' of Shakespeare's politics. In the eighteenth century Shakespeare's religion was a more controversial issue than his politics. Malone printed in his 1790 edition of the plays John Shakespeare's 'Spiritual Testament', a Catholic profession of faith which had supposedly been discovered in 1757 behind the rafters of the 'birthplace'

---

[2] See *Guardian*, 5 Sept. 1983. Lawson's central text is also Tillyard's: 'Take but degree away . . .'. When asked for another example, he cited *Coriolanus* as being 'written from a Tory point of view'.

house in Henley Street; although Malone, after initially accepting the document's authenticity, later denounced it as a fabrication, the Testament lent support to the claim that Shakespeare came from a Catholic family. But even if we went further and supposed that Shakespeare was himself a Catholic, that would not make his plays crypto-Catholic. So too, supposing we were to discover an authentic 'William Shakespeare's Political Testament', we would be no wiser as to the politics of the plays. Drama is not propaganda, even though it may be used for propagandistic purposes. The well-known events surrounding *Richard II* and the Essex plot are decisive in this respect: Shakespeare's company was paid by the Essex faction to perform *Richard II* the night before the rebellion, as if to prepare the public for an act of deposition; the players were examined during the trial of the rebels, but cleared of any complicity in the conspiracy. Sir Gilly Meyrick was executed for, among other things, procuring the performance of *Richard II*, but the dramatist and players were not held responsible. The Lord Chief Justice and Chief Justice of Common Pleas ruled, in effect, that the politics of usurpation were not contained within the play text, but had been imposed upon it. Shakespeare was not implicated in the first recorded political appropriation of his work.

It is also worth noting that it was the players who were examined on this occasion. The dramatist was not called. That an Elizabethan play text is collaborative and that it is given to the public by a group of actors rather than an individual writer are further reasons for contesting the view that Shakespeare's texts belong to Shakespeare. Furthermore, recent scholarship (pre-eminently Taylor and Warren 1983) has called into question the stability of Shakespeare's texts, the very notion of his plays having a single identity. Whether it was revised in the playhouse or by the hand of the author, haphazardly or systematically, *King Lear* exists in (at least) two distinct versions. The play admired by Hazlitt as the greatest product of Shakespeare's genius in fact seems to have been the product of eighteenth-century editors conflating the two texts.

We are on a very slippery slope here. All plays are subject to playhouse revision during the course of rehearsal and performance; if a dramatist respects his actors, he will trust them to discover what does not work on stage and to suggest improvements. So it is that critics who wish to purge Shakespeare's text, to exonerate the dramatist from the indecorums it contains, can make the players into scapegoats, as Coleridge did when, embarrassed by the 'lowness' of the porter scene in *Macbeth*, he dismissed it as an interpolation for the benefit of the 'mob'. But Coleridge's notion of authorship was a Romantic one whereby the text evolves in the mind of the solitary creative genius. Elizabethan playhouse practice was very different:

the creation of a play was a collaborative process, with the author by no means at the center of the collaboration. The company commissioned the play, usually stipulated the subject, often provided the plot, often parcelled it out, scene by scene, to several playwrights. The text thus produced was a working model, which the company then revised as seemed appropriate. The author had little or no say in these revisions: the text belonged to the company, and the authority represented by the text . . . is that of the company, the owners, not that of the playwright, the author. (Orgel 1981, p. 3)

An historically informed view of the circumstances in which Shakespeare's plays were originally produced must accept the 'authority' of revisions undertaken by the actors. In all probability, the company sometimes worked on the plays when Shakespeare was not present in the playhouse. From accepting playhouse revisions undertaken while Shakespeare was away in Stratford, it is a short step to accepting those undertaken after he was dead. The progression from the Q-F revision to the Q/F-Tate revision would then be of degree, not of kind.

Each revision is a preparation for performance of a script that is only completed in performance; there is no such thing as a unitary 'ideal' text because in freeing a play from playhouse 'contamination' one is destroying its peculiar identity as a play, for a play, unless it folds after one night and is never revived, is intrinsically multiple and constantly open to revision and re-creation. It follows that 'Shakespeare' is separated out from William Shakespeare. 'Shakespeare' becomes a history of stagings—each of them different from every other in particulars of text, business, and interpretation—and of editions and of readings and of appropriations in the culture at large.

If all interpretations are appropriations, then a special value should be attached to those that acknowledge themselves as such. Bertolt Brecht's 'Study of the First Scene of Shakespeare's *Coriolanus*' is a strong analysis because it concerns itself with a self-consciously appropriative production. 'Can we amend Shakespeare?' asks one of the actors; 'I think we can amend Shakespeare if we can amend him', replies Brecht. The analysis reaches a number of conclusions related to the proposition that 'the position of the oppressed classes can be strengthened by the threat of war and weakened by its outbreak'. Another actor asks, 'Do you think that all this and the rest of it can be read in the play?'; 'Read in it and read into it', says Brecht, nicely eliding the *reading in* of interpretation and the *reading into* of appropriation (Brecht 1964, pp. 259, 264).

Few would argue with the proposition that theatrical productions are appropriative, but traditional textual scholarship would deny that an edition is an appropriation. It would claim that printing-house errors can be detected and a text that is true to the author's intentions reconstructed. The problems inherent in this position are manifold (see McGann 1983*a*), but in the case of Shakespeare we do not even have to address them: since Shakespeare did not authorize publication of his plays, if we are to be true to his intentions there can be no 'authoritative' published text. For the strict intentionalist, all printed texts of Shakespeare's plays must be 'stolne, and surreptitious copies'. Because he was shareholder, actor, and house dramatist in his company, Shakespeare had more say in the production of his plays than most of his contemporaries did of theirs, but he was not a Jonson, overseeing a published text which laid claim to an authority that the acting versions lacked. There is obviously value in reconstructing Shakespeare's working copy, though such a reconstruction must recognize that it is dealing not in a stable text but in raw material that is to be worked upon in the theatre—which is to say, material that is designed to be appropriated. Jonathan Goldberg provocatively articulates a possible consequence of the instability of Shakespeare's text: 'The historical construction of Shakespeare is not a statement about the intrinsic value of the Shakespearean text. It doesn't even identify a Shakespearean text; Shakespeare may epitomize English literature, yet no two editions of Shakespeare are identical. There is no Shakespeare, no single Shakespeare, that is, but only a divided kingdom' (Goldberg 1986, p. 214).

It is beginning to sound as if we can say anything we want, as if 'Shakespeare' exists only in the mind of the appropriator. Many people would want to resist the pull towards the deconstructionist position that all texts are open to an infinite number of interpretations, no one of which has more 'authority' than any other. Most of us feel instinctively that if an author has gone to the trouble of writing something he or she should be allowed some say in the interpretation of it. Coleridge has a revealing phrase in his note on the *Macbeth* porter's soliloquy: he conjectures that it was written 'by some other hand, perhaps with Shakespeare's consent' (Coleridge 1960, i. 67). Many readers set great store by the idea of authorial 'consent'. A 'true' revision or interpretation, it might be said, is one to which Shakespeare would 'consent', which is true to the 'spirit' of the 'original'—one could imagine Shakespeare giving his posthumous assent to the Kean–Hazlitt revision of Shylock or, more locally, Theobald's alteration of F's 'and a Table of greene fields' to 'and a' babbled of green fields' (*Henry V*, II. iii. 17). The rub lies in 'one could imagine': opinions about what Shakespeare would or would not consent to are circumscribed by the opiner's preconceptions about Shakespeare. Coleridge's note about the porter's speech goes on to complain about the absence from it of 'the ever-present being of Shakespeare'. The oxymoron of an absent presence conceals a contradiction in Coleridge's position: if one is to argue that Shakespeare is 'ever-present' and 'universal', that he is all things, then no reading can be excluded, no policing of the text is admissible.

Is there, then, a middle ground between an untenable deference to authorial 'consent' ('authority') and an anarchy of appropriation? If we cannot ascribe the 'meaning' of Shakespeare to William Shakespeare, do we have to go to the opposite extreme and say that the text is a mere cipher given meaning by each actor, reader, and alluder? Of course we do all impose our own predilections on Shakespeare and make the plays mean what we want them to mean. It is not really surprising that a contributor to the *Gentleman's Magazine* during the wars against France should conclude that Shakespeare was a true John Bull. But this does not always happen, for sometimes the plays will unsettle instead of confirm. Hazlitt's reading of *Coriolanus* is again exemplary: if interpreters merely imposed their own ideologies and dispositions on the text, Hazlitt would have developed a radicalized reading like Brecht's. That he does not suggests that a series of reciprocal relationships may be at work in the encounter between interpreter and multivalent ('classic') text. The interpreter brings his ideals and his ideologies to the text; this is what makes him an appropriator. His ideologies may interrogate the text in such a way as to make it yield up new meanings (Hazlitt's readings of Shylock and Henry V, or Brecht's of *Coriolanus* are strong examples) which have hitherto existed as unrealized potential within the text. But alternatively, or simultaneously, the text may interrogate the interpreter in such a way as to make him see the limitations of his own positions. If

I may be allowed to appropriate Geoffrey Hartman's appropriation of *Hamlet*,

> INTERPRETER. *Who's there?*
> BOOK. *Nay, answer me; stand, and unfold yourself.*

(Hartman 1975, p. 19)

The strong reader—whether actor, critic, director, artist, political polemicist, or whatever—expands the range of signification within the text; the strong text expands the horizon of the reader. We make the classic our own, bring it into our world; but we also give ourselves up to it, enter into its world. Without this reciprocity, appropriation will become misappropriation.

New meanings evolve from the text, but even as it is appropriated the text retains a certain constancy. Jonathan Miller's biological metaphor is helpful: 'In the phylogenetic history of an evolving organism it is always possible to recognize the existence of a morphological prototype and while this may undergo extensive transformation, with the unexpected enlargement of one part accompanied by a proportional shrinkage of another, the structural relationships are preserved so that it is easy to recognize the underlying affinity of many different examples.' Shakespeare may undergo 'changes that are tantamount to anamorphic distortions', yet 'something equivalent to topological propriety is preserved from one instance to the next' (Miller 1986, p. 35).

Shakespeare's 'classic' status is a function of both his infinite appropriability—he speaks to all occasions and all predilections—and his occasional intractability. You cannot always make him say what you want him to say; he can sometimes make you say something you don't like saying. He is both familiar and strange, both present and past, both of us and not of us. To say this is to modify but also to reiterate, if in a less reverential tone of voice, Matthew Arnold's response to Shakespeare: 'Others abide our question. Thou art free.' Everyone takes possession of Shakespeare, yet he remains elusive, refuses to yield himself up. 'We ask and ask: Thou smilest and art still, | Out-topping knowledge', Arnold continues his sonnet, suggesting that there is something Mona Lisa-like about Shakespeare. In Thomas Hardy's tercentenary poem, Shakespeare has been read for three hundred years but 'Still shalt remain at heart unread eternally'. The Shakespearean text is what Roland Barthes would call 'pensive':

36. Anonymous caricature of King George III as Prospero (1798)

37. Isaac Cruikshank, *The Tempest* as a 'prophecy' of contemporary politics (1795)

"— off, off, ye lendings."

38. James Gillray, Citizen Stanhope as Lear and the Fool (1794)

Ordains the REVOLUTIONS of the times!

A thing of no bowels———
——— from the crown to the toe, topfull
Of direst cruelty.—His Realm a slaughter-house—
The swords of soldiers are his teeth——
Iron for NAPLES, hid with English *gilt*.

SHAKSPEARE.

THE END.

Printed by W. Hone, Ludgate Hill, London.

39. George Cruikshank, Spenser's Iron Man and the art of political quotation—Tailpiece to *The Right Divine of Kings to Govern Wrong!* (1821)

replete with meaning, it still keeps some ultimate meaning in reserve. 'At its discreet urging, we want to ask the classic text: *What are you thinking about?* but the text, wilier than all those who try to escape by answering *about nothing*, does not reply, giving meaning its last closure: suspension' (Barthes 1974, p. 217).

Hans-Georg Gadamer's propositions about the nature of 'the classic' in *Truth and Method* accordingly seem to me to tell only half of the story. The following pronouncements do ample justice to Shakespeare's historical presence in ages after his own, but fail to speak of *difference*, of the classic's inscrutability: 'What we call "classical" is something retrieved from the vicissitudes of changing time and its changing taste'; the classical 'says something to the present as if it were said specially to it'; 'What we call "classical" does not first require the overcoming of historical distance, for in its own constant communication it does overcome it. The classical, then, is certainly "timeless", but this timelessness is a mode of historical being'; 'the work belongs to our world'; 'This is just what the word "classical" means, that the duration of the power of a work to speak directly is fundamentally unlimited' (Gadamer 1975, pp. 256–8). The relationship with the classic proposed here is altogether too comfortable; what is omitted is a sense of how the classic may speak to the present in such a way as to perplex or disturb it. Paradoxically, the endurance of the classic tells us something about temporality: the permanence of its validity is dependent on its capacity not only to speak to a future age as if it were written prophetically, specifically for that age, but also to reveal the impermanence of the ideologies (what Hazlitt would call the 'spirit') of every age and every individual. The really challenging moments in interpretation occur when ideology runs aground—when *Coriolanus* will not yield to Hazlitt's liberal politics, when *King Lear* will not submit to Dr Johnson's desire for poetic justice (with the result that Johnson submits to Tate's morally and politically comfortable revision).

I think again of that sense in which Hazlitt does *not* appropriate *King Lear*, and I am in wholehearted agreement with the argument of Harriett Hawkins's iconoclastic book, *The Devil's Party: Critical Counter-Interpretations of Shakespearian Drama*:

Although one certainly can see the point of Frank Kermode's eloquent arguments that the survival of a masterpiece like *King Lear* may finally depend on its malleability, its inclusiveness, its capacity to accommodate successive, and diametrically opposite, interpretations, it could, conversely, be argued that the inclusiveness of Shakespeare's plays works both ways, and that the status and survival of *King Lear* as an independent and primary source of wisdom and insight into the ways of our world (as opposed to an eminently pliable subject for successive critical commentaries on and theatrical adaptations of it) may well depend on its exceptions, its resistance, its ability to challenge and ultimately refute, and thus outlive, by defying and denying, *all* the one-sided interpretations that have been, and may yet be, imposed upon it.[3] (Hawkins 1985, p. 10)

I would only quarrel with this in so far as it comes close to implying that 'wisdom and insight' are timeless and that 'the ways of our world' are unchanging. Here, I would recall Gadamer's remark that the 'timelessness' of the classic is 'a mode of historical being'. Shakespeare transcends his own particular history through his capacity to live in subsequent history, but at no time is he outside history. Once we are aware of the history of his influence, we can no longer contain him within his own world or believe in his unmediated presence in our own. Nor can we speak naïvely of him reflecting the assumptions of his readers, for he is capable of both shaping and modifying those assumptions.

I am conscious that this book has itself been an act of mediation: mediation between Shakespeare's life in 1590 and his life in 1990 through his life in 1790; mediation between his life on the stage, on the page, and in an age more generally; mediation between coercion of Shakespeare and submissiveness to him, notably in Hazlitt's way of sometimes taking strong feelings from him while at other times carefully feeling into him; mediation between a criticism that is politicized and a criticism that is sceptical of dogma. So perhaps it would be appropriate to end by quoting a man in the middle, Thomas Love Peacock's Mr Jenkison, 'one who from equal measures can always produce arguments on both sides of a question, with so much nicety and exactness, as to keep the said question eternally pending'.[4] Of the 'truth' of Shakespeare, one may say with Jenkison that everyone who has known him 'sees his own truth. Truth is that which a man *troweth* [believes]. Where there is no man there is no truth. Thus

---

[3] I do not think that Kermode would dissent from this: as he writes in *Forms of Attention*, 'however a particular epoch or a particular community may define a proper mode of attention or a licit area of interest, there will always be something else and something different to say' about a classic text (Kermode 1985, p. 62; *Hamlet* is the exemplar here).

[4] *Headlong Hall* (1816), ch. 1.

the truth of one is not the truth of another.'[5] His 'truth' cannot be defined or pinned down. He is always being appealed to, but he does not exist in an Authorized Version. He is open to perpetual reinterpretation and reappropriation. Shakespeare is like the English Constitution.

[5] *Headlong Hall*, ch. 7. The footnote is more partial than the body of the text: Peacock acknowledges that his source is the radical etymologist Horne Tooke. To lean on Tooke or, as I do for much of this book, on Hazlitt is to adopt a political position. To put it another way, Coriolanus does not believe that truth is plural.

Bibliography

Unless otherwise stated, all books are published in London; titles of periodicals are abbreviated according to standard practice.

ALBRECHT, W. P. (1965), *Hazlitt and the Creative Imagination*. Lawrence, Kans.

ARAC, JONATHAN (1987), 'The Media of Sublimity: Johnson and Lamb on *King Lear*', *SIR* 26: 209–20.

ARCHENHOLTZ, JOHANN VON (1790), *A Picture of England*, tr. from the French. Dublin.

ASHBEE, C. R. (1928), *Caricature*.

ATHERTON, H. M. (1974), *Political Prints in the Age of Hogarth*. Oxford.

AUSTEN, JANE (1955), *Letters 1796–1817*, sel. and ed. R. W. Chapman. Oxford.

AVERY, EMMETT L. (1938), 'Cibber, *King John*, and the Students at Law', *MLN* 53: 272–5.

—— (1939), 'The *Craftsman* of July 2, 1737, and Colley Cibber', *Research Studies of the State College of Washington*, 7: 90–103.

—— (1956), 'The Shakespeare Ladies Club', *SQ* 7: 153–8.

BABCOCK, R. W. (1931), *The Genesis of Shakespeare Idolatry 1766–1799*. Chapel Hill.

BAGOT, JOSCELINE (1909), *George Canning and his Friends*, 2 vols.

BAKER, HERSCHEL (1942), *John Philip Kemble: The Actor in his Theatre*. Cambridge, Mass.

BALSON, THOMAS (1949), 'John Boydell, Publisher, "The Commercial Maecenas" ', *Signature*, 8: 3–22.

BARNES, THOMAS (1814), 'Theatrical Examiner No. 165', *Examiner*, 27 Feb., 138–9.

BARNET, SYLVAN (1954), 'Charles Lamb and the Tragic Malvolio', *PQ* 33: 178–88.

BARTHES, ROLAND (1974), *S/Z*, tr. Richard Miller. New York.

BATE, JONATHAN (1985), 'Lamb on Shakespeare', *Charles Lamb Bulletin*, NS 51: 76–85.

—— (1986), *Shakespeare and the English Romantic Imagination*. Oxford.

—— (1987), Introduction to *Charles Lamb: Elia and the Last Essays of Elia*. Oxford.

BATE, W. J. (1945), 'The Sympathetic Imagination in Eighteenth-Century Criticism', *ELH* 12: 144–64.

BENJAMIN, WALTER (1973), *Illuminations*, tr. Harry Zohn, ed. Hannah Arendt (repr., originally New York, 1968).

—— (1979), *One-Way Street and Other Writings*, tr. Edmund Jephcott and Kingsley Shorter.

BERTELSEN, LANCE (1977–8), 'David Garrick and English Painting', *Eighteenth-Century Studies*, 11: 308–24.

BOADEN, JAMES (1825), *Memoirs of the Life of John Philip Kemble*, 2 vols.

—— (1827), *Memoirs of Mrs Siddons*, 2 vols.

BOASE, T. S. R. (1947), 'Illustrations of Shakespeare's Plays in the Seventeenth and Eighteenth Centuries', *JWCI* 10: 83–108.

BOYDELL, JOHN, and BOYDELL, JOSIAH (publ.) (1805), *Collection of Prints, from Pictures Painted for the Purpose of Illustrating the Dramatic Works of Shakspeare, by the Artists of Great Britain.* 2 vols., dated 1803 (repr., ed. A. E. Santaniello, New York, 1979).

BRANAM, G. C. (1956), *Eighteenth Century Adaptations of Shakespearean Tragedy.* Berkeley and Los Angeles, Calif.

BRECHT, BERTOLT (1964), *Brecht on Theatre*, tr. John Willett.

BREWER, JOHN (1986), *The Common People and Politics 1750–1790s*, The English Satirical Print 1600–1832, gen. ed. Michael Duffy. Cambridge.

BROADLEY, A. M. (1911), *Napoleon in Caricature 1795–1821*, 2 vols.

BROMLEY, HENRY, pseud. (1793), *A Catalogue of Engraved British Portraits.*

BROMWICH, DAVID (1983), *Hazlitt: The Mind of a Critic.* New York and Oxford.

BROWN, JOHN RUSSELL (1961), 'The Realization of Shylock: A Theatrical Criticism', in *Early Shakespeare*, Stratford-upon-Avon Studies, 3.

BULLITT, J. M. (1945), 'Hazlitt and the Romantic Conception of the Imagination', *PQ* 24: 343–61.

BULWER, EDWARD LYTTON (1836), 'Some Thoughts on the Genius of William Hazlitt', in *Literary Remains of William Hazlitt*, vol. i, pp. lxxiv–lxxxvii.

BURKE, EDMUND (1790), *Reflections on the Revolution in France* (quoted from Everyman edn., 1910).

BYRON, LORD (1973–82), *Letters and Journals*, ed. Leslie A. Marchand, 12 vols.

CAMPBELL, THOMAS (1834), *Life of Mrs Siddons*, 2 vols.

CARLSON, C. L. (1938), *The First Magazine: A History of the* Gentleman's Magazine. Providence, Rhode Island.

CHILD, HAROLD (1935), *The Shakespearean Productions of John Philip Kemble.*

CIBBER, COLLEY (1700), *The Tragical History of King Richard III.*

CLARK, WILLIAM SMITH (1965), *The Irish Stage in the County Towns 1720–1800.* Oxford.

CLARKE, MARY COWDEN (1850–1), *The Girlhood of Shakespeare's Heroines*, 3 vols.

COHN, A. M. (ed.) (1924), *George Cruikshank, A Catalogue* Raisonné.

COLERIDGE, SAMUEL TAYLOR (1835), *Table Talk*, ed. H. N. Coleridge, 2 vols., quoted by date of entry.

—— (1956–71), *Collected Letters*, ed. E. L. Griggs, 6 vols. Oxford.

—— (1960), *Shakespearean Criticism*, ed. T. M. Raysor, 2nd edn., 2 vols.

—— (1970), *The Watchman*, ed. Lewis Patton (*The Collected Works of Samuel Taylor Coleridge*, vol. ii). Princeton, NJ.

—— (1971), *Lectures 1795: On Politics and Religion*, ed. Lewis Patton and Peter Mann (*The Collected Works of Samuel Taylor Coleridge*, vol. i). Princeton, NJ.

—— (1987), *Lectures 1808–1819: On Literature*, ed. R. A. Foakes, 2 vols. (*The Collected Works of Samuel Taylor Coleridge*, vol. v). Princeton, NJ.

COLLINGWOOD, R. G. (1946), *The Idea of History*. Oxford.

[COMBE, WILLIAM] (1801), *The Life, Adventures, and Opinions of Col. George Hanger, Written by Himself*, 2 vols.

CONRAD, PETER (1985), *The Everyman History of English Literature*.

DAGLEY, RICHARD (1821), *Takings*.

DEELMAN, CHRISTIAN (1964), *The Great Shakespeare Jubilee*.

DENNIS, JOHN (1720), *The Invader of his Country: or, The Fatal Resentment*.

DE QUINCEY, THOMAS (1889–90), *Collected Writings*, ed. David Masson, 14 vols. Edinburgh.

DIBDIN, CHARLES, jun. (1826), *History and Illustrations of the London Theatres*.

DIBDIN, THOMAS (1827), *Reminiscences*, 2 vols.

DICKINSON, H. T. (1986), *Caricatures and the Constitution 1760–1832*, The English Satirical Print 1600–1832, gen. ed. Michael Duffy. Cambridge.

DODD, WILLIAM (1752), *The Beauties of Shakespear*, 2 vols.

DOLLIMORE, JONATHAN, and SINFIELD, ALAN (eds.) (1985), *Political Shakespeare: New Essays in Cultural Materialism*. Manchester.

DONOHUE, J. W., jun. (1965), 'Hazlitt's Sense of the Dramatic Actor as Tragic Character', *SEL* 5: 703–21.

—— (1970), *Dramatic Character in the English Romantic Age*. Princeton, NJ.

—— (1975), *Theatre in the Age of Kean*. Oxford.

DRAKE, NATHAN (1817), *Shakspeare and his Times*. 2 vols.

DRYDEN, JOHN (1962), *Of Dramatic Poesy and Other Critical Essays*, ed. George Watson, 2 vols.

EAGLETON, TERRY (1986), *William Shakespeare*. Oxford.

EDWARDS, PHILIP (1986), *Shakespeare: A Writer's Progress*. Oxford.

ENGLAND, M. W. (1964), *Garrick's Jubilee*. Columbus, Ohio.

EVANS, MALCOLM (1986), *Signifying Nothing: Truth's True Contents in Shakespeare's Text*. Brighton.

FARINGTON, JOSEPH (1978–84), *The Diary of Joseph Farington*, ed. Kenneth Garlick, Angus Macintyre, Kathryn Cave, 16 vols. (through pagination).

FARMER, RICHARD (1767), *An Essay on the Learning of Shakespeare*.

FINLAY, JOHN (1835), *Miscellanies*. Dublin.

FOOTE, HORACE (1829), *A Companion to the Theatres; and A Manual of the British Drama.*

FOOTE, SAMUEL (1778), *The Devil upon Two Sticks.*

FORD, H. L. (1935), *Shakespeare 1700–1740: A Collation of the Editions and Separate Plays.* Oxford.

[FORD, THOMAS] (1794), *Confusion's Master-Piece: or, Paine's Labour's Lost. Being a Specimen of Some Well-Known Scenes in Shakespeare's* Macbeth. *Revived and Improved; as Enacted by Some of His Majesty's Servants before the Pit of Acheron. By the Writer of the Parodies in the* Gentleman's Magazine.

FRIEDMAN, W. H. (1976), *Boydell's Shakespeare Gallery.* New York.

FULFORD, ROGER (1967), *The Trial of Queen Caroline.*

GADAMER, HANS-GEORG (1975), *Truth and Method.* New York. Originally *Wahrheit und Methode* (Tübingen, 1960).

GARRICK, DAVID (1785), *Poetical Works.*

—— (1963), *Letters*, ed. D. M. Little and G. M. Kahrl, 3 vols.

—— (1980–2), *Plays*, ed. H. W. Pedicord and F. L. Bergmann, 6 vols. Carbondale, Ill.

GENEST, JOHN (1832), *Some Account of the English Stage*, 10 vols. Bath.

GEORGE, M. DOROTHY (1959), *English Political Caricature: A Study of Opinion and Propaganda*, 2 vols. Oxford.

—— (1967), *Hogarth to Cruikshank: Social Change in Graphic Satire.*

GIFFORD, WILLIAM (1818), 'Hazlitt's *Characters of Shakespear's Plays*', *Quarterly Review*, 18: 458–66.

GILDON, CHARLES (1710), *Remarks on the Plays of Shakespear.*

GILLRAY, JAMES (1830), *Illustrative Description of the Genuine Works of James Gillray.*

—— (1847), *Works*, 2 vols.

GOLDBERG, JONATHAN (1986), 'Textual Properties', *SQ* 37: 213–17.

GOLLANCZ, ISRAEL (ed.) (1916), *Shakespeare Tercentenary Observance.*

GOMBRICH, E. H. (1966), 'The Style *all'antica*: Imitation and Assimilation' and 'Reynolds's Theory and Practice of Imitation', in his *Norm and Form.*

—— (1971), 'Imagery and Art in the Romantic Period', in his *Meditations on a Hobby Horse and Other Essays on the Theory of Art*, 2nd edn.

GONCOURT, EDMOND DE, and GONCOURT, JULES DE (1854), *Histoire de la société française pendant la Révolution.* Paris.

GRAY, C. H. (1931), *Theatrical Criticism in London to 1795.* New York.

GREBANIER, BERNARD (1966), *The Great Shakespearean Forgery.*

GREER, GERMAINE (1986), *Shakespeare.* Oxford.

GREGO, JOSEPH (1873), *The Works of James Gillray, the Caricaturist*, ed. T. Wright.

—— (1880), *Rowlandson the Caricaturist*, 2 vols.

GRIFFITH, ELIZABETH (1775), *The Morality of Shakespeare's Drama Illustrated.*

GUTHRIE, WILLIAM (1747), *An Essay upon English Tragedy.*

HACKETT, J. H. (1959), *Oxberry's 1822 Edition of* King Richard III *with the Descriptive Notes Recording Edmund Kean's Performance Made by James H. Hackett*, ed. A. S. Downer.

HALLIDAY, F. E. (1957), *The Cult of Shakespeare.*

Hansard (publ.) (1806–20), *The Parliamentary History of England*, 36 vols.

HARBAGE, ALFRED (1966), *Conceptions of Shakespeare.* Cambridge, Mass.

HARTMAN, GEOFFREY H. (1975), *The Fate of Reading and Other Essays.* Chicago.

HAWKES, TERENCE (1986), *That Shakespeherian Rag: Essays on a Critical Process.*

HAWKINS, F. W. (1869), *The Life of Edmund Kean*, 2 vols.

HAWKINS, HARRIETT (1985), *The Devil's Party: Critical Counter-Interpretations of Shakespearian Drama.* Oxford.

HAWKINS, WILLIAM (1759), Cymbeline. *A Tragedy, Altered from Shakespeare. As it is Perform'd at the Theatre-Royal in Covent-Garden.*

HAYDON, B. R. (1853), *Life, from his Autobiography and Journals*, ed. Tom Taylor, 3 vols.

—— (1960–3), *Diary*, ed. W. B. Pope, 5 vols. Cambridge, Mass.

HAZLITT, MARGARET (1967), *The Journal of Margaret Hazlitt*, ed. E. J. Moyne. Lawrence, Kan.

HAZLITT, WILLIAM (1930–4), *Complete Works*, ed. P. P. Howe, 21 vols. *Characters of Shakespear's Plays* (1817) is in vol. iv; *A View of the English Stage* (1818) in vol. v; *Political Essays* (1819) in vol. vii; *A Letter to William Gifford, Esq.* (1819) in vol. ix; and *The Spirit of the Age* (1825) in vol. xi.

—— (1979), *Letters*, ed. H. M. Sikes.

HAZLITT, W. CAREW (1867), *Memoirs of William Hazlitt*, 2 vols.

—— (1897), *Four Generations of a Literary Family*, 2 vols.

HIGHET, GILBERT (1962), *The Anatomy of Satire*, ch. 3, 'Parody'. Princeton, NJ.

HILL, DRAPER (1965), *Mr Gillray the Caricaturist.*

—— (1966), *Fashionable Contrasts.*

—— (1976), *The Satirical Etchings of James Gillray.* New York.

HILLEBRAND, H. N. (1933), *Edmund Kean.* New York.

HILTON, TIM (1985), *John Ruskin: The Early Years.* New Haven, Conn.

HOGAN, C. B. (1952–7), *Shakespeare in the Theatre 1701–1800*, 2 vols. Oxford.

HOGARTH, WILLIAM (1970), *Graphic Works*, ed. Ronald Paulson, 2 vols. New Haven, Conn.

HOLDERNESS, GRAHAM (ed.) (1988), *The Shakespeare Myth.* Manchester.

[HOLE, RICHARD] (1796), 'An Apology for the Character and Conduct of Shylock', in *Essays, by a Society of Gentlemen, at Exeter.* Exeter.

HONE, WILLIAM (1818), *The Three Trials of William Hone for Publishing Three Parodies.*

—— (n.d.), *History of Parody*, 11 vols. of manuscript materials, British Library, Add. MSS 40108-18.

HOWARD, JEAN E., and O'CONNOR, MARION F. (eds.) (1987), *Shakespeare Reproduced: The Text in History and Ideology.*

HOWE, P. P. (1949), *The Life of William Hazlitt* (repr., originally 1922). Harmondsworth.

HUNT, LEIGH (1807), *Critical Essays on the Performers of the London Theatres.*

—— (1894), *Dramatic Essays,* ed. William Archer and R. W. Lowe.

—— (1949), *Dramatic Criticism 1808-1831,* ed. L. H. and C. W. Houtchens. New York.

—— (1956), *Literary Criticism,* ed. L. H. and C. W. Houtchens. New York.

IRELAND, W. H. (1803), *Rhapsodies.*

JACKSON, RUSSELL (1971), '*Cymbeline* in the Nineteenth Century', MA dissertation, Birmingham University.

JACOBS, H. E., and JOHNSON, C. D. (1976), *An Annotated Bibliography of Shakespearean Burlesques, Parodies, and Travesties.* New York.

JAMES, C. L. R. (1963), *Beyond a Boundary.*

JAMESON, ANNA [BROWNELL] (1832), *Characteristics of Women, Moral, Poetical, and Historical,* 2 vols.

JAUSS, HANS ROBERT (1982), *Toward an Aesthetic of Reception,* tr. Timothy Bahti. Minneapolis, Minn.

JEFFREY, FRANCIS (1817), 'Hazlitt on Shakespeare', *Edinburgh Review,* 28: 472-88.

JENKIN, FLEEMING (1887), *Papers Literary, Scientific, etc.,* ed. Sidney Colvin and J. A. Ewing, 2 vols.

JERROLD, BLANCHARD (1882), *The Life of George Cruikshank,* 2 vols.

JOHNSON, SAMUEL (1986), *Selections from Johnson on Shakespeare,* ed. B. H. Bronson (from the 2 vols. *On Shakespeare,* ed. Arthur Sherbo, in the Yale Edition of *The Works of Samuel Johnson,* 14 vols., 1958-).

JUMP, JOHN (1972), *Burlesque.*

KAMES, Lord [HENRY HOME] (1762), *Elements of Criticism,* 3 vols.

KEATS, JOHN (1958), *The Letters of John Keats 1814-1821,* ed. Hyder E. Rollins, 2 vols. Cambridge, Mass.

KEMBLE, JOHN PHILIP (1786), *Macbeth Reconsidered.*

—— (1817), *Macbeth, and* King Richard the Third.

KERMODE, FRANK (1971), *Shakespeare, Spenser, Donne: Renaissance Essays.*

—— (1975), *The Classic.*

—— (1985), *Forms of Attention.* Chicago, Ill.

KINNAIRD, J. W. (1978), *William Hazlitt: Critic of Power.* New York.

KLINGBERG, F. J., and HUSTVEDT, S. B. (eds.) (1944), *The Warning Drum: The British Home Front Faces Napoleon: Broadsides of 1803.* Berkeley and Los Angeles, Calif.

KLINGENDER, F. D. (1944), *Hogarth and English Caricature.*

KRUMBHAAR, E. B. (ed.) (1966), *Isaac Cruikshank: A Catalogue* Raisonné. Philadelphia, Penn.

LAMB, CHARLES, and LAMB, MARY (1912), *Works*, ed. E. V. Lucas, 4 vols. (repr., originally 1903–5, 7 vols.).

—— (1935), *Letters*, ed. E. V. Lucas, 3 vols.

LANDSEER, JOHN (1831), 'Mr Landseer's Apology for James Gillray', *Athenaeum*, 15 Oct., 667–8.

LANDSEER, THOMAS (1871), *Life and Letters of William Bewick*, 2 vols.

LANGFORD, PAUL (1986), *Walpole and the Robinocracy*, The English Satirical Print 1600–1832, gen. ed. Michael Duffy. Cambridge.

LENNOX, CHARLOTTE (1753–4), *Shakespear Illustrated: or, The Novels and Histories, on which the Plays of Shakespear are Founded, Collected and Translated from the Original Authors. With Critical Remarks*, 3 vols.

LICHTENBERG, C. G. (1938), *Visits to England as Described in his Letters and Diaries*, tr. M. L. Mare and W. H. Quarrell. Oxford.

—— (1966), *Commentaries on Hogarth's Engravings*, tr. I. and G. Herdan.

LIESENFELD, VINCENT J. (1984), *The Licensing Act of 1737*. Madison, Wis.

LILLO, GEORGE (1738), *Marina: A Play . . . Taken from Pericles Prince of Tyre*.

LOFTIS, JOHN (1963), *The Politics of Drama in Augustan England*. Oxford.

London Stage, 1660–1800, The (1965–79), ed. William van Lennep, Emmett L. Avery, Arthur H. Scouten, G. W. Stone, jun., and C. B. Hogan, 12 vols. Carbondale, Ill.

LUDERS, ALEXANDER (1813), *The Character of Henry V when Prince of Wales*.

MACREADY, WILLIAM CHARLES (1875), *Reminiscences*, ed. Sir Frederick Pollock, 2 vols.

MAIR, JOHN (1938), *The Fourth Forger*.

MALCOLM, J. P. (1813), *An Historical Sketch of the Art of Caricaturing*.

MALCOLMSON, R. W. (1973), *Popular Recreation in English Society 1700–1850*. Cambridge.

MALONE, EDMOND (1796), *Inquiry into the Authenticity of Certain Miscellaneous Papers and Legal Instruments*.

MCFARLAND, THOMAS (1987), *Romantic Cruxes: The English Essayists and the Spirit of the Age*. Oxford.

MCGANN, JEROME J. (1983*a*), *A Critique of Modern Textual Criticism*. Chicago, Ill.

—— (1983*b*), *The Romantic Ideology*. Chicago, Ill.

MERCHANT, W. M. (1959), *Shakespeare and the Artist*.

MILLER, JONATHAN (1986), *Subsequent Performances*.

MITCHELL, HANNAH (1978), 'Art and the French Revolution: An Exhibition at the Musée Carnavalet', *History Workshop*, 5: 123–45.

Modern Characters from Shakespear, The (1778).

MONTAGU, ELIZABETH (1769), *Essay on the Writings and Genius of Shakespear*.

MOORE, THOMAS (1825), *Memoirs of the Life of Sheridan*, 3rd edn., 2 vols.

—— (1853–6), *Memoirs, Journal, and Correspondence*, ed. Lord John Russell, 8 vols.

MORGANN, MAURICE (1777), *An Essay on the Dramatic Character of Sir John Falstaff.*

MORITZ, C. P. (1795), *Travels, Chiefly on Foot, through Several Parts of England, in 1782.*

NICHOLS, JOHN (1812–15), *Literary Anecdotes of the Eighteenth Century*, 9 vols.

—— (1821), *The Rise and Progress of the* Gentleman's Magazine.

NICOLL, ALLARDYCE (1952–9), *A History of the English Drama 1600–1900*, 6 vols. Cambridge.

ODELL, G. C. D. (1921), *Shakespeare from Betterton to Irving.* 2 vols.

ORGEL, STEPHEN (1981), 'What is a Text?', *RORD* 24: 3–6.

OULTON, W. C. (1818), *A History of the Theatres of London*, 3 vols.

PARK, ROY (1971), *Hazlitt and the Spirit of the Age.* Oxford.

—— (1982), 'Lamb, Shakespeare, and the Stage', *SQ* 33: 164–77.

PASTON, GEORGE, pseud. (1905), *Social Caricature in the Eighteenth Century.*

PATMORE, P. G. (1817–18), 'Notices on the Acted Drama in London. No. I', *Blackwood's Magazine*, 2: 426–31.

PAULSON, RONALD (1971), *Hogarth: His Life, Art, and Times*, 2 vols. New Haven, Conn.

—— (1975), *Emblem and Expression: Meaning in English Art in the Eighteenth Century.*

—— (1982), *Book and Painting: Shakespeare, Milton and the Bible: Literary Texts and the Emergence of English Painting.* Knoxville, Tenn.

—— (1983), *Representations of Revolution (1789–1820).* New Haven, Conn.

PERKIN, HAROLD (1969), *The Origins of Modern English Society 1780–1880.*

PIPER, DAVID (1982), *The Image of the Poet: British Poets and their Portraits.* Oxford.

Poetical Epistle from Florizel to Perdita; with Perdita's Answer. And a Preliminary Discourse on the Education of Princes (1781).

POOLE, JOHN (1810), *Hamlet Travestie.*

PORTER, ROY (1982), *English Society in the Eighteenth Century.* Harmondsworth.

—— (1988), 'Seeing the Past', *Past and Present*, 118: 186–205.

PRAWER, S. S. (1976), *Karl Marx and World Literature.* Oxford.

PROCTER, B. W. (1830), 'My Recollections of the Late William Hazlitt', *New Monthly Magazine*, pt. II: 469–82.

—— (1833), 'Death of Edmund Kean', *Athenaeum*, 18 May, 313–15.

—— (1835), *The Life of Edmund Kean*, 2 vols.

—— (1936), *The Literary Recollections of Barry Cornwall*, ed. R. W. Armour. Boston, Mass.

RABKIN, NORMAN (1981), *Shakespeare and the Problem of Meaning.* Chicago, Ill.

REDGRAVE, RICHARD, and REDGRAVE, SAMUEL (1981), *A Century of British Painters.* Oxford (repr., originally London, 1866).

REID, G. W. (ed.) (1871), *George Cruikshank: A Descriptive Catalogue*, 3 vols.

REIMAN, D. H. (ed.) (1972), *The Romantics Reviewed: Contemporary Reviews of British Romantic Writers*, 9 vols. New York.

[REPTON, HUMPHREY] (1789), *The Bee; or A Companion to the Shakespeare Gallery: Containing a Catalogue*-Raisonné *of All the Pictures; with Comments, Illustrations, and Remarks.*

RICHARDSON, WILLIAM (1797), *A Philosophical Analysis and Illustration of Some of Shakespeare's Remarkable Characters*, 5th edn. (originally 1774).

RICKWORD, EDGELL (ed.) (1971), *Radical Squibs and Loyal Ripostes: Satirical Pamphlets of the Regency Period, 1819–1821*. Bath.

ROBERDEAU, J. P. (1804), *Fugitive Verse and Prose*, 2nd edn.

ROBINSON, HENRY CRABB (1869), *Diary, Reminiscences and Correspondence*, ed. T. Sadler, 3 vols.

—— (1938), *On Books and their Writers*, ed. E. J. Morley, 3 vols. (through pagination).

—— (1966), *The London Theatre, 1811–1866, Selections from the Diary*, ed. Eluned Brown.

ROBINSON, MARY (1796), *The Sicilian Lover. A Tragedy.*

ROBINSON, R. E. (1959), *William Hazlitt's* Life of Napoleon Buonaparte. Geneva and Paris.

ROE, A. S. (1971), 'The Demon behind the Pillow: A Note on Erasmus Darwin and Reynolds', *Burlington Magazine*, 113: 460–70.

ROSENBLUM, ROBERT (1967), *Transformations in Late Eighteenth-Century Art.* Princeton, NJ.

ROSENFELD, SYBIL (1939), *Strolling Players and Drama in the Provinces 1660–1765.* Cambridge.

ROSTRON, DAVID (1972), 'Contemporary Political Comment in Four of J. P. Kemble's Shakespearean Productions', *Theatre Research*, 12: 113–19.

RUSKIN, JOHN (1872), *Munera Pulveris: Six Essays on the Elements of Political Economy.*

RYMER, THOMAS (1692), *A Short View of Tragedy*, dated 1693.

SALUSINSZKY, IMRE (1987), *Criticism in Society: Interviews with Jacques Derrida, Northrop Frye, Harold Bloom* [*et al.*].

SAUER, THOMAS G. (1981), *A. W. Schlegel's Shakespearean Criticism in England 1811–1846*. Bonn.

SAYERS, JAMES (n.d.), *Satirical Prints*, British Museum Banks Collection II, with manuscript annotations.

SCHLEGEL, A. W. von (1846), *A Course of Lectures on Dramatic Art and Literature*, tr. John Black (originally 2 vols., 1815), rev. A. J. W. Morrison.

SCHNEIDER, E. W. (1933), *The Aesthetics of William Hazlitt*. Philadelphia, Penn.

SCHNÖCKELBORG, G. (1931), *Schlegels Einfluss auf Hazlitt als Shakespeare-Kritiker*. Münster.

SCHOENBAUM, SAMUEL (1970), *Shakespeare's Lives*. Oxford.

SCOUTEN, A. H. (1945), 'Shakespeare's Plays in the Theatrical Repertory when Garrick Came to London', in *Texas Studies in English*, 257–68. Austin, Tex.

—— (1956), 'The Increase in Popularity in Shakespeare's Plays in the 18th Century: A Caveat for Interpreters of Stage History', *SQ* 7: 189–202.

Shakespeare's History of the Times (1778).

SHARP, R. FARQUHARSON (1920), 'Travesties of Shakespeare's Plays', *Library*, 1: 1–20.

SHATTUCK, C. H. (ed.) (1974), *John Philip Kemble Promptbooks*, 11 vols. Charlottesville, Va.

SHELLEY, P. B. (1909), *Literary and Philosophical Criticism*, ed. John Shaw-cross.

SHERBO, ARTHUR (1986), *The Birth of Shakespeare Studies*. East Lansing, Mich.

SIDDONS, SARAH (1834), 'Remarks on the Character of Lady Macbeth', in vol. ii of Campbell, above.

SMITH, HORACE, and SMITH, JAMES (1812), *Rejected Addresses or The New Theatrum Poetarum* (quoted from New Universal Library edn., n.d.).

SMITH, OLIVIA (1984), *The Politics of Language 1791–1819*. Oxford.

SOUTHEY, ROBERT, and COLERIDGE, S. T. (1969), *Omniana*. Fontwell, Sussex (repr., originally 1812, 2 vols.).

SPENCER, HAZELTON (1927), *Shakespeare Improved*. Cambridge, Mass.

SPRAGUE, A. C. (1945), *Shakespeare and the Actors*. Cambridge, Mass.

—— (1953), *Shakespearian Players and Performances*. Cambridge, Mass.

STEPHENS, F. G., and GEORGE, M. DOROTHY (eds.) (1870–1954), *Catalogue of Political and Personal Satires Preserved in the Department of Prints and Drawings in the British Museum*, 11 vols.

STONE, G. W., jun. (1934), 'Garrick's Long Lost Alteration of *Hamlet*', *PMLA* 49: 890–921.

—— (1948), 'The God of his Idolatry: Garrick's Theory of Acting and Composition with Especial Reference to Shakespeare', in *J. Q. Adams Memorial Studies*, 115–28. Washington DC.

—— (1950), 'David Garrick's Significance in the History of Shakespearean Criticism', *PMLA* 65: 183–97.

—— and KAHRL, G. M. (1979), *David Garrick: A Critical Biography*. Carbondale, Ill.

TALFOURD, T. N. (1836), 'Thoughts upon the Intellectual Character of the Late William Hazlitt', in *Literary Remains of William Hazlitt*, vol. i, pp. lxxxviii–cxxxiv.

—— (1848), *Final Memorials of Charles Lamb*, 2 vols.

TATE, NAHUM (1681), *The History of King Lear*.

—— (1682), *The Ingratitude of a Common-Wealth: Or, The Fall of Caius Martius Coriolanus*.

TAYLOR, GARY (ed.) (1982), *The Oxford Shakespeare: Henry V.* Oxford.

—— and WARREN, MICHAEL (eds.) (1983), *The Division of the Kingdoms: Shakespeare's Two Versions of* King Lear. Oxford.

TEGG, THOMAS (1810), *The Rise, Progress, and Termination of the O.P. War.*

THELWALL, JOHN (1795–6), *The Tribune,* 3 vols.

THOMPSON, E. P. (1968), *The Making of the English Working Class.* Harmondsworth (repr., originally 1963).

TRILLING, LIONEL (1950), *The Liberal Imagination.* New York.

TWISS, HORACE (1814), *Posthumous Parodies.*

—— (1844), *Life of Lord Eldon,* 3 vols.

UPTON, JOHN (1746), *Critical Observations on Shakespeare.*

VICKERS, BRIAN (1981), 'The Emergence of Character Criticism, 1774–1800', *ShS* 34: 11–21.

—— (ed.) (1974–81), *Shakespeare: The Critical Heritage 1623–1801,* 6 vols.

WALPOLE, HORACE (1910), *The Last Journals of Horace Walpole,* ed. A. F. Steuart, 2 vols.

WARDLE, RALPH (1971), *Hazlitt.* Lincoln, Nebr.

WARDROPER, JOHN (1973), *Kings, Lords, and Wicked Libellers: Satire and Protest 1760–1837.*

—— (1977), *The Caricatures of George Cruikshank.*

WEIMANN, ROBERT (1977), *Structure and Society in Literary History* (repr., originally Charlottesville, 1976).

—— (1978), *Shakespeare and the Popular Tradition in the Theater.* Baltimore, Md.

—— (1982–3), ' "Appropriation" in Renaissance Narrative', *NLH* 14: 459–95.

WELLS, STANLEY (1963), 'Shakespeare in Planché's Extravaganzas', *ShS* 16: 103–17.

—— (1980), 'Shakespeare in Leigh Hunt's Theatre Criticism', *Essays and Studies,* 33: 119–38.

—— (1982), 'Shakespeare in Hazlitt's Theatre Criticism', *ShS* 35: 43–55.

—— (ed.) (1977–8), *Nineteenth-Century Shakespeare Burlesques,* 5 vols.

WHATELY, THOMAS (1785), *Remarks on Some of the Characters of Shakespeare.*

WHITE, HAYDEN (1978), *Tropics of Discourse: Essays in Cultural Criticism.* Baltimore, Md.

WHITE, JAMES (1796), *Original Letters, etc. of Sir John Falstaff.*

WHITLEY, ALVIN (1955), 'Hazlitt and the Theatre', *University of Texas Studies in English,* 34: 67–100.

WING, VINCENT (1864), *Reminiscences of the Rev. Thomas Ford.* Melton Mowbray.

WORDSWORTH, WILLIAM (1974), *Wordsworth's Literary Criticism,* ed. W. J. B. Owen.

WRAXALL, NATHANIEL (1884), *Historical and Posthumous Memoirs, 1772–1784,* ed. H. B. Wheatley, 5 vols.

WRIGHT, THOMAS (1865), *A History of Caricature and Grotesque in Literature and Art.*

—— and EVANS, R. H. (1851), *Historical and Descriptive Account of the Caricatures of James Gillray.*

Index